NSW Targeting Maths

Year 4

Garda Turner

PASCAL PRESS

Contents

New Edition

Targeting Maths Australia's Favourite Maths Program

Australian Curriculum/ NSW Alignment

This NEW Edition fully aligns each student page with both the new NSW Syllabus (2024) and the new Australian Curriculum: Mathematics F-10 version 9.0. The NSW Syllabus outcome codes and content groups appear with the Australian Curriculum strand and code on each student page.

iPad Apps

With an app for each year, from Foundation/Kindergarten to Year 6, the Targeting Maths Apps include all the essential maths content that children need to know in an amazing app that makes learning maths fun, motivating and full of rewards. Look for it in Apple's App Store today! Made especially for the iPad and aligned to each student page in this book.

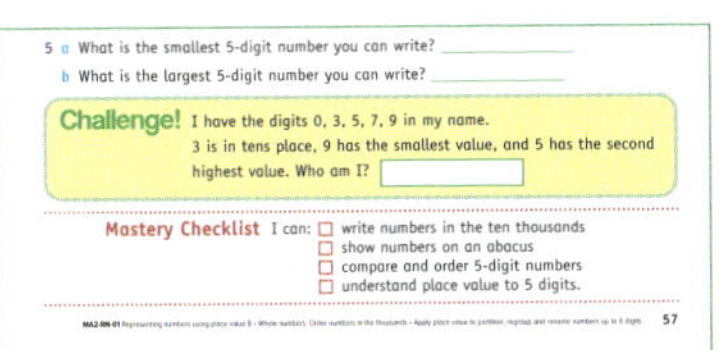

Mastery Checklists

Each unit has a Mastery Checklist. These checklists engage students in visible learning as they recognise and reflect on the specific maths skills learnt in each unit.

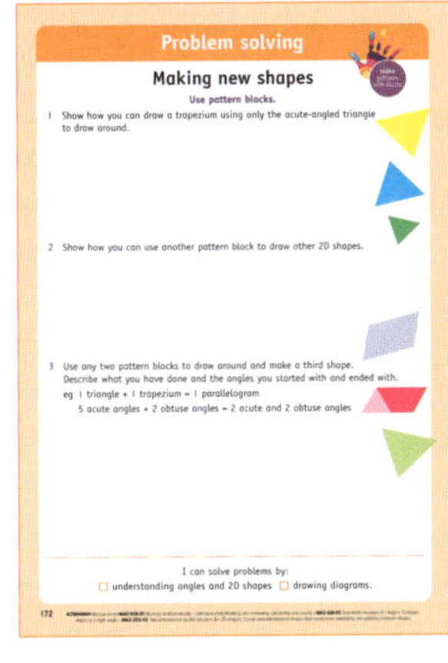

Integrated Problem-solving Program

Includes an integrated problem-solving program that actively builds students' problem solving capabilities.

In-stage Topic Alignment for Composite Classes

Great for composite classes too, the contents of each book in one stage, eg Year 3 and Year 4, match topic by topic.

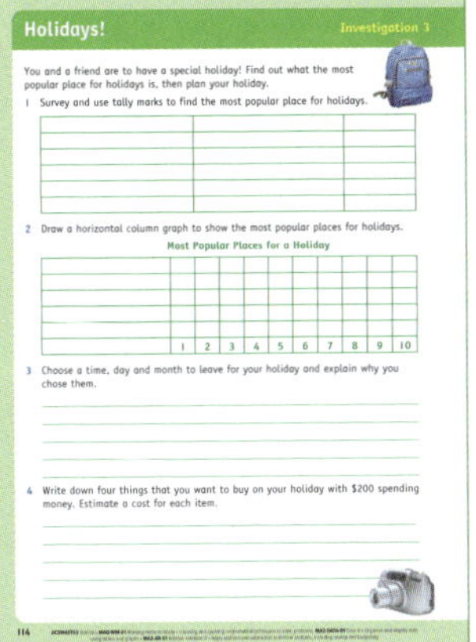

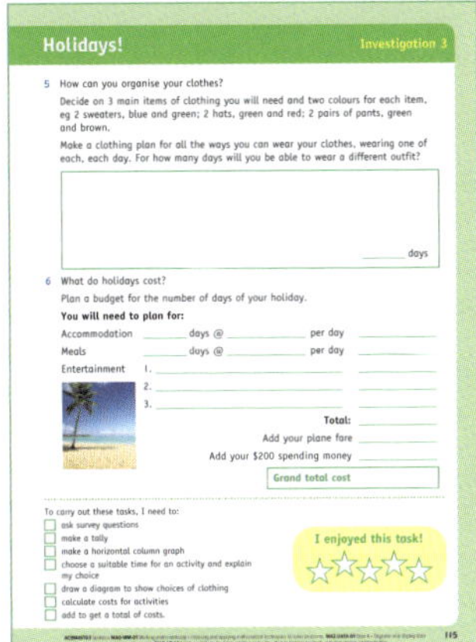

Term Investigations

Each term includes an investigation that will get students planning and working through an extended problem.

Regular Revision

Revision pages appear both at mid term and at the end of each term to revise key concepts.

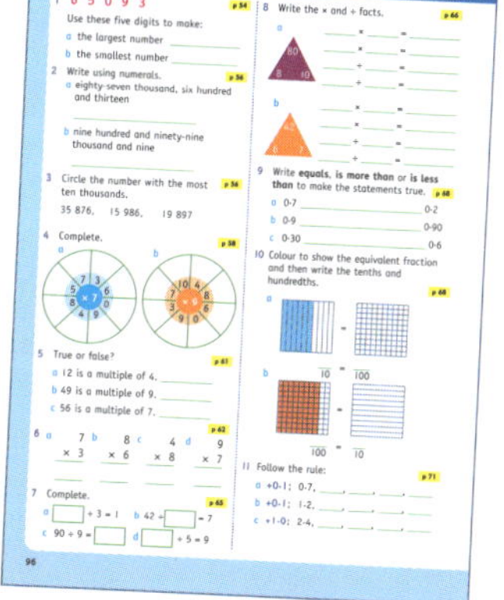

Hands-on Activities

Various hands-on activities are included in each term, asking students to measure and make, count and compare, using objects from around the classroom or home.

Year 4 Outcomes

	NSW Syllabus Outcomes	Student pages
Working Mathematically	**MA1-WM-01** develops understanding and fluency in mathematics through exploring and connecting mathematical concepts	2–184
	MA1-WM-01 develops understanding and fluency in mathematics through choosing and applying mathematical techniques to solve problems	12, 20, 30, 37, 43, 63, 72, 79, 92, 105, 109, 153, 162, 174
	MA1-WM-01 develops understanding and fluency in mathematics through communicating their thinking and reasoning coherently and clearly	20, 63, 79, 92, 105, 109, 114, 125, 130, 144, 157, 172, 174
Number and Algebra	**Representing numbers**	
	MA2-RN-01 applies an understanding of place value and the role of zero to represent numbers to at least tens of thousands	2, 3, 13, 54, 55, 56, 57, 98, 99, 113
	MA2-RN-02 represents and compares decimals up to 2 decimal places using place value	18, 19, 68, 69, 71, 112, 154, 155, 156, 157
	Additive relations	
	MA2-AR-01 selects and uses mental and written strategies for addition and subtraction involving 2- and 3-digit numbers	4, 5, 6, 8, 9, 10, 11, 12, 26, 70, 76, 77, 78, 79, 82, 100, 101, 102, 103, 114, 121, 122, 123, 124, 125, 139, 145, 146, 147, 148, 149, 150, 151, 152, 153
	MA2-AR-02 completes number sentences involving addition and subtraction by finding missing values	4, 7, 11, 103, 118, 119, 120
	Multiplicative relations	
	MA2-MR-01 represents and uses the structure of multiplicative relations to 10 × 10 to solve problems	25, 27, 28, 29, 30, 58, 59, 60, 61, 62, 63, 64, 66, 72, 80, 81, 104, 105, 106, 108, 109, 118, 121, 130, 142, 143, 144, 150, 166, 167, 168
	MA2-MR-02 completes number sentences involving multiplication and division by finding missing values	24, 25, 65, 66, 67, 83, 107, 119, 120
	Fractions	
	MA2-PF-01 represents and compares halves, quarters, thirds and fifths as lengths on a number line and their related fractions formed by halving (eighths, sixths and tenths)	16, 17, 110, 111, 112, 154, 155
Measurement and Space	**Geometric measure**	
	MA2-GM-01 uses grid maps and directional language to locate positions and follow routes	175, 176, 177, 178
	MA2-GM-02 measures and estimates lengths in metres, centimetres and millimetres	13, 14, 15, 20, 159
	MA2-GM-03 identifies angles and classifies them by comparing to a right angle	169, 170, 171, 172
	Two-dimensional (2D) spatial structure	
	MA2-2DS-01 compares two-dimensional shapes and describes their features	84, 85
	MA2-2DS-02 performs transformations by combining and splitting two-dimensional shapes	86, 87, 88, 131, 132, 133, 134, 172
	MA2-2DS-03 estimates, measures and compares areas using square centimetres and square metres	158, 159, 160, 161, 162
	Three-dimensional (3D) spatial structure	
	MA2-3DS-01 makes and sketches models and nets of three-dimensional objects including prisms and pyramids	34, 35, 36, 37
	MA2-3DS-02 estimates, measures and compares capacities (internal volumes) using litres, millilitres and volumes using cubic centimetres	89, 90, 91, 92, 93
	Non-spatial measure	
	MA2-NSM-01 estimates, measures and compares the masses of objects using kilograms and grams	126, 127, 128, 129
	MA2-NSM-02 represents and interprets analog and digital time in hours, minutes and seconds	31, 32, 33, 162, 172, 173
Statistics and Probability	**Data**	
	MA2-DATA-01 collects discrete data and constructs graphs using a given scale	38, 41, 42, 95, 114, 135, 136, 137
	MA2-DATA-02 interprets data in tables, dot plots and column graphs	39, 40, 95, 136, 138
	Chance	
	MA2-CHAN-01 records and compares the results of chance experiments	41, 42, 43, 94, 179, 180, 181

	Australian Curriculum Content Descriptions *Students learn to:*	Student pages
Number and Algebra	**Number**	
	AC9M4N01 recognise and extend the application of place value to tenths and hundredths and use the conventions of decimal notation to name and represent decimals	18, 19, 68, 69, 70, 71, 72, 76, 77, 78, 79, 112, 113, 123, 154, 155, 156, 157
	AC9M4N02 explain and use the properties of odd and even numbers	26, 67
	AC9M4N03 find equivalent representations of fractions using related denominators and make connections between fractions and decimal notation	13, 16, 17, 71, 112
	AC9M4N04 count by fractions including mixed numerals; locate and represent these fractions as numbers on number lines	17, 68, 69, 110, 111, 154, 155
	AC9M4N05 solve problems involving multiplying or dividing natural numbers by multiples and powers of 10 without a calculator, using the multiplicative relationship between the place value of digits	61, 67, 80, 81, 143
	AC9M4N06 develop efficient strategies and use appropriate digital tools for solving problems involving addition and subtraction, and multiplication and division where there is no remainder	5, 6, 7, 8, 9, 10, 11, 12, 64, 65, 66, 83, 100, 101, 105, 106, 109, 121, 142, 145, 146, 147, 148, 149, 150, 151, 152, 153, 157
	AC9M4N07 choose and use estimation and rounding to check and explain the reasonableness of calculations including the results of financial transactions	5, 9, 77, 78, 102, 103, 107, 113, 124, 125, 142, 152
	AC9M4N08 use mathematical modelling to solve practical problems involving additive and multiplicative situations including financial contexts; formulate the problems using number sentences and choose efficient calculation strategies, using digital tools where appropriate; interpret and communicate solutions in terms of the situation	10, 11, 12, 70, 76, 79, 83, 92, 100, 101, 103, 105, 106, 107, 108, 109, 122, 123, 124, 125, 130, 145
	AC9M4N09 follow and create algorithms involving a sequence of steps and decisions that use addition or multiplication to generate sets of numbers; identify and describe any emerging patterns	8, 27, 30, 80, 81, 120, 121, 144, 166, 167, 168
	Algebra	
	AC9M4A01 find unknown values in numerical equations involving addition and subtraction, using the properties of numbers and operations	4, 82, 118, 119
	AC9M4A02 recall and demonstrate proficiency with multiplication facts up to 10 x 10 and related division facts; extend and apply facts to develop efficient mental strategies for computation with larger numbers without a calculator	24, 25, 28, 29, 58, 59, 60, 62, 63, 104
Measurement and Geometry	**Measurement**	
	AC9M4M01 interpret unmarked and partial units when measuring and comparing attributes of length, mass, capacity, duration and temperature, using scaled and digital instruments and appropriate units	14, 31, 32, 33, 89, 90, 91, 93, 126, 127, 128, 129
	AC9M4M02 recognise ways of measuring and approximating the perimeter and area of shapes and enclosed spaces, using appropriate formal and informal units	15, 20, 158, 159, 160, 161, 162
	AC9M4M03 solve problems involving the duration of time including situations involving "am" and "pm" and conversions between units of time	31, 32, 33, 162, 173, 174
	AC9M4M04 estimate and compare angles using angle names including acute, obtuse, straight angle, reflex and revolution, and recognise their relationship to a right angle	84, 85, 169, 170, 171, 172
	Space	
	AC9M4SP01 represent and approximate composite shapes and objects in the environment, using combinations of familiar shapes and objects	34, 35, 87, 88
	AC9M4SP02 create and interpret grid reference systems using grid references and directions to locate and describe positions and pathways	175, 176, 177, 178
	AC9M4SP03 recognise line and rotational symmetry of shapes and create symmetrical patterns and pictures, using dynamic geometric software where appropriate	86, 88, 131, 132, 133, 134
Statistics and Probability	**Statistics**	
	AC9M4ST01 acquire data for categorical and discrete numerical variables to address a question of interest or purpose using digital tools; represent data using many-to-one pictographs, column graphs and other displays or visualisations; interpret and discuss the information that has been created	38, 39, 40, 43, 95, 136, 137, 139
	AC9M4ST02 analyse the effectiveness of different displays or visualisations in illustrating and comparing data distributions, then discuss the shape of distributions and the variation in the data	95, 136, 138
	AC9M4ST03 conduct statistical investigations, collecting data through survey responses and other methods; record and display data using digital tools; interpret the data and communicate the results	114, 135
	Probability	
	AC9M4P01 describe possible everyday events and the possible outcomes of chance experiments and order outcomes or events based on their likelihood of occurring; identify independent or dependent events	94, 179, 180, 181
	AC9M4P02 conduct repeated chance experiments to observe relationships between outcomes; identify and describe the variation in results	41, 42, 180, 181

How to Solve a Problem

Read • Plan • Work • Check

Read the problem carefully. Read it again. Underline important words.

Plan what you are going to do — add, subtract, multiply or divide.

Work Write the steps you take to work out the answer. Write your answer in full.

Check your answer! Make sure that your answer makes sense and that you answered the question.

Draw a diagram

Draw a simple picture.
Use symbols if you can.

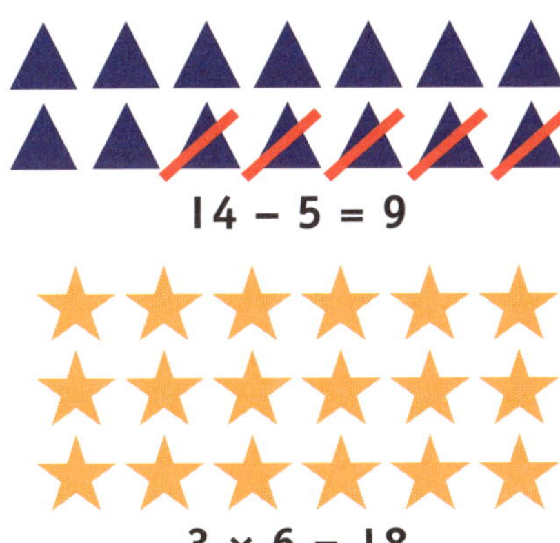

Trial and Error

Make a guess and write it down. Check if it is right. If not, work out if your guess should be higher or lower. Make another guess and write it down. Check if it's right. Keep going until you have the correct answer.

Look for patterns

Study the numbers in the problem.
Write them down in a list.
Can you see a pattern?
What comes next in the pattern.
Write it as your answer.

Cindy cycles 3 km, then 6 km, then 9 km on 3 days. How far should she cycle on the 4th day to keep to her pattern?

3, 6, 9, ?   3, 6, 9, 12

Cindy should cycle 12 km.

Use a table

Put the information from the problem in columns. Can you see the pattern? The information is clearer in a table.

Use this to work out the answer.

Jerry	5 mins	10 cakes	2 in 1 min.
Cam	4 mins	8 cakes	2 in 1 min.
Tilly	3 mins	9 cakes	3 in 1 min.

Who eats the fastest?

Answer: Tilly eats fastest.

Work backwards

Read the problem all the way through. Find one piece of information. Write it down. Find another piece of information that relates and put them together. Write it down. Keep working backwards until you solve all the pieces of the problem.

Kell has $2 more than Matt, who has $3 less than Jan. Jan has $10. How much do they each have?

Jan = $10

Matt = $10 – $3 = $7

Kell = $7 + $2 = $9

Dictionary

am (ante meridiem)
The time from midnight to midday

angle
The amount of turning between two lines that meet at a point

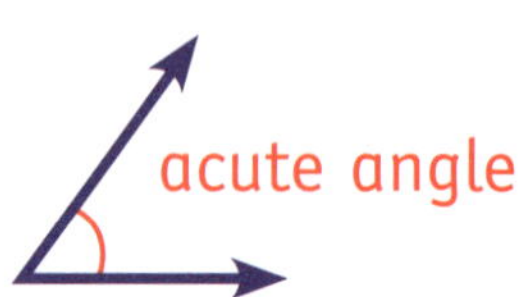

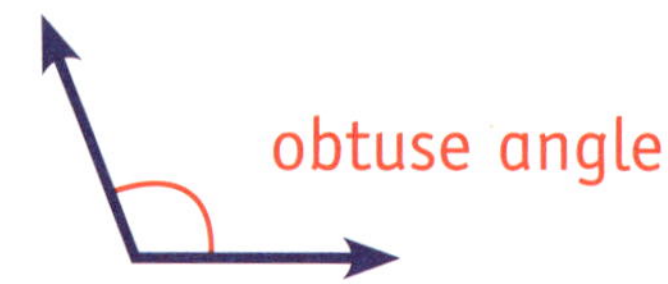

ascending order
In order from smallest to largest

1, 7, 11, 19, 32

capacity
The amount a container can hold

The capacity of this bottle is 1 litre.

centimetre (cm)
A unit of length
10 mm = 1 cm
100 cm = 1 m

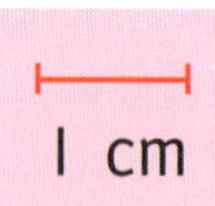

certain
Something that is definite.
It will happen.

cone
A solid shape that tapers to a point and has a circular base

cube
A solid shape which has six square faces

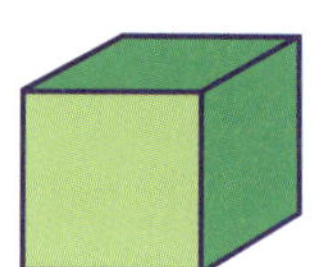

cylinder
A solid shape which has two circular ends and a curved surface

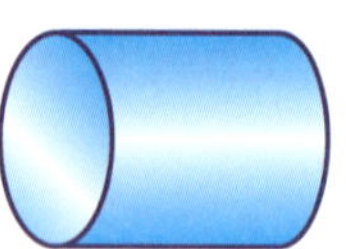

data
A collection of information

Favourite sports		
Sport	Votes	Total
Soccer	卌 卌 ||	12
Netball	卌 |	6
Football	卌 |||	8
Chess	卌 卌 |	11

decimal number
A number that has a decimal point

eg 0·3, 75·16

descending order
In order from largest to smallest

96, 84, 61, 37, 11

diagonal
A line that joins two corners in a polygon but does not make a side

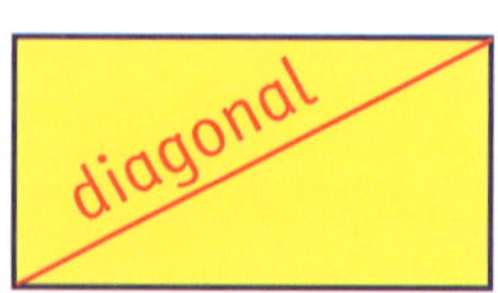

digit
The numerals that are used to write numbers: 0, 1, 2, 3, 4, 5, 6, 7, 8, 9

Dictionary

division (÷)

Sharing into equal groups

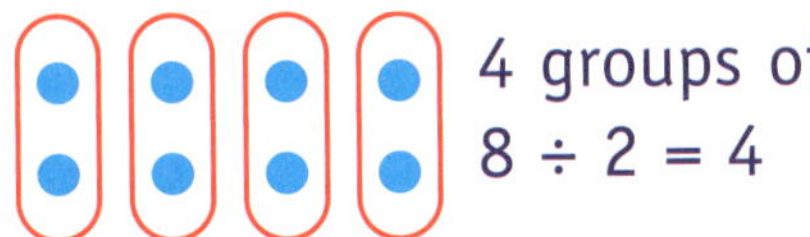

4 groups of 2

$8 \div 2 = 4$

edge

Where two flat surfaces meet

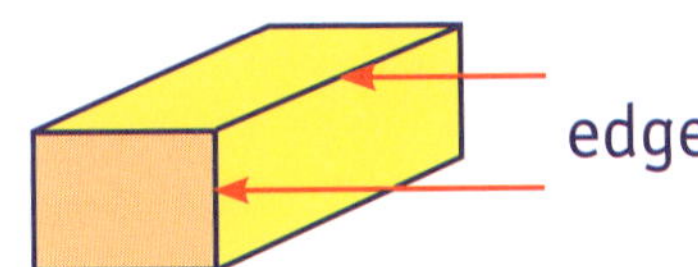

face

A flat surface of a solid shape

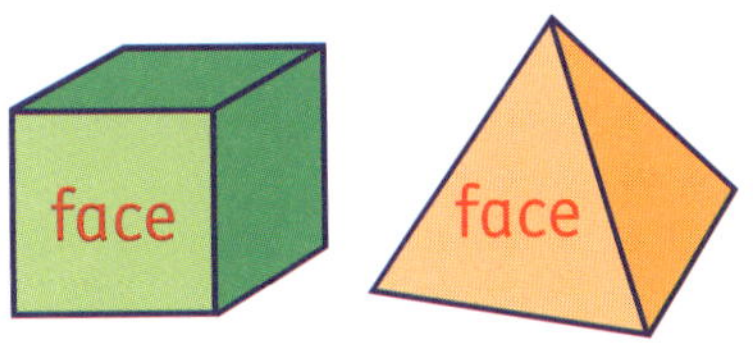

fraction

A part of a whole or a group

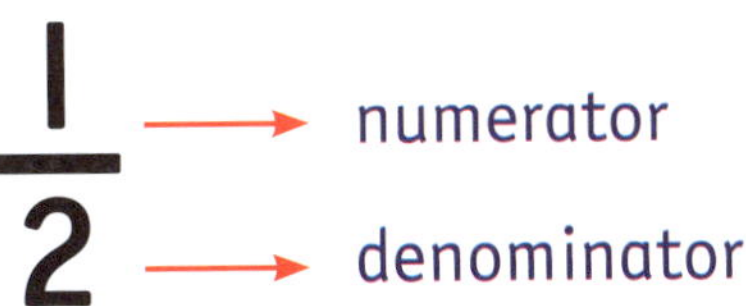

graph

A diagram that shows a collection of data

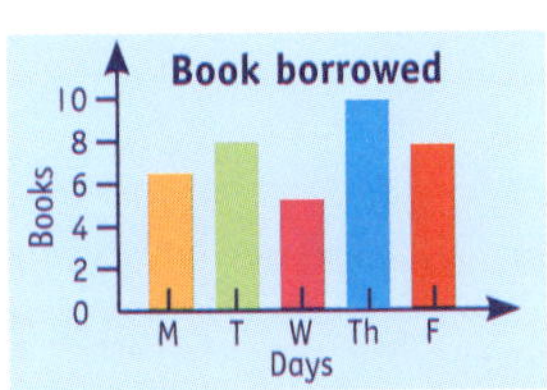

column graph

Money saved

Sam	$$$$$$
Mary	$$$
Jo	$$$$$

picture graph

hexagon

A 2D shape with 6 straight sides

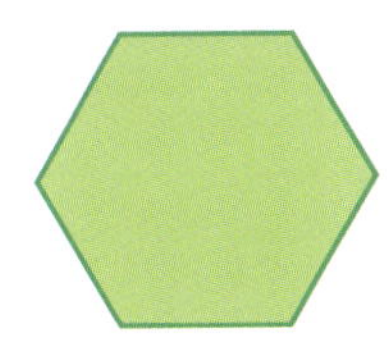

regular hexagon

irregular hexagon

kilogram (kg)

A unit of mass for weighing things

1 kilogram = 1000 grams

1000 kilograms = 1 tonne

line

straight line

parallel lines

curved line

litre (L)

A unit of capacity

1 L = 1000 millilitres (mL)

mass

The amount of material that makes up an object. Measured in grams, kilograms and tonnes.

metre (m)

A unit of length

1 m = 100 cm

1000 m = 1 km

millimetre (mm)

A unit of length

10 mm = 1 cm

multiple

$3 \times 2 \times 4 = 24$

24 is a multiple of 2, 3 and 4.

Dictionary

multiplication (×)

Find the total of a number of equal groups or equal rows

$5 \times 4 = 20$

$4 \times 6 = 24$

octagon

A 2D shape with 8 straight sides

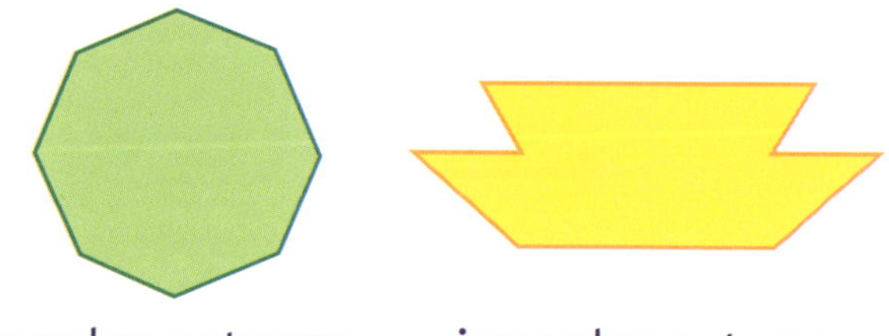

regular octagon irregular octagon

parallelogram

A quadrilateral with opposite sides parallel

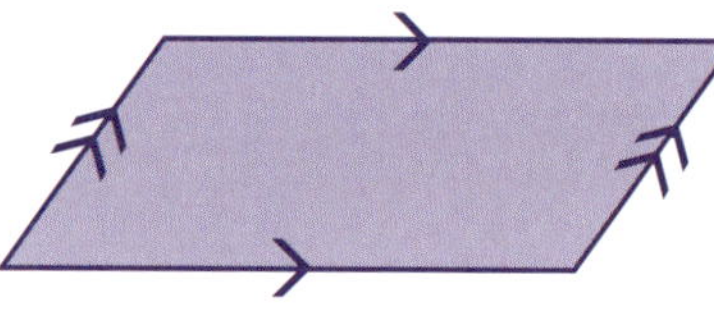

pentagon

A 2D shape with 5 straight sides

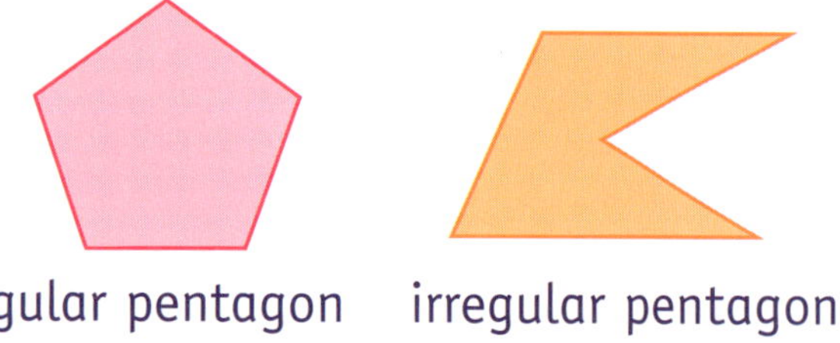

regular pentagon irregular pentagon

place value

The value of a numeral depending on its position in a number

396 = 300 + 90 + 6

754 = 7 hundreds + 5 tens + 4 ones

8·57 = 8 ones + 5 tenths + 7 hundredths

pm (post meridiem)

The time from midday to midnight

polygon

A shape with 3 or more straight sides

eg

prism

A 3D object with identical ends. All other faces are rectangles. The ends give a prism its name.

triangular prism

probability

The chance of something happening, eg certain, impossible, likely, unlikely.

product

When numbers are multiplied, the answer is called the product.

pyramid

A 3D object with one flat base. All other faces are triangles coming to a point at the apex. The base shape gives a pyramid its name.

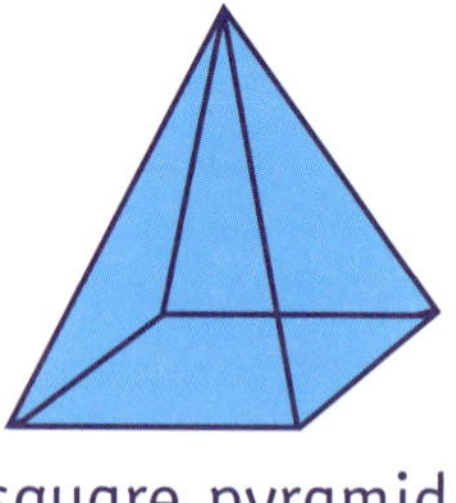

square pyramid

quadrilateral

A 2D shape with 4 straight sides

Dictionary

rhombus

A quadrilateral with all sides equal and opposite sides parallel. It is a special parallelogram.

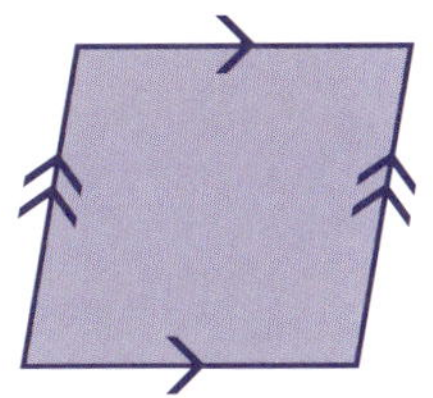

rounding (to nearest 10)

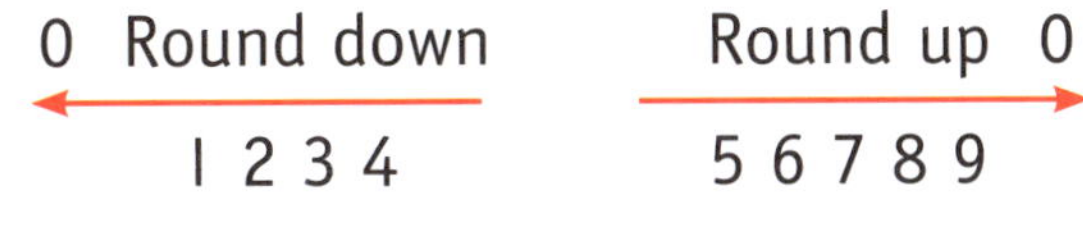

eg 675 ⟶ 700
(rounded to the nearest 100)
4492 ⟶ 4000
(rounded to the nearest 1000)

tally

Count and record in groups of 5

𝍸 = 5   𝍸 𝍸 ||| = 13

three-dimensional objects (3D)

Solid shapes that have length, width and height

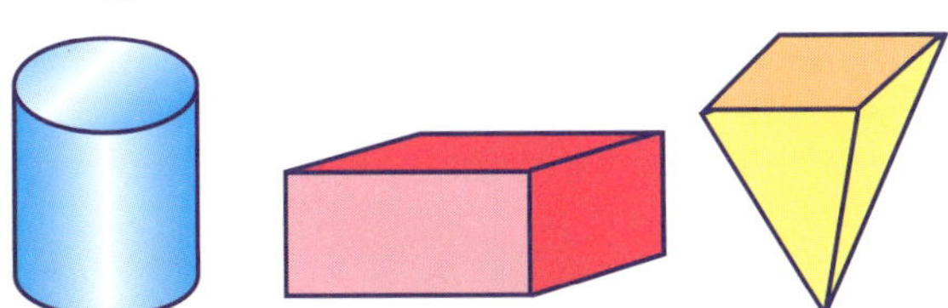

time

analogue

digital

1 hour = 60 minutes

1 minute = 60 seconds

trapezium

A quadrilateral that has one pair of parallel sides

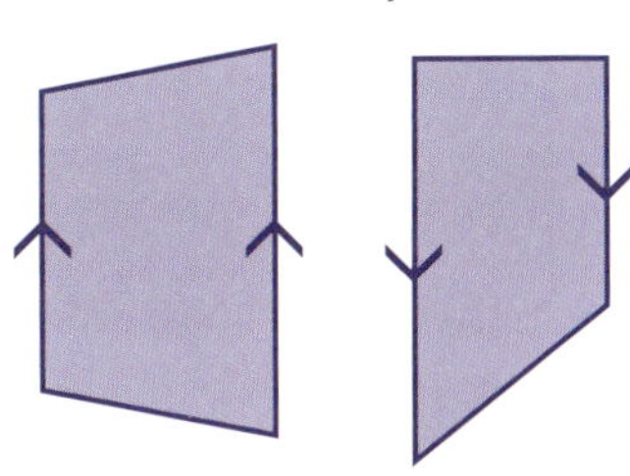

triangle

A 2D shape with 3 straight sides

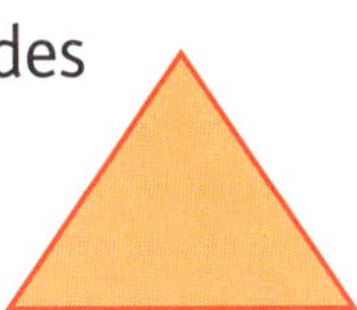

two-dimensional shapes (2D)

Shapes that only have length and width

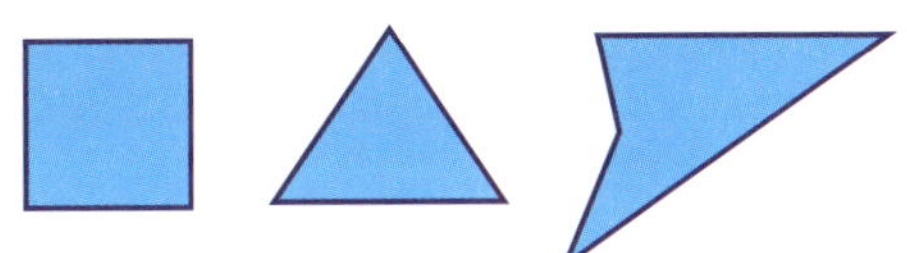

vertex

The point where the arms of an angle meet

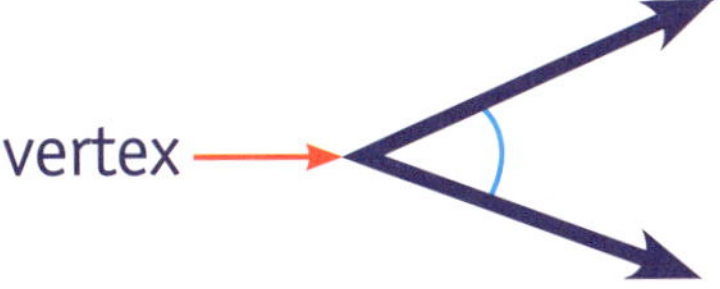

volume

The amount of space a solid object takes up

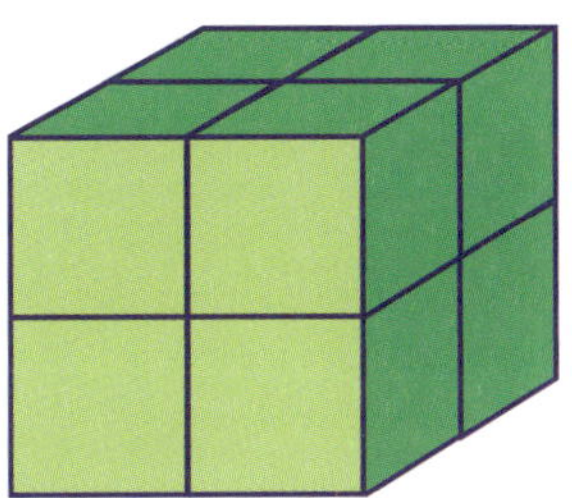

Unit 1 Place value with four-digit numbers

Place value

1 The zeros are missing!
Rewrite the numbers with zeros in the correct positions.

a	57	five hundred and seven	
b	31	three hundred and one	
c	426	four thousand and twenty-six	
d	72	seven thousand and twenty	
e	89	eight thousand and nine	
f	15	one thousand, five hundred	

Zeros are place holders. They keep numbers in their correct place value positions.

2 Write these numbers on the place value chart.

	Th	H	T	O
a seventy-two				
b one thousand, thirty-five tens and eight				
c nine thousand and six				
d six thousand, four tens and seven				
e eight thousand, five hundred and nine				
f two hundred and thirteen				
g twenty-eight				
h five thousand, one hundred and nine tens				

3 From the place value chart write:

a the largest number. ___________

b the smallest number. ___________

c a number with 35 tens. ___________

d a number with 90 hundreds. ___________

e a number with 0 ones. ___________

f an even number. ___________

g a number between 5000 and 5900. ___________

h an odd number. ___________

i a number with 5 in the hundreds place and 9 in the ones place. ___________

Challenge! Write 6 examples from real life where numbers in the thousands are used.

Unit 1 Position on a number line

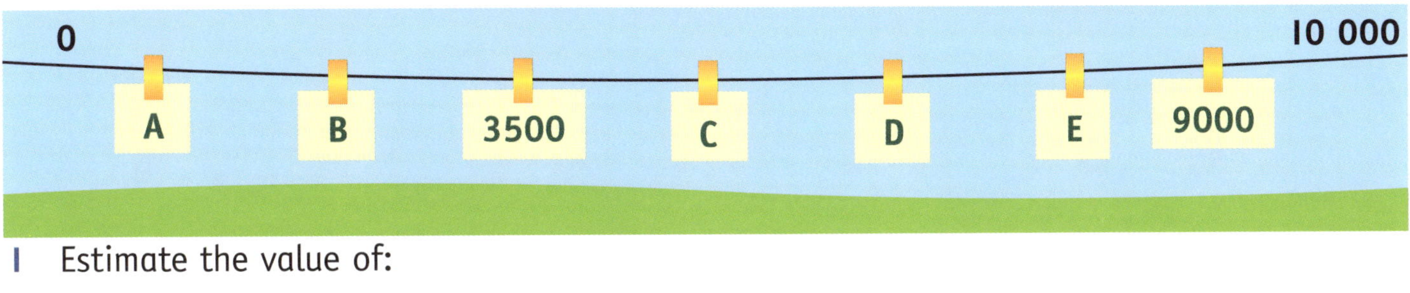

1 Estimate the value of:

A ________ B ________ C ________ D ________ E ________

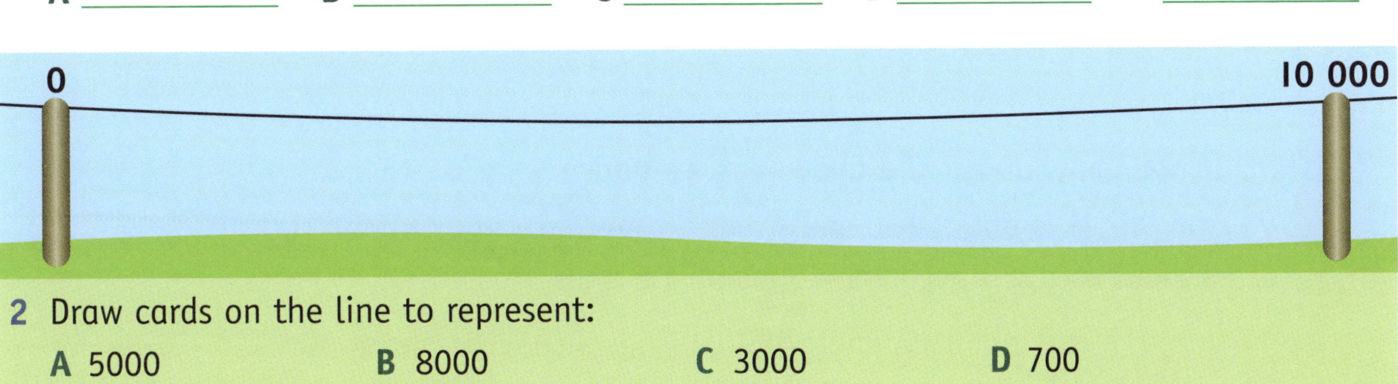

2 Draw cards on the line to represent:

A 5000 **B** 8000 **C** 3000 **D** 700

E 6300 **F** 1800 **G** 9950 **H** 2472

3 Write the new score for each contestant.

	Name	Score	New points	New score
a	Zoe	1720	100	
b	Lin	2010	170	
c	Sara	1850	200	
d	Micky	2100	130	
e	Ju	1990	110	

f Write the contestants' scores in ascending order. ______ ______ ______ ______ ______

4 Write a description of each number.

eg **4300** Is an even number between 4000 and 5000. It has three hundreds.	a **7063**
b **1004**	c **9999**

Mastery Checklist I can: ☐ understand zeroes in place value
☐ use place value to 10 000.

Unit 2 Addition

What do we know about the answer if we add:

1 74 and 96? It is about 100 more than 74 because 96 is about 100.
It will end with a 0 because 4 ones plus 6 ones are 10.

2 17 and 47? It is about 50 more than 17 because 47 is about 50.
It will end with a 4 because 7 plus 7 is 14.
It is about 50 plus 20.
It will be 50 plus 14. Take 3 off the 17 to make the 47 into 50.

3 74 and 21? It is 1 more than 74 and 20.

4 Two numbers to equal 43?
Look for 7 and 6, or 8 and 5, or 2 and 1, or 9 and 4 in the ones to end with a 3.

1 Use compensation strategies plus your addition facts to answer these questions.

a 74 + ______ = 83 b ______ + 47 = 64 c 63 + ______ = 88

d ______ + 47 = 59 e 96 + ______ = 105 f 15 + ______ = 53

2 Use the clues and facts to find two numbers that total:

a 24 = ______ + ______ b 55 = ______ + ______ c 91 = ______ + ______

d 25 = ______ + ______ e 90 = ______ + ______ f 99 = ______ + ______

g 26 = ______ + ______ h 62 = ______ + ______ i 78 = ______ + ______

3 Find three numbers that total:

a 144 = ______ + ______ + ______ b 86 = ______ + ______ + ______

4 What strategies and facts helped you in question 3?

____

____

____

AC9M4A01 Algebra **MA2-AR-01 • MA2-AR-02** Additive relations A • Select strategies flexibly to solve addition and subtraction problems of up to 3 digits
Additive relations B • Complete number sentences involving additive relations to find unknown quantities

Unit 2 Addition strategies

1 Partition numbers and use the jump strategy.

a 48 + 15 = ______ b 66 + 35 = ______ c 54 + 27 = ______
d 87 + 36 = ______ e 33 + 49 = ______ f 68 + 83 = ______
g 124 + 35 = ______ h 118 + 67 = ______ i 136 + 49 = ______

2 Partition numbers and use the split strategy.

a 58 + 14 = 50 + 10 + 8 + 4 = ______
b 75 + 45 = ______ + ______ + ______ + ______ = ______
c 46 + 86 = ______ + ______ + ______ + ______ = ______
d 93 + 75 = ______ + ______ + ______ + ______ = ______
e 127 + 67 = ______ + ______ + ______ + ______ + ______ = ______
f 155 + 36 = ______ + ______ + ______ + ______ + ______ = ______
g 137 + 43 = ______ + ______ + ______ + ______ + ______ = ______

3 Partition numbers and use the compensation strategy.

a 42 + 39 = 42 + 40 − 1 = ______
b 63 + 32 = ______ + ______ + ______ = ______
c 18 + 78 = ______ + ______ − ______ = ______
d 54 + 19 = ______ + ______ − ______ = ______
e 146 + 59 = ______ + ______ + ______ − ______ = ______
f 316 + 68 = ______ + ______ + ______ − ______ = ______

4 Double these numbers.

11	12	13	14	15	16	17	18	19	20

5 Use doubles to help.

a 14 + 15 = ______ b 16 + 15 = ______ c 11 + 12 = ______ d 20 + 19 = ______
e 17 + 16 = ______ f 14 + 12 = ______ g 19 + 17 = ______ h 13 + 15 = ______

Challenge! Add these mentally!

a 53 + 59 ☐ b 237 + 212 ☐ c 408 + 353 ☐
d 294 + 106 ☐ e 556 + 147 ☐ f 527 + 495 ☐

Unit 2 Addition using a number line

1 What must be added to make 100? Count on tens first, then ones.

a 63 ______ b 46 ______ c 28 ______ d 55 ______ e 71 ______

2 What must be added to make $1? Count on.

a 12c ______ b 39c ______ c 65c ______

d 82c ______ e 97c ______

3 Use the number lines for these.

a 143 + 28 = ______

143 153 163 171

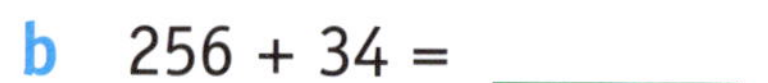

b 256 + 34 = ______

c 195 + 66 = ______

d 318 + 74 = ______

e 534 + 128 = ______

4 Add the ones first, then the tens, then the hundreds. Use one of your strategies to check your answer.

a
```
   63
 + 24
 ----
```
b
```
   85
 + 12
 ----
```
c
```
   79
 + 20
 ----
```
d
```
  231
+ 356
-----
```
e
```
  410
+ 379
-----
```
f
```
  105
+ 573
-----
```
g
```
  327
+ 512
-----
```
h
```
  282
+ 614
-----
```
i
```
  135
+ 464
-----
```
j
```
  783
+ 105
-----
```
k
```
  416
+  83
-----
```
l
```
  922
+  57
-----
```

5 There are 231 jelly beans in one bowl and 267 in another. How many jelly beans altogether?

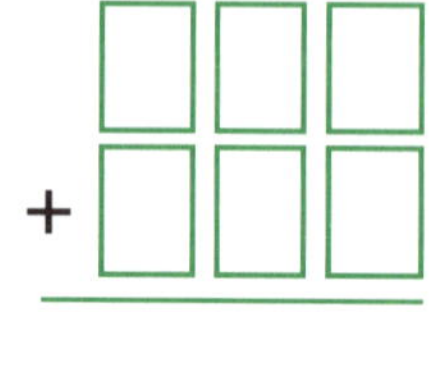

6 At the fish market Joe sold 82 fish and Jill sold 307 fish. How many were sold altogether?

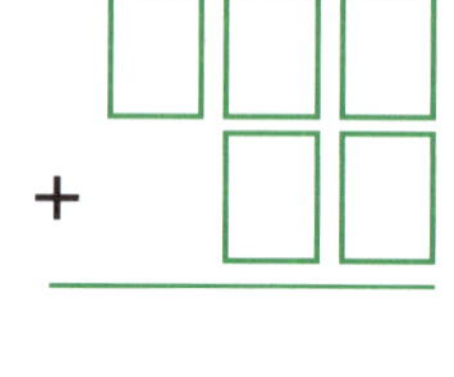

 AC9M4N06 Number MA2-AR-01 Additive relations A • Select strategies flexibly to solve addition and subtraction problems of up to 3 digits • Additive relations B • Partition, rearrange and regroup numbers to at least 1000 to solve additive problems

Unit 2 Addition with trading

1 Cross off 10 ones and add 1 ten in each diagram.

eg

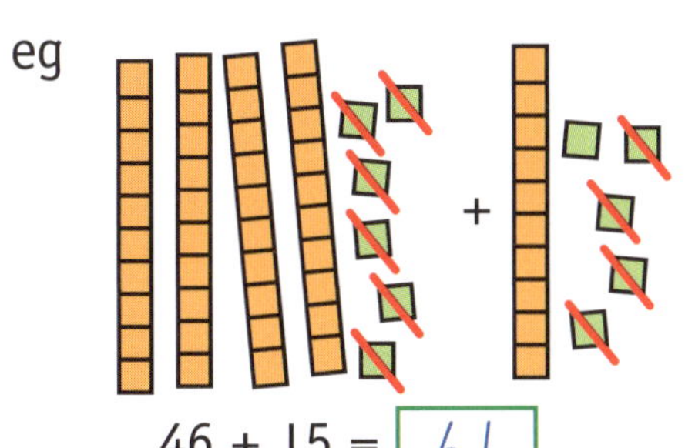

46 + 15 = 61

a

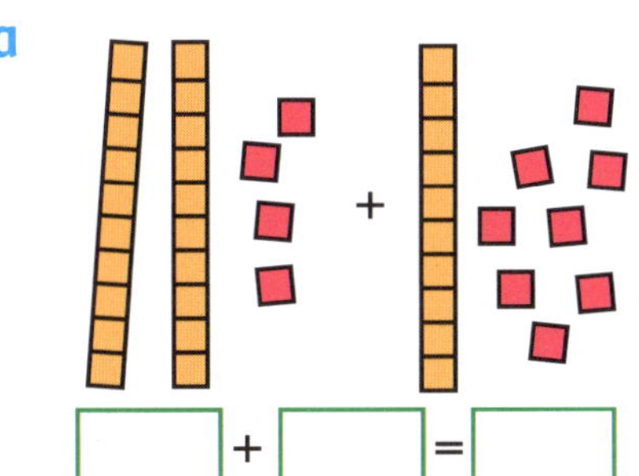

☐ + ☐ = ☐

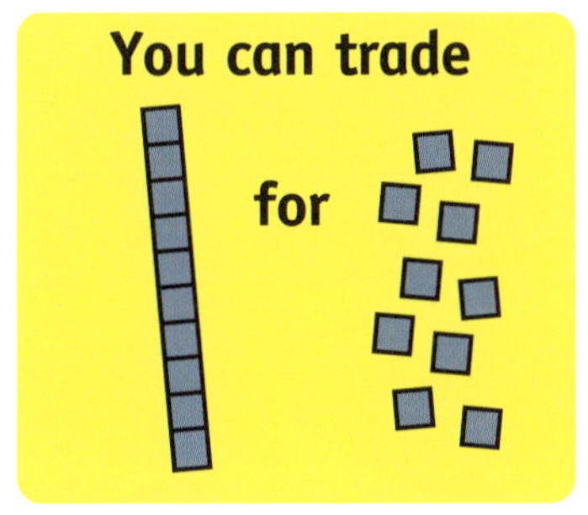

b

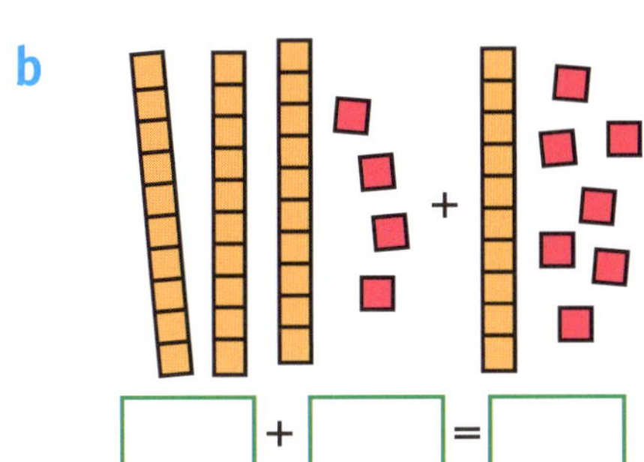

☐ + ☐ = ☐

c

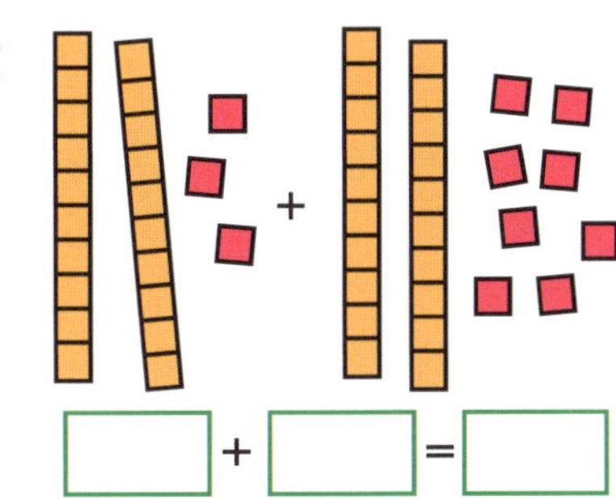

☐ + ☐ = ☐

d

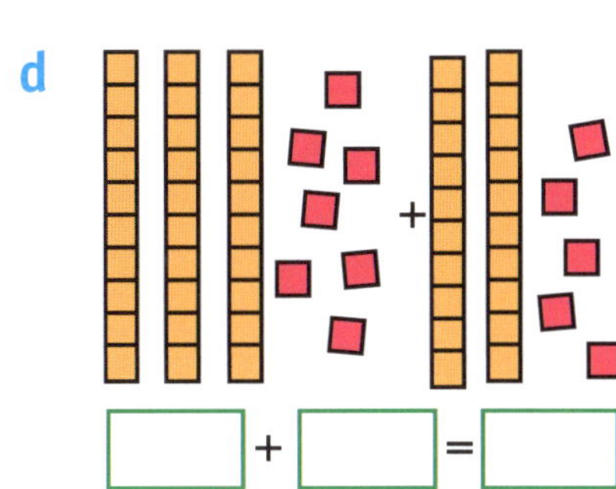

☐ + ☐ = ☐

2

a

	Tens	Ones
	5	7
+		9

b

	Tens	Ones
	6	4
+		8

c

	Tens	Ones
	3	5
+		6

d

	Tens	Ones
	8	3
+		8

Setting out

	Tens	Ones
	1	
	2	9
+	2	3
	5	2

10 ones have been traded for 1 ten.

e

	Tens	Ones
	4	9
+	2	7

f

	Tens	Ones
	3	5
+	3	7

g

	Tens	Ones
	2	8
+	4	8

h

	Tens	Ones
	7	8
+	1	5

i

	Tens	Ones
	3	6
+	2	7

j

	Tens	Ones
	1	6
+	4	6

k

	Tens	Ones
	5	6
+	2	9

l

	Tens	Ones
	7	9
+	1	4

m

	Tens	Ones
	3	5
+	5	9

Mastery Checklist

I can:
- ☐ use different strategies to add
- ☐ partition numbers
- ☐ use a number line to add
- ☐ trade ones for ten to add.

Work backwards

The children have 68 marbles altogether. John has 8 less than Tim. Tim has 3 more than Ali who has half as many as Von. Von has 28 marbles. How many do John, Tim and Ali have?

Unit 3 Two-digit subtraction

Jerry

78 − 23 = 45	69 − 15 = 54
85 − 23 = 62	77 − 45 = 42
59 − 27 = 22	48 − 16 = 32

Mark ______

Josie

64 − 31 = 33	72 − 30 = 40
99 − 63 = 35	59 − 15 = 44
36 − 15 = 21	47 − 27 = 27

Mark ______

1 Jerry and Josie finished their maths tests.

a Mark their work. **b** Give each of them a mark.

c Rewrite the ones that are wrong and work out the correct answer.

2 Complete these number patterns.

a
7 − 2 = ______
70 − 20 = ______
700 − 200 = ______

b
9 − 4 = ______
90 − ______ = ______
900 − ______ = ______

c
8 − 3 = ______
______ − ______ = ______
______ − ______ = ______

d
9 − 7 = ______
______ − ______ = ______
______ − ______ = ______

e
5 − 2 = 3
15 − 2 = ______
25 − 2 = ______
85 − 2 = ______

f
7 − 4 = ______
17 − 4 = ______
27 − 4 = ______
67 − 4 = ______

g
8 − 4 = ______
18 − 4 = ______
28 − 4 = ______
58 − 4 = ______

h
6 − 3 = ______
16 − 3 = ______
26 − 3 = ______
96 − 3 = ______

Unit 3 Subtraction strategies

Mixed 

1 Use strategy A.

a $53 - 28 =$ 53-30+2
$=$ ____

b $64 - 29 = 64 -$ ____ + ____
$=$ ____

c $46 - 19 = 46 -$ ____ + ____
$=$ ____

d $85 - 57 = 85 -$ ____ + ____
$=$ ____

e $97 - 68 = 97 -$ ____ + ____
$=$ ____

f $73 - 36 = 73 -$ ____ + ____
$=$ ____

Strategy A
$64 - 18 =$
$64 - 20 + 2 = 46$

Strategy B
$71 - 24 =$
$71 - 20 - 4 = 47$

2 Use strategy B.

a $67 - 43 = 67 - 40 - 3$
$=$ ____

b $91 - 52 = 91 -$ ____ − ____
$=$ ____

c $52 - 24 = 52 -$ ____ − ____
$=$ ____

d $75 - 31 = 75 -$ ____ − ____
$=$ ____

e $80 - 33 = 80 -$ ____ − ____
$=$ ____

f $41 - 24 = 41 -$ ____ − ____
$=$ ____

Partition
91 is 90 and 1.
Take away 90 then take away another 1.
Check answers by counting on.

3

	−	56	73	64	49	76	62	81	50
a	27								
b	38								

4

	−	61	91	70	62	87	74	90	83
a	32								
b	53								

5 Farmer Fred had 64 sheep. How many were left when he sold 39?

6 Ciara had 880 jelly beans. She was sick when she ate 132. How many were left?

Challenge!

Make up a subtraction problem about kites where the answer is 37.

Unit 3 Subtraction on a number line

To use a number line for subtraction, start from the right.

72 – 37

You can use little jumps

or big jumps.

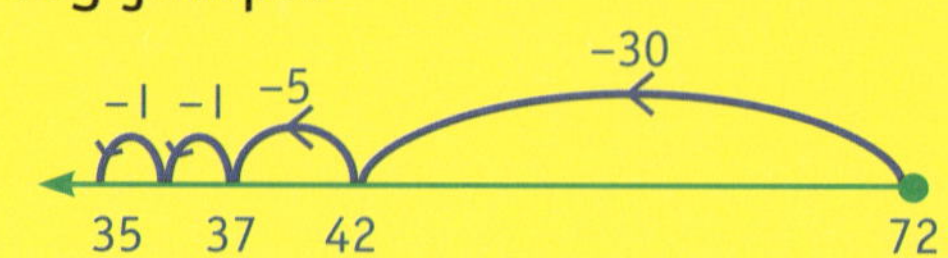

1 Subtract.

a 16 – 9 = ______ b 15 – 8 = ______
c 14 – 6 = ______ d 12 – 7 = ______
e 11 – 5 = ______ f 16 – 8 = ______
g 15 – 9 = ______ h 13 – 6 = ______
i 14 – 5 = ______ j 17 – 8 = ______

2 Use the number lines.

a 53 – 26 = ______ (number line ending at 53)

b 71 – 43 = ______ (number line ending at 71)

c 85 – 37 = ______ (number line ending at 85)

d 92 – 48 = ______

e 80 – 35 = ______

f 264 – 149 = ______

g 376 – 123 = ______

h 457 – 243 = ______

3 Jin loves olives. He had 73 jars in the pantry. Thieves broke in and stole 47 jars.

a How many did he have left? ______

b How did you work out your answer? ______

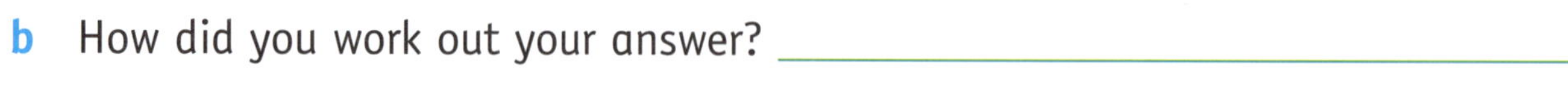

c Show another way. ______

d Which way was best? ______

e How can you check if you are correct? ______

Unit 3 Three-digit subtraction

3-digit subtraction

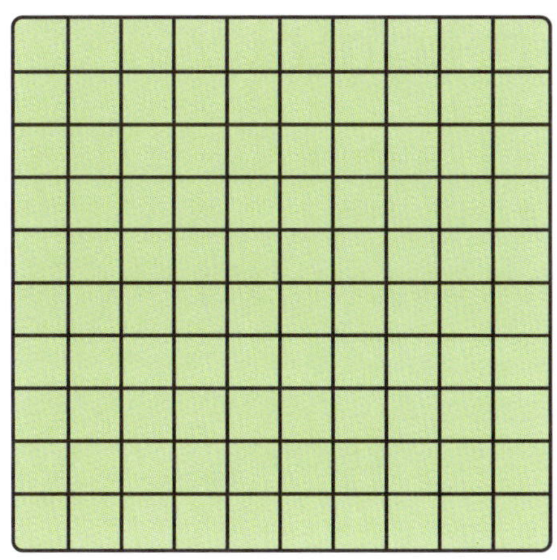

1 Use the hundred square to help.

a $100 - 56 =$ ______, $56 +$ ______ $= 100$

b $100 - 23 =$ ______, $23 +$ ______ $= 100$

c $100 - 49 =$ ______, $49 +$ ______ $= 100$

d $100 - 64 =$ ______, $64 +$ ______ $= 100$

e $100 - 11 =$ ______, $11 +$ ______ $= 100$

f $100 - 77 =$ ______, $77 +$ ______ $= 100$

2 Change from $1?

a ______

37c

b ______

c ______

d ______

e ______

3

a	b	c	d	e
346 − 125	877 − 542	539 − 413	621 − 320	959 − 426

f	g	h	i	j
148 − 23	273 − 153	759 − 532	485 − 165	907 − 506

k	l	m	n	o
986 − 144	890 − 770	679 − 238	748 − 341	485 − 21

Mastery Checklist

I can:
- ☐ subtract 2-digit numbers
- ☐ use different strategies to subtract
- ☐ use a number line to subtract
- ☐ subtract 3-digit numbers.

Work backwards

If I subtract 13 from a number, then double the answer, I get 28.

What is the number? ______

Problem solving

Work backwards, use a table

Four children brought home fish for dinner. Tam caught the smallest fish, 25 cm shorter than Grace's. Grace's fish was 10 cm longer than Teddy's. Teddy's fish was 12 cm longer than Harry's fish, which was 25 cm long. How long were the other fish?

Harry ⟶ Teddy ⟶ Grace ⟶ Tam

Harry's fish = 25 cm

Teddy's fish = 25 + 12 = ________

Grace's fish = ________

Tam's fish = ________

Check backwards: 22 + 25 – ______ – ______ = ______ cm = Harry's fish

1 The temperature in Dubbo on Wednesday was 5 degrees higher than in Wellington. Wellington was 8 degrees cooler than Parkes, which was 2 degrees hotter than Forbes. Forbes' temperature was 34 degrees, so what temperatures were reported at the other towns?

Forbes = ________

Parkes = ________

Wellington = ________

Dubbo = ________

2 In the maths test, Dee gained a better score than last week, but still 10 less than Kay. Kay's score was 5 less than her friend, Len. Len gained 12 more than Rod, who scored 85. Whose mark was highest and what were the other's scores?

____

____

____

3 Write your own problem with this ending.
Pete's house is 32 km from school. Who lives farthest from school?

____

____

____

I can solve problems by:

☐ finding unknown amounts ☐ writing algorithms to solve a problem.

Unit 4 Length

Guesses

Name	Height of snowman		
Ren	1 m 28 cm	128 cm	1·28 m
Jack	1 m 37 cm		
Josh		119 cm	
Asha		1·08 m	
Teri		124 cm	
Kim	1 m 10 cm		
Vito			1·42 m

At the Winter Carnival there was a competition to guess the height of the snowman.

1 Complete the guessing chart.

2 Write the guesses in descending order using the numbers in the middle column.

____

3 The snowman was 1 m 31 cm tall.

a Whose guess was the closest? _______________

b How close was it? _______________

c Whose guess was the furthest away? _______________

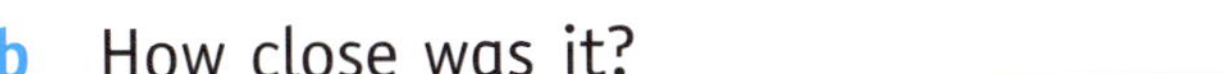

4 What is the difference in cm between the highest and lowest guesses? _______________

5 Write your height three ways. _______________ _______________ _______________

Challenge!

Using the Internet, find the heights of the (a) tallest and (b) shortest man and woman. Write their heights three ways.

Man	a		b	
Woman	a		b	

Unit 4 mm, cm, m

estimate and measure to check

metre m
centimetre cm
millimetre mm

1 Estimate in metres the:

a width of your classroom. ____________

b height of the board. ____________

c height of the classroom door. ____________

d length of the classroom. ____________

e width of the windows. ____________

Estimate in centimetres the:

f width of your desk. ____________

g length of this page. ____________

h length of your arm. ____________

i width of the door. ____________

Estimate in millimetres the:

j width of your pencil. ____________

k length of your thumbnail. ____________

l length of your pencil. ____________

m width of your hand. ____________

2 With a partner, measure the above items.

a ____________ b ____________ c ____________ d ____________ e ____________

f ____________ g ____________ h ____________ i ____________ j ____________

k ____________ l ____________ m ____________

3 Tick the answers that are close to your estimate.

4 Match each item to the unit of measurement you would use to find their length.

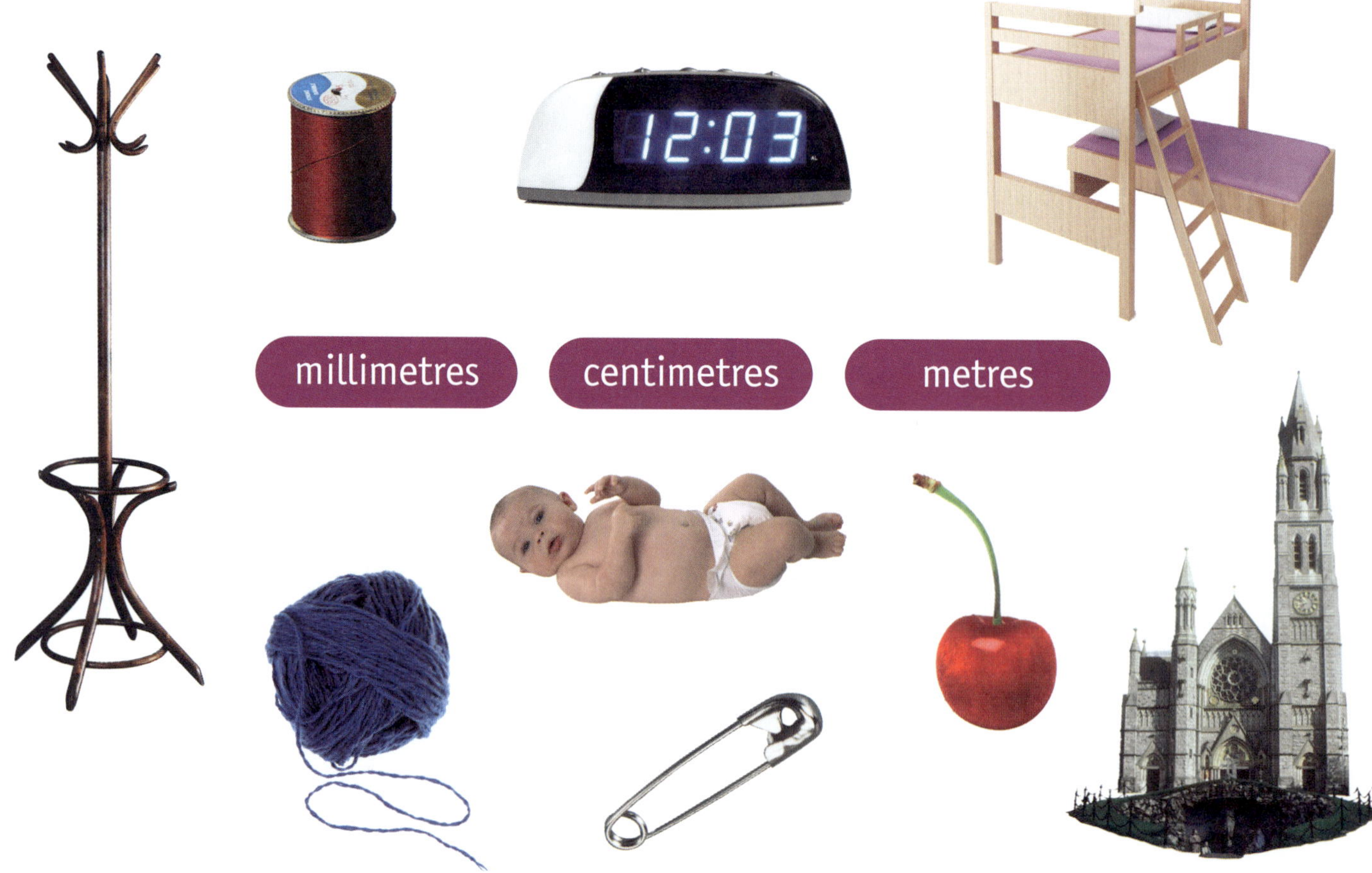

Unit 4 Perimeter

10 mm = 1 cm
100 cm = 1 m
1000 mm = 1 m

23 mm = 2·3 cm
356 cm = 3·56 m

Perimeter is the distance around the outside.
Add the lengths of all the sides.

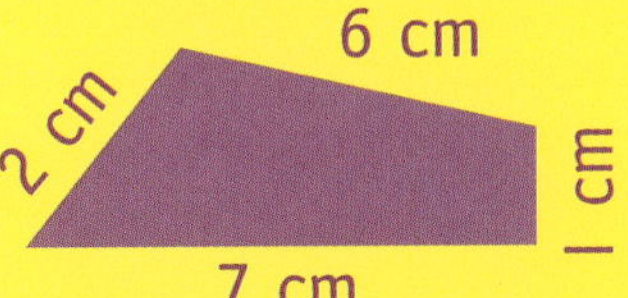

P = 6 + 1 + 7 + 2
= 16 cm

1 Write as centimetres.

a 50 mm ______ b 70 mm ______
c 80 mm ______ d 10 mm ______
e 100 mm ______ f 1 m ______ g 5 m ______
h 8 m ______ i 2·36 m ______ j 4·85 m ______

2 Write as metres.

a 300 cm ______ b 800 cm ______ c 700 cm ______
d 400 cm ______ e 200 cm ______ f 1000 mm ______
g 3000 mm ______ h 9000 mm ______ i 6000 mm ______
j 500 mm ______ k 2300 mm ______ l 842 cm ______

3 Find the perimeters.

a

P = ☐ + ☐ + ☐ + ☐
= ☐ cm

b

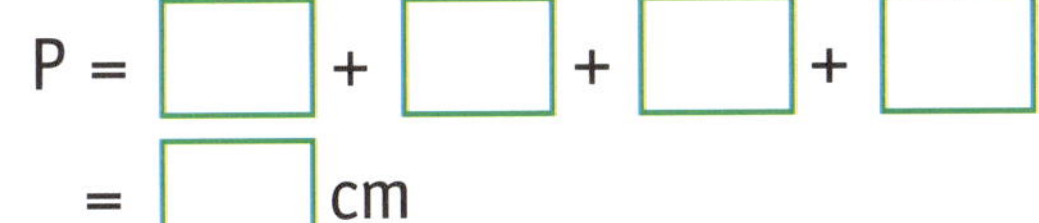

P = ☐ + ☐ + ☐ + ☐
= ☐ cm

c

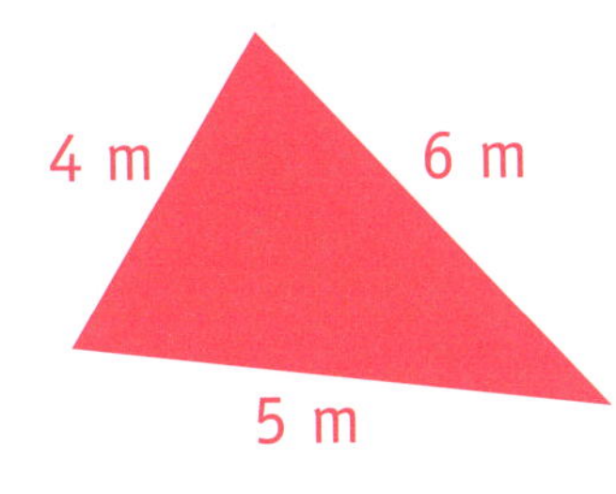

P = ☐ + ☐ + ☐
= ☐ m

d

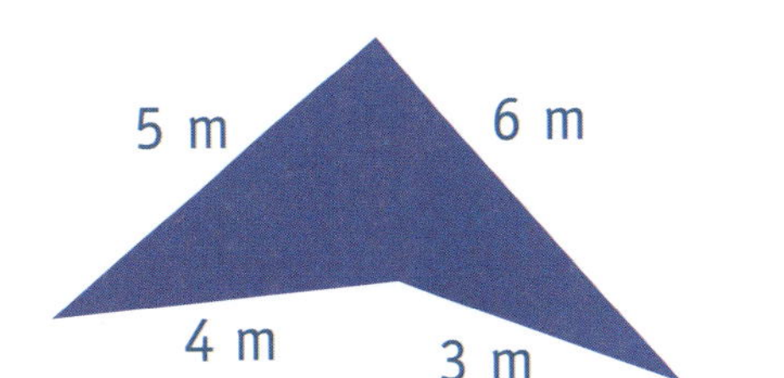

P = ☐ + ☐ + ☐ + ☐
= ☐ m

Mastery Checklist

I can: ☐ record lengths in metres and centimetres in different ways
☐ estimate lengths
☐ measure using mm, cm and m
☐ add to find perimeters.

Challenge!

Farmer Jones has a small paddock with a perimeter of 58 m. Two sides are 12 m each and another side is 16 m.

How long is the fourth side? ☐

Unit 5 Animal fractions

1 How many:

a dogs? ______ b cats? ______ c sheep? ______ d animals? ______

2 How many is $\frac{1}{4}$ of the:

a dogs? ______ b cats? ______ c sheep? ______ d animals? ______

3 Of which animal group can we find:

a an eighth? ______ b a quarter? ______ c a sixth? ______

4 What fraction of the dogs is:

a 6 dogs? ______ b 4 dogs? ______ c 3 dogs? ______

5 What fraction of the total number of animals is:

a the dogs? ______ b the cats? ______ c the sheep? ______

AC9M4N03 Number MA2-PF-01 Partitioned fractions A • Create fractional parts of a length using techniques other than repeated halving

Unit 5 Naming fractions

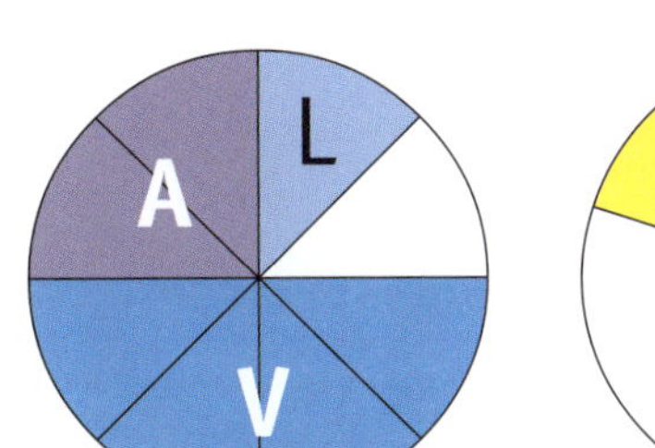

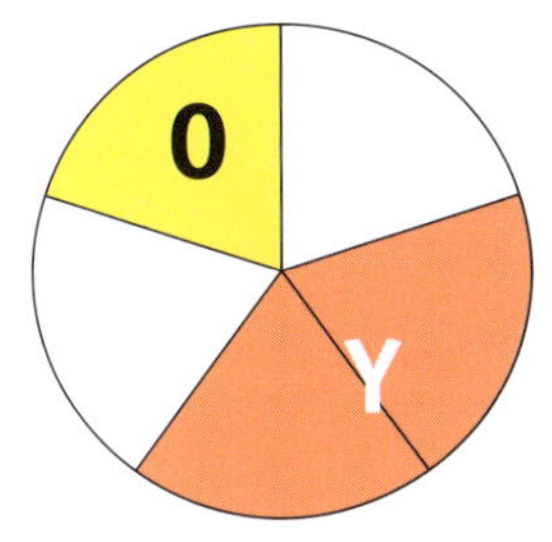

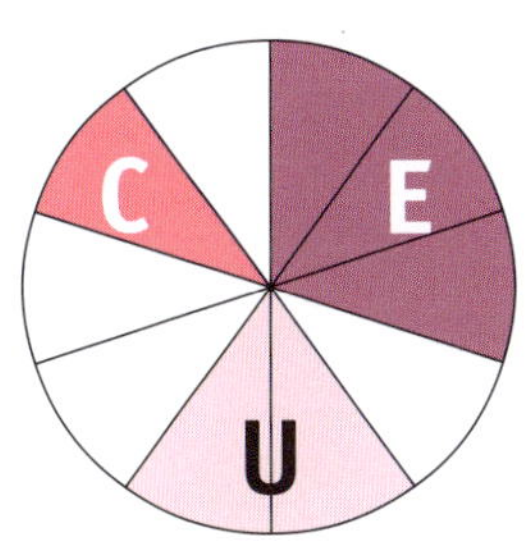

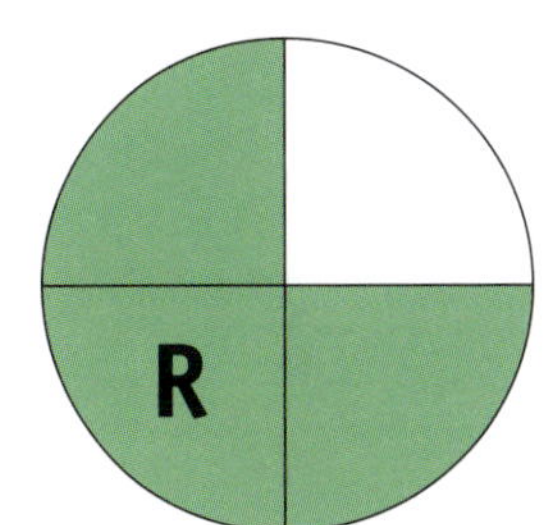

1 Find the fraction part to match the fraction. Write its letter in the box.

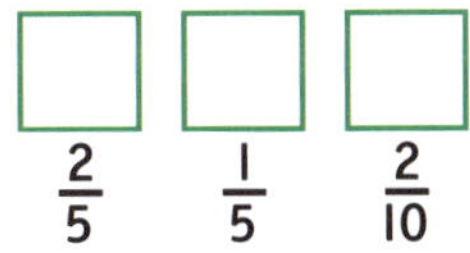

$\frac{2}{5}$ $\frac{1}{5}$ $\frac{2}{10}$

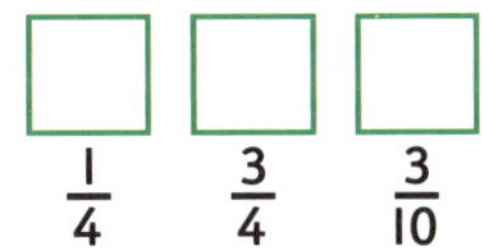

$\frac{1}{4}$ $\frac{3}{4}$ $\frac{3}{10}$

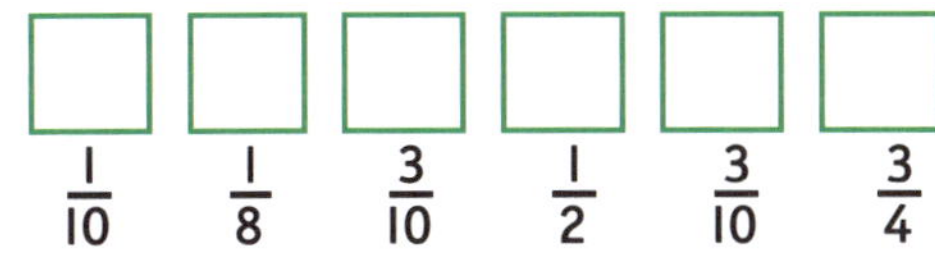

$\frac{1}{10}$ $\frac{1}{8}$ $\frac{3}{10}$ $\frac{1}{2}$ $\frac{3}{10}$ $\frac{3}{4}$

2 Fractions add to make a whole.

eg

red + blue

$\frac{3}{4} + \frac{1}{4} = 1$

a

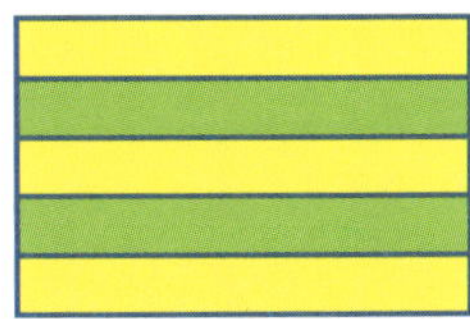

green + yellow

b

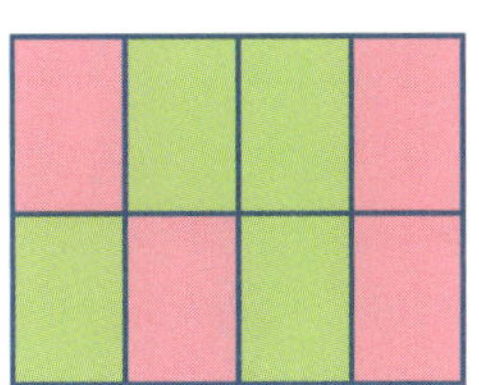

pink + green

c

orange + purple

d

red + yellow

e

green + blue

f

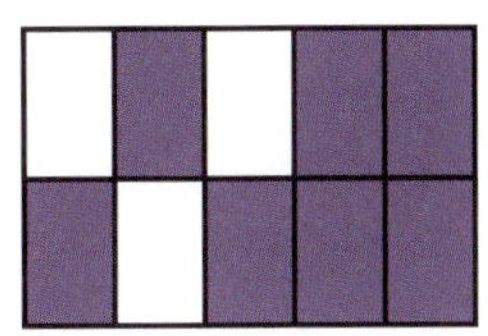

purple + white

g

pink + orange

h

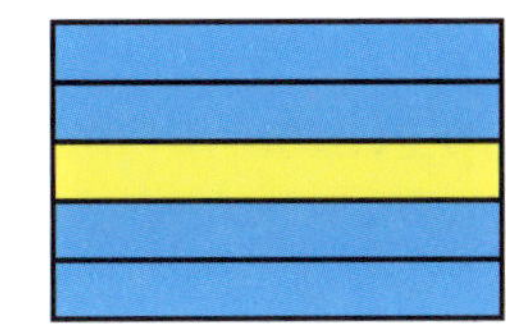

yellow + blue

Challenge! Use the animals on page 16.

a $\frac{5}{6}$ of dogs = ☐ b $\frac{3}{4}$ of cats = ☐ c $\frac{1}{4}$ of cats plus sheep = ☐

d $\frac{3}{4}$ of sheep plus cats = ☐ e $\frac{3}{4}$ of cats plus dogs = ☐

Unit 5 Tenths

A B C D E F G H I

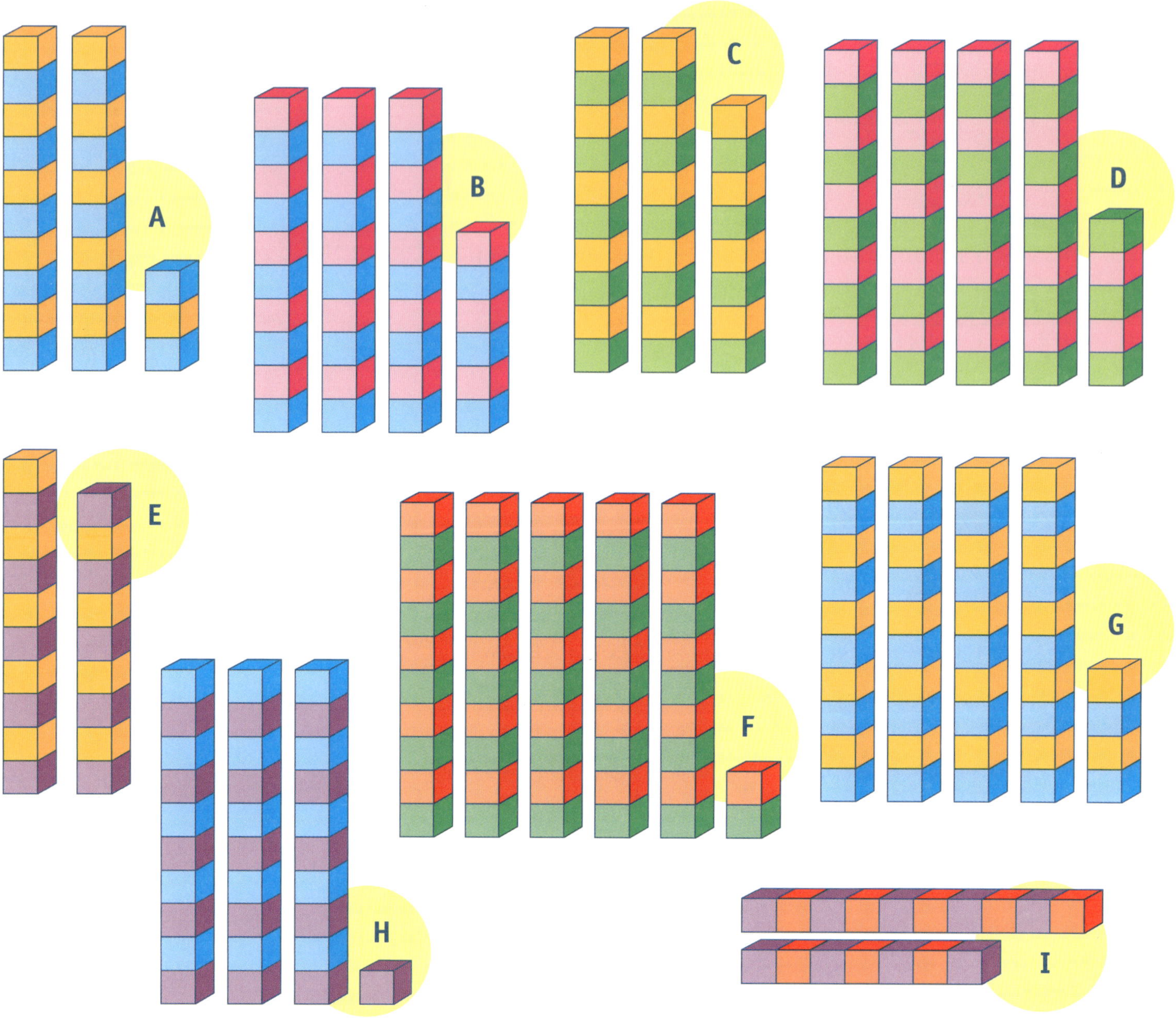

Each complete tower has 10 cubes. **A** has 23 cubes. 2 complete towers and $\frac{3}{10}$. $2\frac{3}{10}$ or 2·3

1 Write each group as a fraction and a decimal.

Group	Fraction	Decimal
B		
C		
D		
E		

Group	Fraction	Decimal
F		
G		
H		
I		

2 How many cubes are needed to build each group?

A ______ B ______ C ______ D ______ E ______ F ______ G ______ H ______ I ______

Unit 5 Tenths and hundredths

10ths and 100ths

1 Write the tenths and the decimal.

a 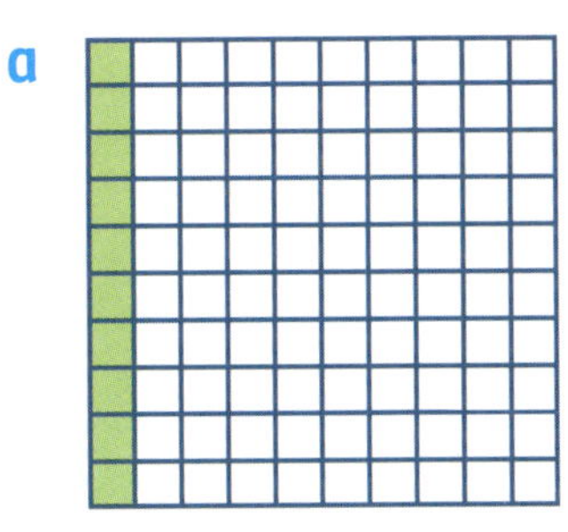

_____ = 0· _____

b

_____ = _____

c 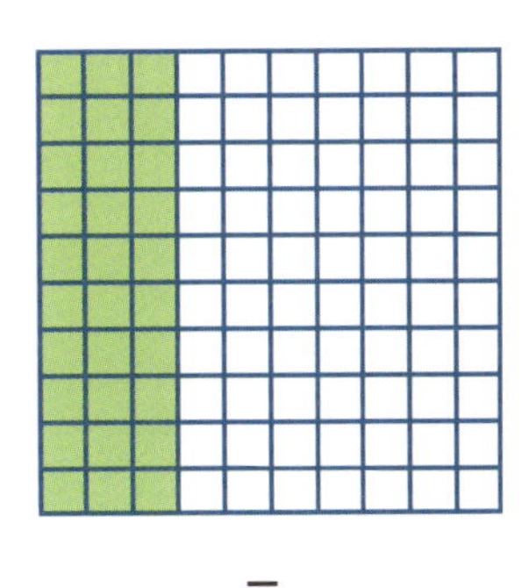

_____ = _____

d 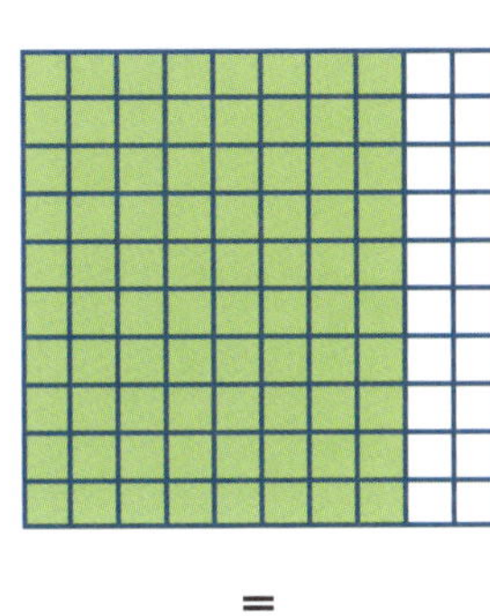

_____ = _____

2 Write the tenths and the hundredths and the decimal.

a 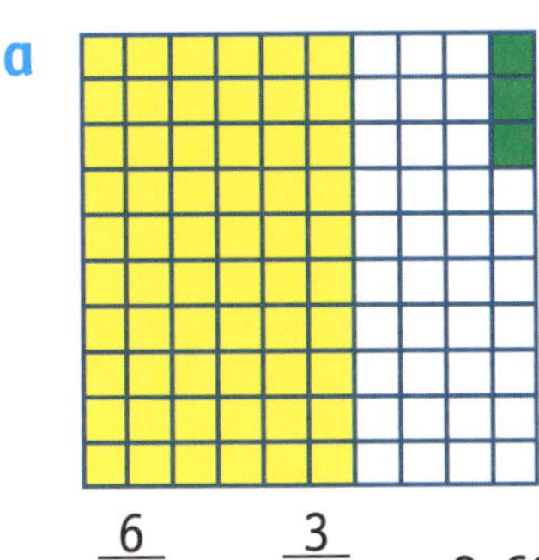

$\frac{6}{10} + \frac{3}{100} = 0{\cdot}63$

b

_____ + _____ = _____

c 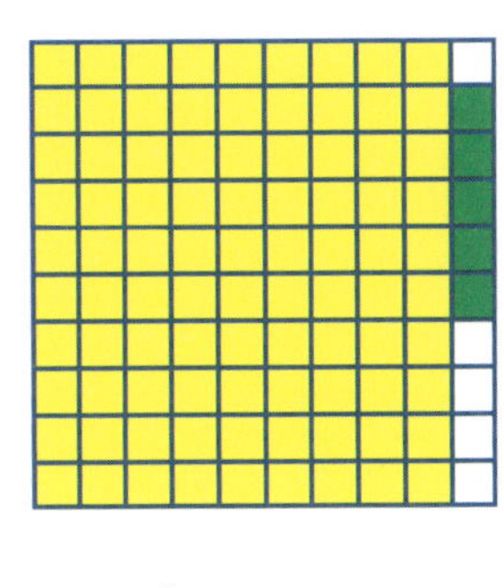

_____ + _____ = _____

d 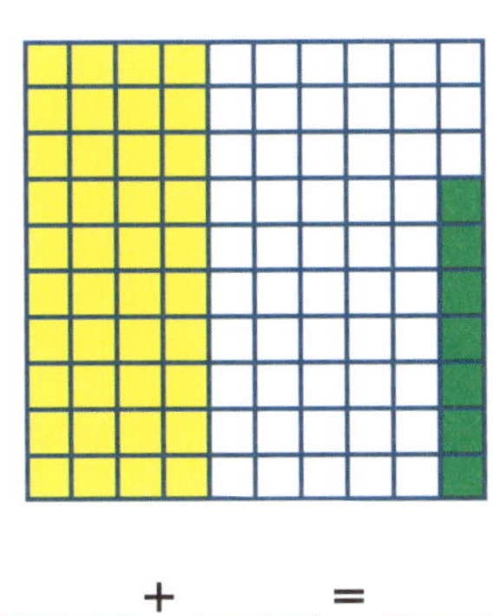

_____ + _____ = _____

3 Colour the tenths and the hundredths separately to show:

a 0·54 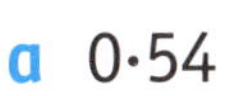 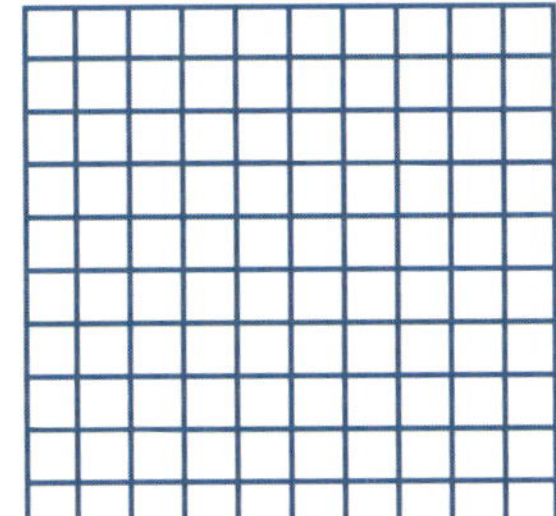

b 0·28 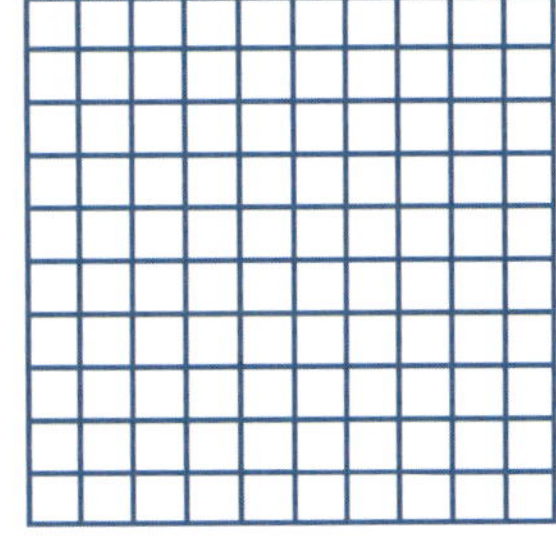

c 0·07 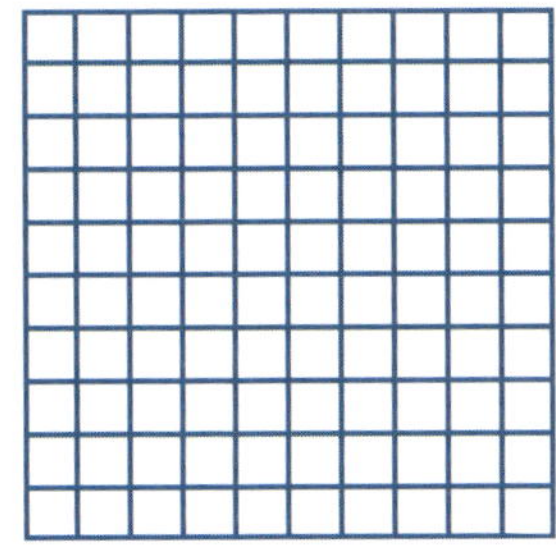

4 Circle the number in the tenths place.

a 0·47 b 1·35 c 7·99 d 13·58

5 Underline the number in the hundredths place.

a 2·57 b 9·05 c 24·74 d 19·32

6 Write these decimals from largest to smallest. 0·18 0·61 0·09 0·35 0·23 0·59

____

7 Write these decimals on the number line. 0·47 0·67 0·7 0·25 0·97 0·5

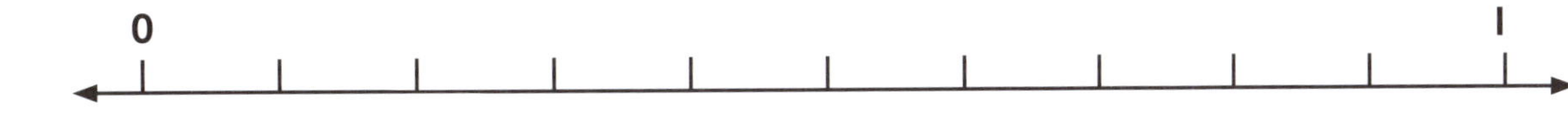

Mastery Checklist I can:
- ☐ find fractions of groups
- ☐ identify and match fractions
- ☐ make connections between fractions and decimals
- ☐ use tenths and hundredths.

AC9M4N01 Number MA2-RN-02 Representing numbers using place value B • Decimals: Extend the application of the place value system from whole numbers to tenths and hundredths • Make connections between fractions and decimal notation

Measure length

Investigation 1

Investigate how to measure a large area and record its dimensions accurately.

Choose a play area of your school ground to measure. Choose a partner to work with.

1 Name the area you choose to measure. ______

2 Which measuring tools will you use? ______

3 What other tools will you use? ______

4 Draw a sketch of the area here. Do not draw it to scale, but try to show the shape.

5 Are there any unusual shapes to measure? What are they? ______

______

6 Estimate the size of the area before you start to measure.

Length ______ Width ______

7 Which part will you measure first? ______

8 Write how you and your partner measure the area you chose.

a ______

b ______

c ______

d ______

e ______

9 Write how you checked your measurements.

______

______

10 What difficulties have you found? ______

______

AC9M4M02 Measurement **MAO-WM-01** Working mathematically • choosing and applying mathematical techniques to solve problems • communicating thinking and reasoning coherently and clearly • **MA2-GM-02** Geometric measure B • Length: Use scaled instruments to measure and compare lengths

Measure length

Investigation 1

measure large areas

11 Record the measurements of your chosen area here, using decimal notation, eg Width of the larger area, 2·35 m.

12 Draw the school ground area again here.

13 Label the drawing with your measurements.

14 Compare your measurements with others in the class. Why might they be different?

To carry out these tasks, I need to:

- [ ] use measuring tools
- [ ] measure length accurately
- [ ] use decimal notation to record length
- [ ] understand why two people may have different results
- [ ] work well with a partner.

I enjoyed this task!

☆☆☆☆☆

Revision

1 What is the number?

308 tens and 7

3807  3087 3078 3870

---

2 Which is the same as:

62 + 47

62 + 70 + 4 | 60 + 20 + 47 | 62 + 40 + 7 | 62 + 42 + 7

---

3 You would measure the length of your classroom in:

metres | **centimetres** | **millimetres** | **books**

---

4 How many tenths are coloured?

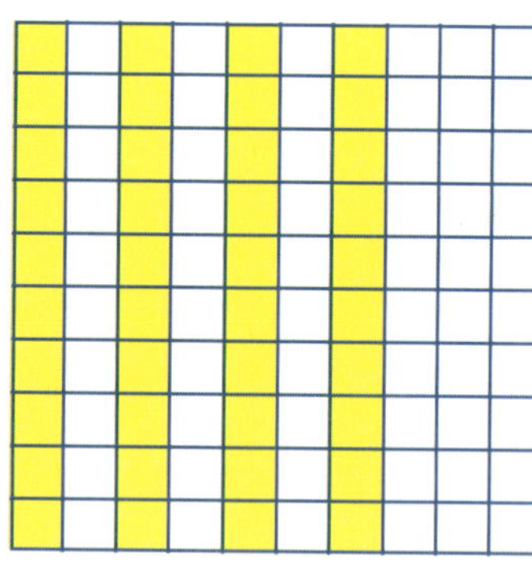

2 | 4 | 40 | 10

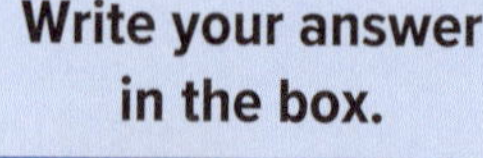

5 Alex has 0·4, or four ☐ of his money in the bank.

Revision

6 Which number belongs in the star?

Shade one bubble.

43 ◯ 37 ◯ 23 ◯ 33 ◯

7 Carl had 336 jelly beans. Mum let him eat 124. How many were left?

212 ◯ 202 ◯ 112 ◯ 252 ◯

8 What fraction is coloured red?

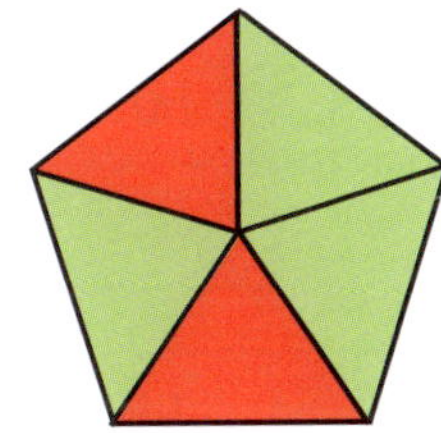

$\frac{3}{5}$ ◯ $\frac{2}{5}$ ◯ $\frac{2}{3}$ ◯ $\frac{3}{2}$ ◯

9 Which of the following shows the correct tenths + hundredths and the decimal?

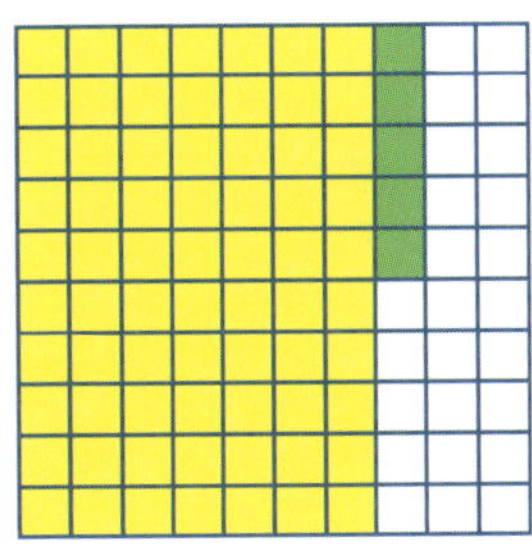

$\frac{7}{10} + \frac{5}{100}$, 0·75 ◯ $\frac{7}{10} + \frac{2}{100}$, 0·72 ◯ $\frac{3}{10} + \frac{8}{100}$, 0·38 ◯ $\frac{3}{10} + \frac{2}{100}$, 0·32 ◯

10 The perimeter of this rectangle is:

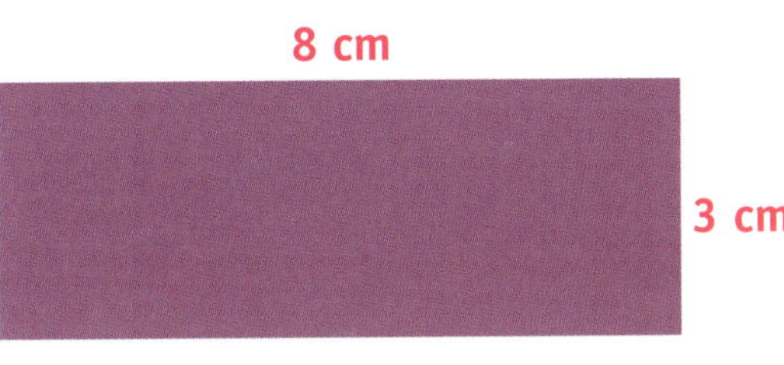

24 cm ◯ 11 cm ◯ 22 cm ◯ 38 cm ◯

Unit 6 Number facts 3×, 4×, 5×, 10×

1

Across	Down
a 5 × 10	a 6 × 9
b 6 × 0	c 6 × 6
c 1 × 3	d 5 × 5
d 3 × 8	e 3 × 6
e 4 × 4	f 6 × 7
f 5 × 9	g 4 × 6
g 4 × 7	
h 4 × 8	
i 2 × 7	

2 Complete.

a

×	0	7	1	8	6	2	4	10	3	9	5
3											

b

×	7	3	9	6	0	5	1	8	2	10	4
4											

c

×	1	10	3	8	0	4	2	6	9	5	7
5											

d

×	6	0	10	1	5	7	2	8	4	9	3
10											

3 Fill in the missing numbers.

a 5 × ______ = 55 b 8 × ______ = 24 c ______ × 4 = 28 d 5 × ______ = 0

e 4 × ______ = 32 f 6 × 5 = ______ g 4 × ______ = 4 h 5 × 9 = ______

i ______ × 4 = 16 j 7 × ______ = 21 k ______ × 9 = 36 l ______ × 3 = 27

Challenge!

Jo-Jo had 2 mice.

Every month the number of mice doubled.

In how many months would there be 2048? 

Unit 6 Number facts

1 a $2 \times 3 \times 4 =$ ______ b $2 \times 4 \times 3 =$ ______ c $3 \times 2 \times 4 =$ ______

d $3 \times 4 \times 2 =$ ______ e $4 \times 2 \times 3 =$ ______ f $4 \times 3 \times 2 =$ ______

2 Do you know your 14 times table?
It is easy if you know the 4 times table and 10 times table.

14 times table

a	1 × 10 = 10	1 × 4 = 4	1 × 14 = 10 + 4 =
b	2 × 10 = 20	2 × 4 = 8	2 × 14 = + =
c	3 × 10 =	3 × 4 =	3 × 14 = + =
d	4 × 10 =	4 × 4 =	4 × 14 = + =
e	5 × 10 =	5 × 4 =	5 × 14 = + =
f	6 × 10 =	6 × 4 =	6 × 14 = + =
g	7 × 10 =	7 × 4 =	7 × 14 = + =
h	8 × 10 =	8 × 4 =	8 × 14 = + =
i	9 × 10 =	9 × 4 =	9 × 14 = + =
j	10 × 10 =	10 × 4 =	10 × 14 = + =

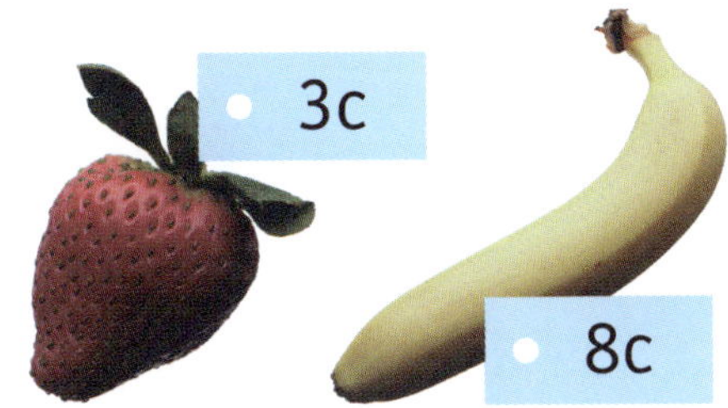

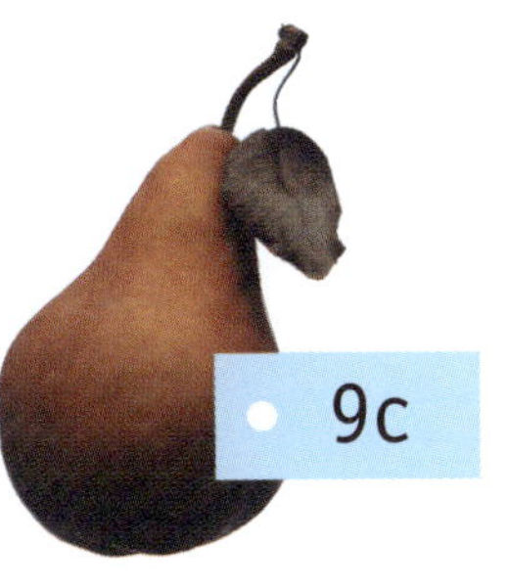

3 How much for:

	4	2	5	3	10
a strawberries					
b bananas					
c apples					
d pears					
e oranges					
f tomatoes					
g grapes					
h cherries					

Unit 6 Odds and evens (+ −)

Answer the sums and complete the rules.

1 a 9 + 9 = ______ b 11 + 15 = ______
c 13 + 7 = ______ d 121 + 1 = ______
e 5 + 217 = ______ f 313 + 25 = ______

Rule
odd + odd
= ______

2 a 4 + 8 = ______ b 10 + 12 = ______
c 28 + 14 = ______ d 18 + 118 = ______
e 120 + 326 = ______ f 622 + 442 = ______

Rule
even + even
= ______

3 a 11 + 6 = ______ b 14 + 3 = ______
c 124 + 9 = ______ d 31 + 16 = ______
e 232 + 15 = ______ f 315 + 114 = ______

Rule
odd + even
= ______

4 a 29 − 3 = ______ b 15 − 7 = ______
c 125 − 7 = ______ d 125 − 11 = ______

Rule
odd − odd
= ______

5 a 16 − 10 = ______ b 22 − 6 = ______
c 128 − 18 = ______ d 336 − 12 = ______

Rule
even − even
= ______

6 a 70 − 15 = ______ b 69 − 18 = ______
c 84 − 23 = ______ d 37 − 14 = ______
e 246 − 217 = ______ f 444 − 13 = ______

Rule
odd − even = ______
even − odd = ______

7 Write odd or even as the answer.

a 765 + 1432 = ______ b 2040 + 738 = ______ c 7841 − 965 = ______

Mastery Checklist I can:
- ☐ use 3×, 4×, 5× and 10× tables
- ☐ use different strategies to multiply
- ☐ identify rules to add and subtract odd and even numbers

Unit 7 Patterns on a hundred square

Pattern A

a 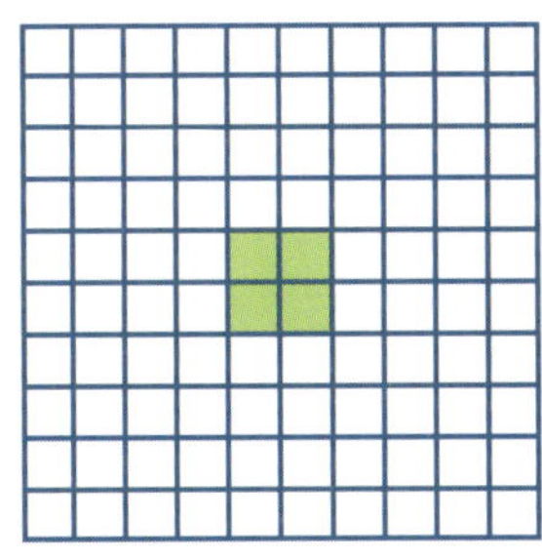 b 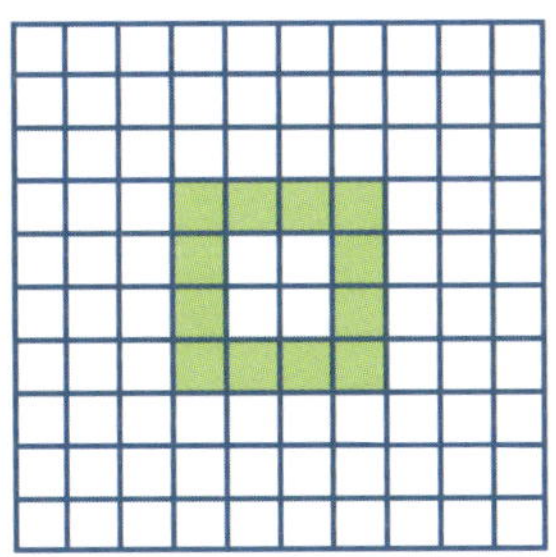 c 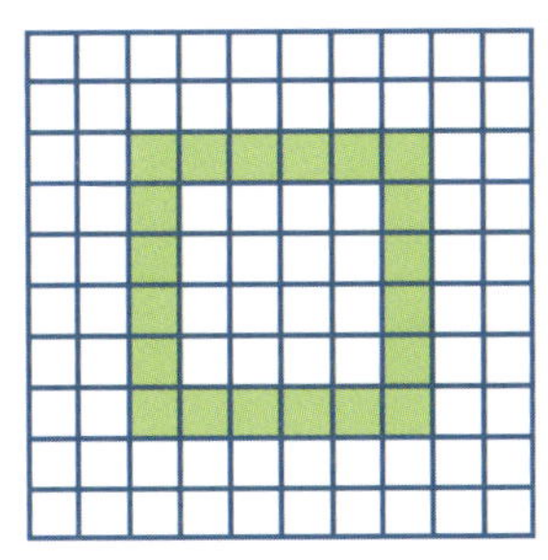 d 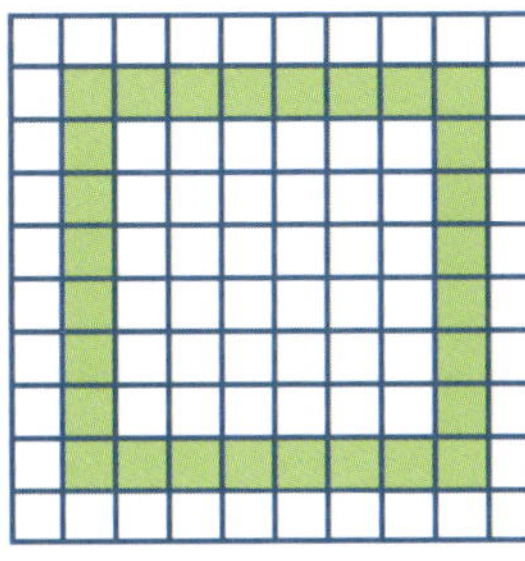

Pattern B

a 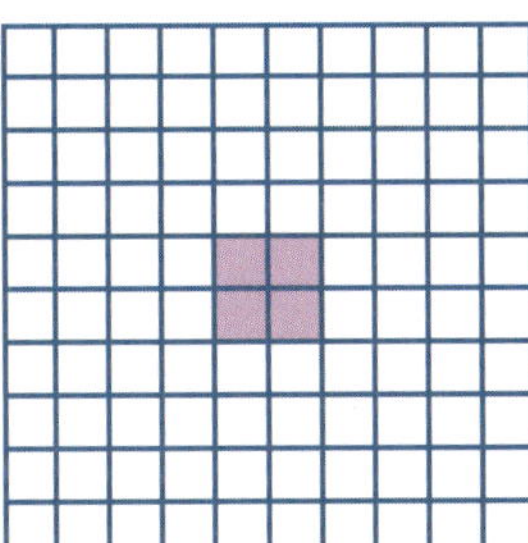 b 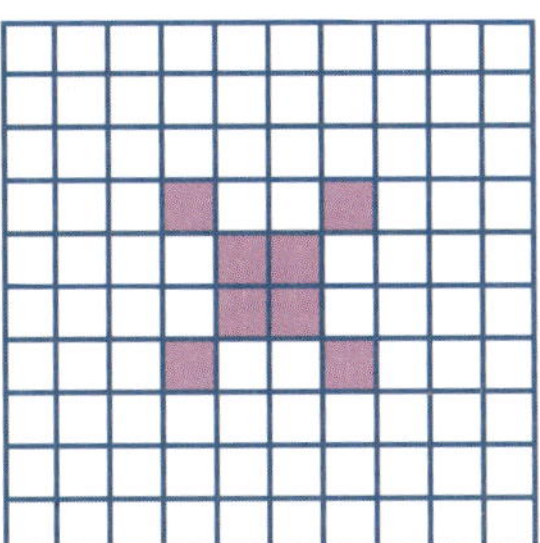 c 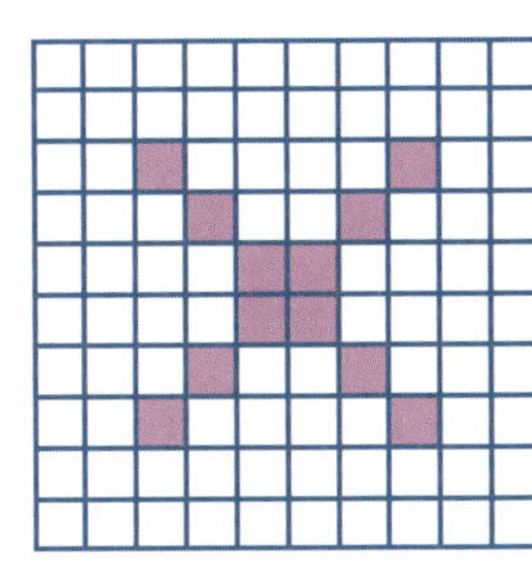 d 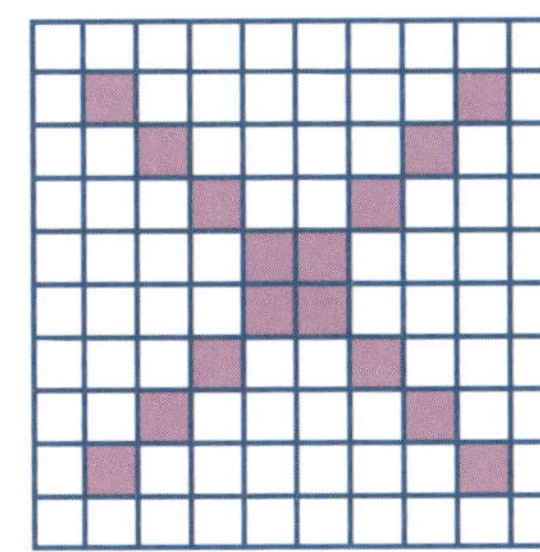

1 In pattern A how many squares are coloured?

a ________ b ________ c ________ d ________

e Do these numbers show a pattern? ____________

f Write the rule. ____

g Write the next three numbers in the pattern. ________________________

2 In pattern B how many squares are coloured?

a ________ b ________ c ________ d ________

e Do these numbers show a pattern? ____________

f Write the rule. ____

g Write the next three numbers in the pattern. ________________________

Challenge!

Draw another pattern.

a 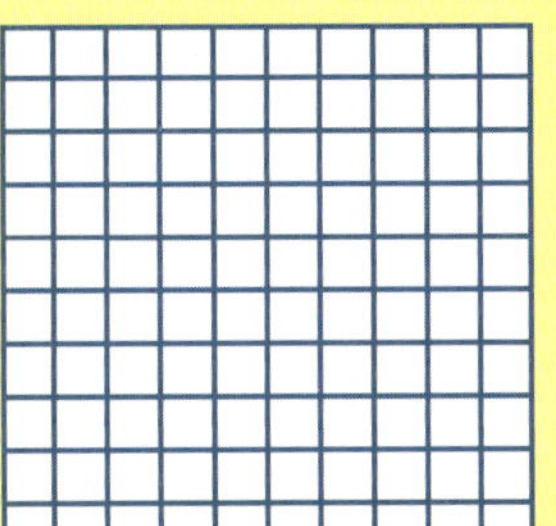 b 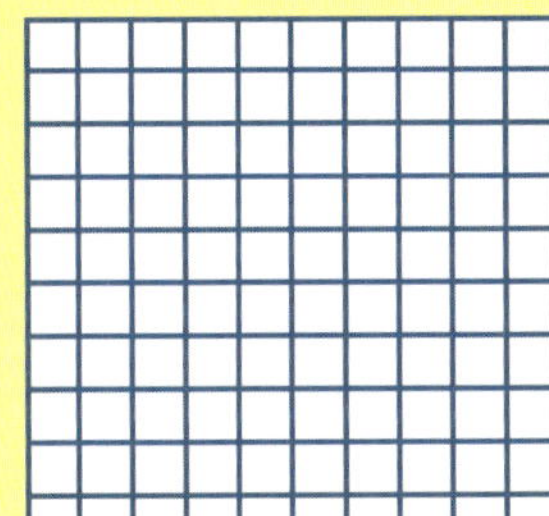 c 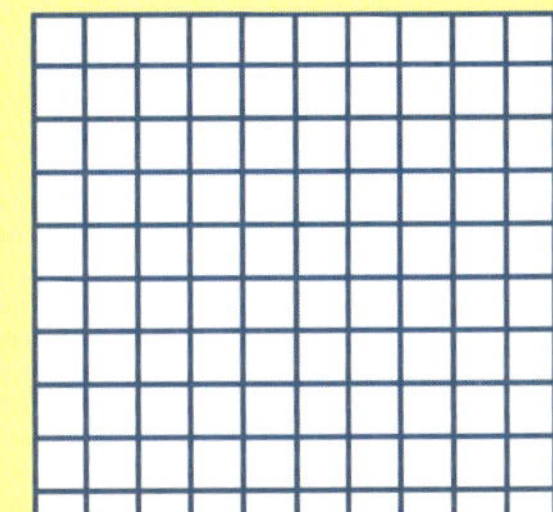 d 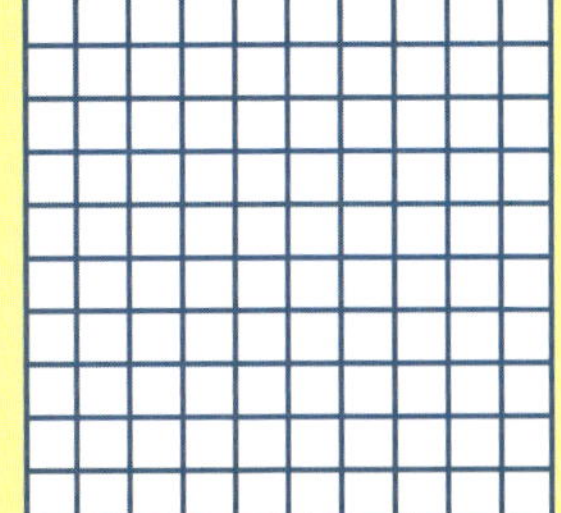

e What shape is your pattern? ____

Unit 7 Patterns of multiples

Number patterns

1 These pattern rows are made by multiplying a number in the top row by a number in the first column. Find the missing numbers to complete each multiplication sequence.

×	1	2	3	4	5	6	7	8
			15					
					20			
	2							
							21	
				32				
		14				42		

2 These are multiplication sequences. Find the rule for each sequence and fill in the missing terms.

eg 12, 16, 20, 24, 28, 32, 36, 40, 44, 48

Rule: multiples of 4 up to 50, starting at 12.

a ______, 24, 27, ______, ______, ______, ______

Rule: ____________________

b 25, ______, 35, ______, ______, ______, ______

Rule: ____________________

c ______, ______, ______, 16, 20, ______, ______

Rule: ____________________

d 18, 24, ______, ______, ______, ______

Rule: ____________________

3 Find all the numbers that are multiples of seven from 0 to 50. Circle them and join them in a line from smallest to largest to make a sequence.

14 36 7 35 15 32 45 42

5 21 24 25 18 28 27 49 48

Unit 7 Multiplication patterns

1 Circle the 3× tables pattern up to 100. Describe the pattern.

______

2 Cross the 6× tables pattern up to 100. Describe it in terms of the 3× tables pattern.

______

3 Colour the 9× tables pattern red. Describe it in terms of the other two tables patterns.

______

______

______

4 What other tables would match answers as in the 3×, 6× and 9×?

______

______

Why? ______

______

1	11	21	31	41	51	61	71	81	91
2	12	22	32	42	52	62	72	82	92
3	13	23	33	43	53	63	73	83	93
4	14	24	34	44	54	64	74	84	94
5	15	25	35	45	55	65	75	85	95
6	16	26	36	46	56	66	76	86	96
7	17	27	37	47	57	67	77	87	97
8	18	28	38	48	58	68	78	88	98
9	19	29	39	49	59	69	79	89	99
10	20	30	40	50	60	70	80	90	100

5 Continue each pattern and write the 10th term. Use the tables square.

a 21, 24, 27, ______, ______, ______. 10th term: ______

b 42, 39, 36, ______, ______, ______. 10th term: ______

c 30, 36, 42, ______, ______, ______. 10th term: ______

d 27, 36, 45, 54, ______, ______, ______. 10th term: ______

e 99, 90, 81, 72, ______, ______, ______. 10th term: ______

Words to use when explaining
begin, end,
count by,
multiples of,
forward,
backward

6 Describe these patterns, including where they start and finish.

a 30, 33, 36, 39, ... 54. ______

______

b 78, 72, 66, 60 ... 42. ______

______

Mastery Checklist

I can:
- ☐ identify, continue and make patterns
- ☐ identify multiples
- ☐ multiply to continue patterns
- ☐ identify patterns in the 3×, 6× and 9× tables.

Challenge! Get describing:

18, 27, 36, 45, 54, 63, 72, 81, 90

The ones digits ☐

The tens digits ☐

The digit sums ☐

Problem solving

Lucky numbers

1 You can choose your own lucky numbers for the *Multiple Luck of the Draw*.
The numbers are multiples of 3, 5, 6, 8 and 10.
Buy numbers that appear most often. You can buy 3 numbers.
Which tickets between 0 and 100 will you choose?

Lucky Number 20

Write down the multiples of each number. Then find the most common numbers.

3 ______________________________

5 ______________________________

6 ______________________________

8 ______________________________

10 ______________________________

Which numbers will you choose? Write them here.

☐ ☐ ☐ ☐ ☐

2 Digit patterns. Connect all the ones digits from the multiples to see a design.

eg Pattern of 3

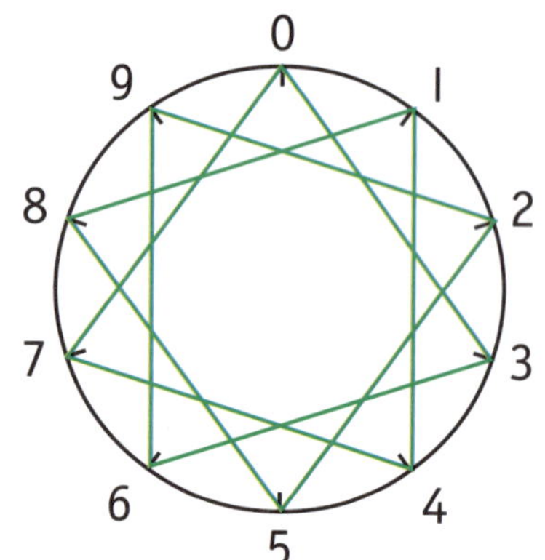

Pattern of 8

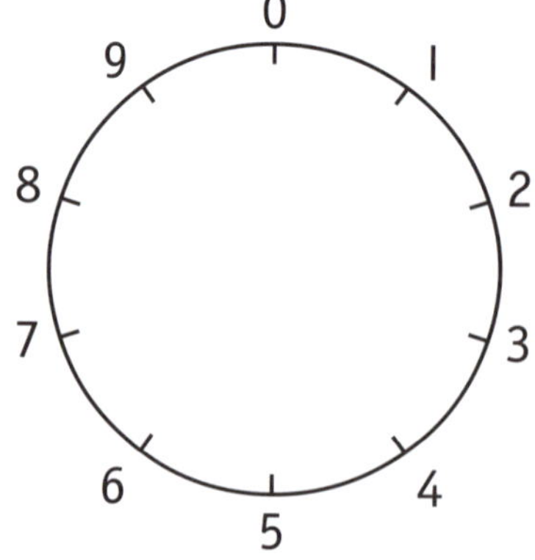

Pattern of 6

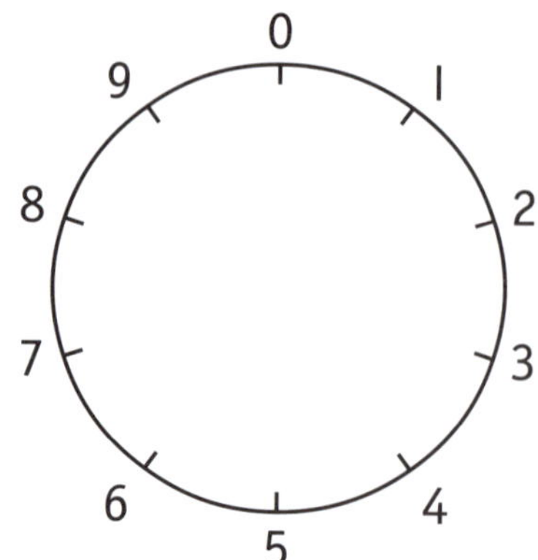

I can solve problems by:

☐ multiplying numbers ☐ creating a pattern using multiples.

AC9M4N09 Number **MAO-WM-01** Working mathematically • choosing and applying mathematical techniques to solve problems • **MA2-MR-01** Multiplicative relations A • Generate and describe patterns

Unit 8 Seconds

Clock hands
Short hand – hours
Long hand – minutes
Thin hand – seconds

60 seconds = 1 minute
60 minutes = 1 hour
24 hours = 1 day
7 days = 1 week

1 Use your pencil as a hand on the clock to show where the second hand will be at:
a 10 seconds. b 40 seconds. c 20 seconds. d 5 seconds. e 55 seconds.

2 Use two pencils to show:
a 5 min 30 sec. b 30 min 15 sec. c 50 min 20 sec.
d 10 min 45 sec. e 40 min 10 sec. f 35 min 50 sec.

3 How many minutes?
a 60 seconds ______ b 120 seconds ______ c 600 seconds ______

4 How many hours?
a 60 minutes ______ b 180 minutes ______ c 600 minutes ______

5 How many days?
a 24 hours ______ b 48 hours ______ c 240 hours ______

Use a table

Days	Hours	Minutes	Seconds
1	24	1440	
2	48	2880	
3	72	4320	
4	96	5760	

a Use a calculator to complete the seconds column.

b How many days in 259 200 seconds? ______

c How many hours in 86 400 seconds? ______

Unit 8 am or pm?

1 Does each event happen in **am** or **pm** time?

a wake up ______ b bedtime ______
c homework ______ d breakfast ______
e sunset ______ f playtime ______
g lunch ______ h dinner ______
i fireworks ______ j dawn ______

2 Write the digital time. Add **am** or **pm** to each.

a 6 o'clock (morning) [:] ______
b $\frac{1}{2}$ past 4 (afternoon) [:] ______
c $\frac{1}{4}$ to 12 (night) [:] ______
d 27 past 6 (evening) [:] ______
e 4 past midday [:] ______
f 2 minutes past midnight [:] ______

3 Add 3 hours and 10 minutes to each time. Write **am** or **pm**.

a 6:24 am ______ b 11:45 am ______
c 1:41 pm ______ d 12:01 pm ______
e 11:01 am ______ f 9:18 pm ______

4 Order these times from earliest to latest.

3:25 pm 4:40 am 8:25 pm 4:13 am

______

5 Circle the longer time.

a 14 days 3 weeks
b 1 minute 50 seconds
c 5 minutes 200 seconds
d 5 weeks 2 months

Challenge!

Use a calculator to work out:

a how many hours in April. [ ]
b how many seconds in April. [ ]

AC9M4M01 • AC9M4M03 Measurement MA2-NSM-02 Non-spatial measure B • Time: Represent and interpret digital time displays

Unit 8 Telling time

Working with time

1 Write the letters of the clocks beside the correct label.

A

B

C

D

E

F

a 6 past 4 ________ b 6 to 3 ________ c 10 past 10 ________

d 25 past 2 ________ e 6 to 12 ________ f 20 to 5 ________

2 Talia takes photos of her clock throughout the day. Write the times.

a

b

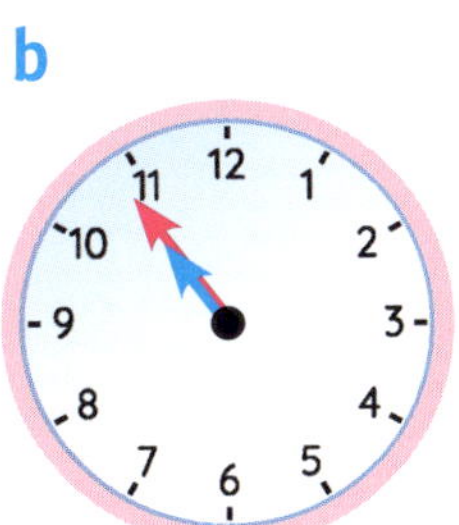

c

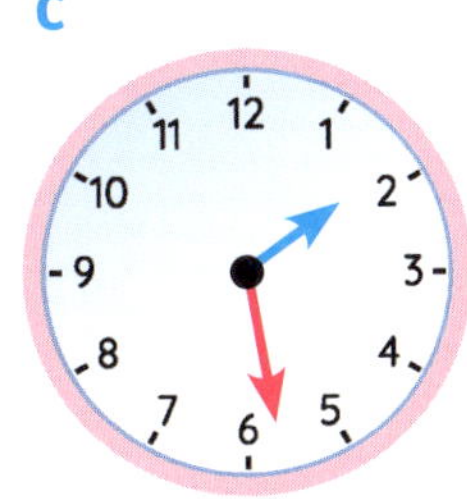

d

e

________ ________ ________ ________ ________

3 How much time passed between these clocks? Answer in hours and minutes.

a 2a and 2b ____________________ b 2a and 2c ____________________

c 2c and 2d ____________________ d 2d and 2e ____________________

e 2a and 2e ____________________

Mastery Checklist I can:

- ☐ convert between units of time
- ☐ use am and pm
- ☐ solve time problems
- ☐ tell time to the minute.

Unit 9 Pyramids

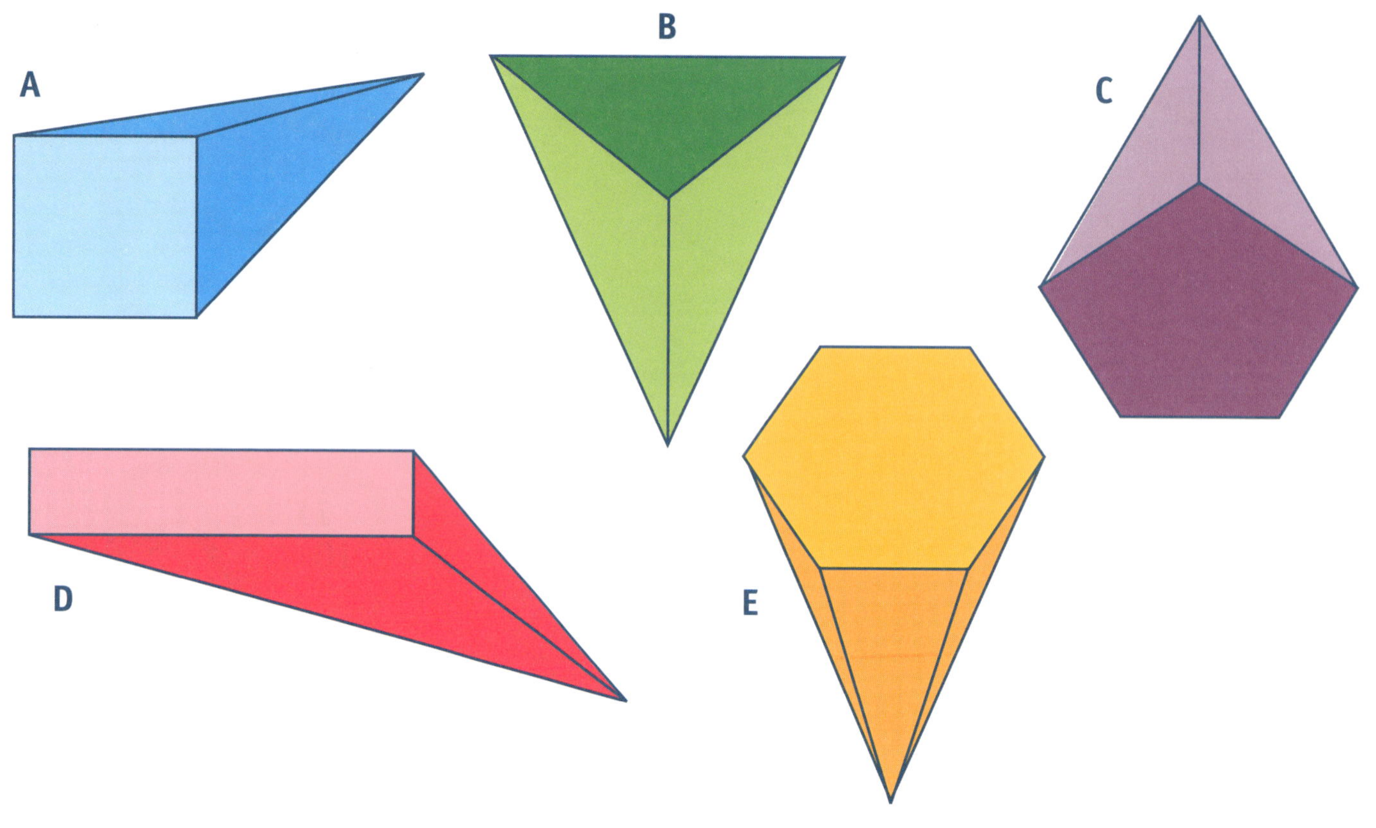

1 Name the shape of each end face (base).

A ______ B ______ C ______

D ______ E ______

2 What shape are all the other faces? ______

3 Name each pyramid.

A ______ B ______ C ______

D ______ E ______

4 How many faces has:

A? ______ B? ______ C? ______ D? ______ E? ______

5 Draw something in your environment that has a pyramid as part of it.

Unit 9 3D objects

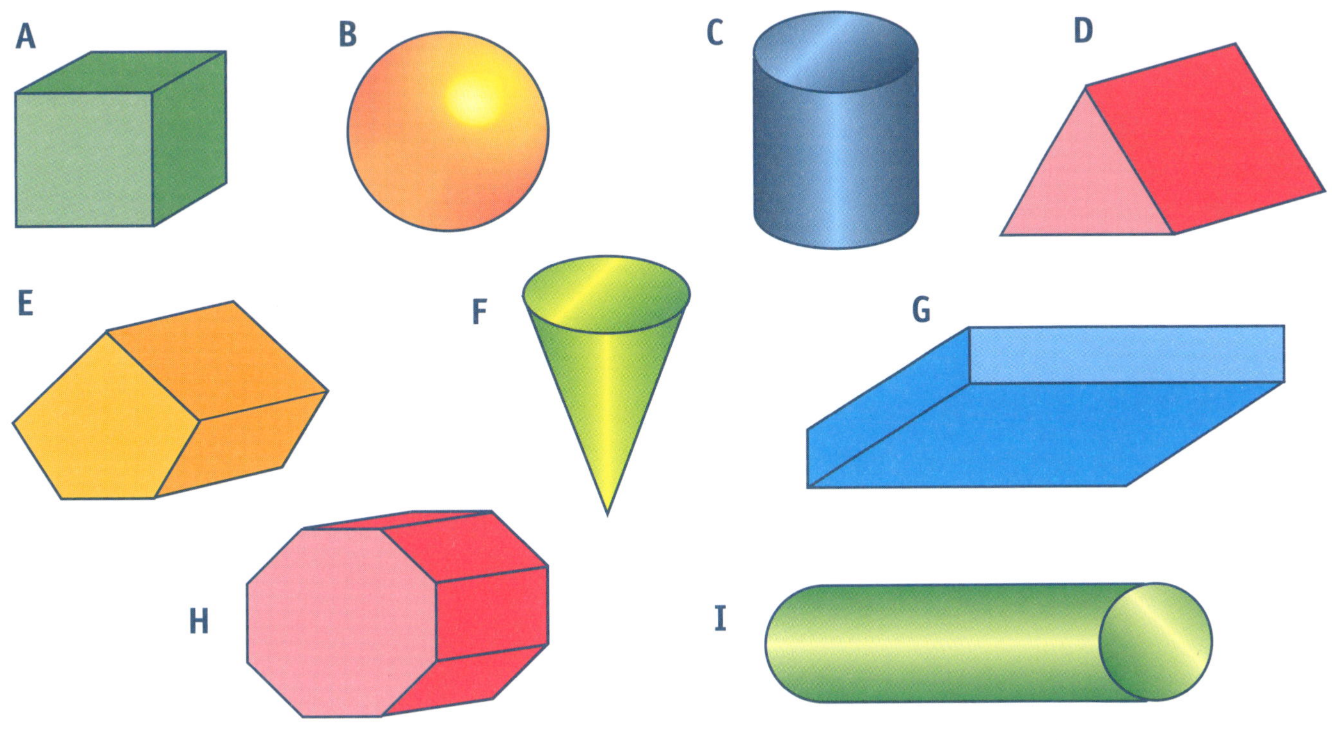

1 Name each object.

A ______________ B ______________ C ______________

D ______________ E ______________ F ______________

G ______________ H ______________ I ______________

2 Draw two things in your environment that are like one of the 3D objects above.

Unit 9 Nets

Nets are flat patterns that can be used to make 3D models.

1 Name the 3D object each net will make when it is folded.

a
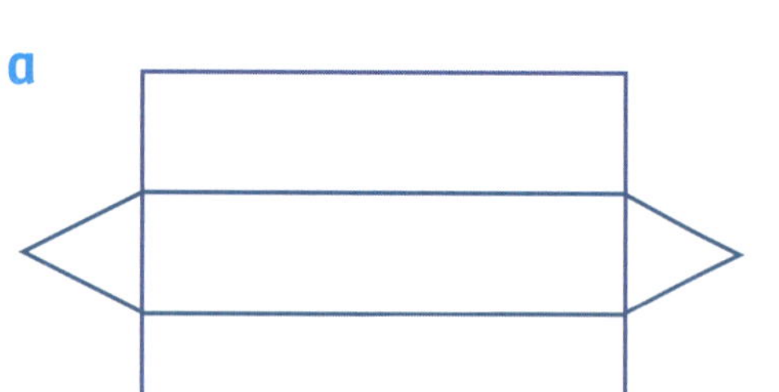

b

c
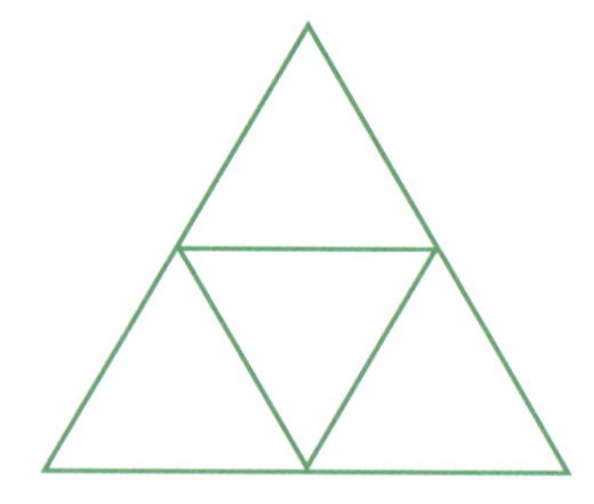

d
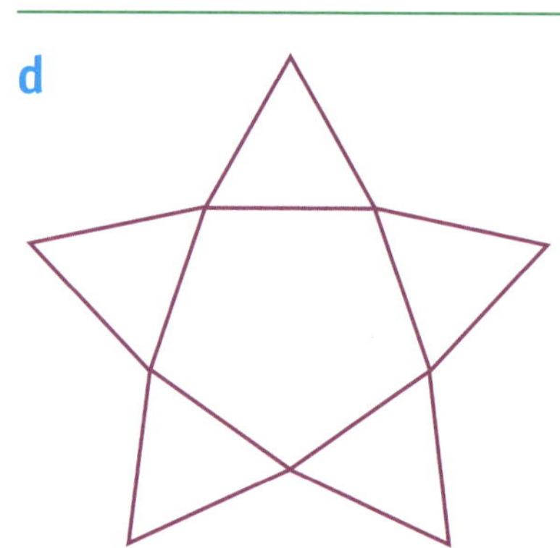

e
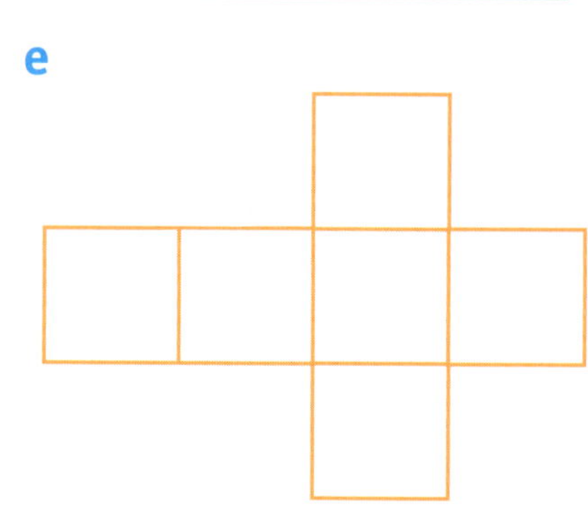

f
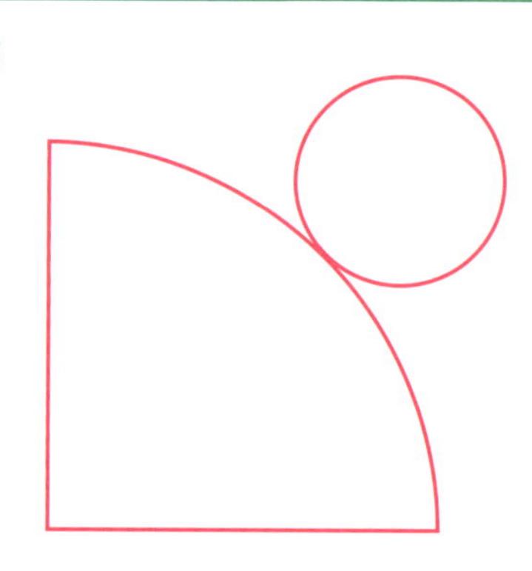

2 Make your own net of a cube. Use a page of one centimetre grid paper. Make sure the squares you draw have sides of 5 cm. Cut out your net, decorate it and make it into a cube. Practise drawing one here.

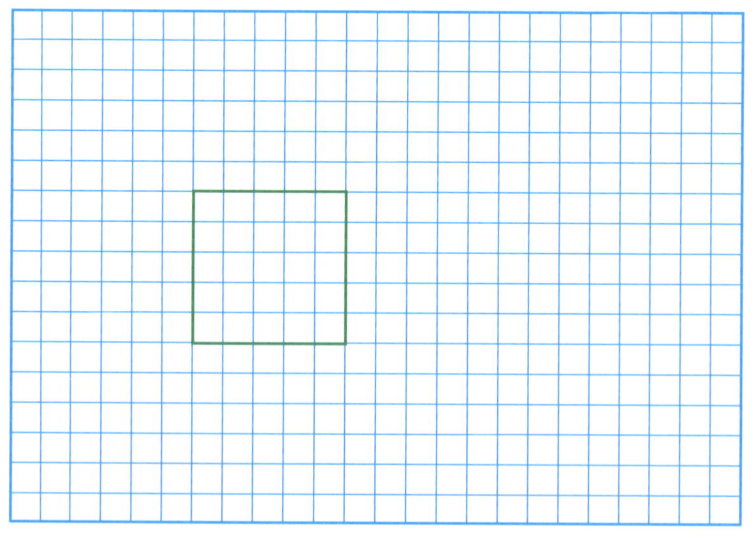

Mastery Checklist I can:
- ☐ identify features of pyramids
- ☐ identify features of prisms
- ☐ match nets to 3D objects.

MA2-3DS-01 Three-dimensional spatial structure A • 3D objects: Make models of three-dimensional objects to compare and describe key features

Problem solving

Different nets

There are many ways to make the nets of 3D objects.

All the following nets can make a cube.

How many different nets can you make for a triangular prism?

Sketch them here.

Choose one net, copy it onto card and make a triangular prism.

Draw two different views of it.

I can solve problems by:

☐ drawing a diagram ☐ using visual thinking.

Unit 10 A survey

Data 

1 Some friends counted the taxis they saw on the way home from school. They drew this graph to show their survey.

Taxis seen on the way home	
Song	
Max	
Asha	
Piper	
George	
Liam	

Key [taxi] = 2 taxis

a How many friends counted taxis? ______

b Why do you think they decided to count taxis?

______

______

c Why do you think Piper didn't count any taxis?

______

______

______

______

2 a Complete this table.

Child	Tally	Total
Song	||||	
Max	卌 ||	
Asha		
Piper		
George		
Liam		

b How many taxis did they count altogether? ______

c How many more taxis did Max count than Liam? ______

d Who might live furthest from the school? ______

How do you know? ______

______

3 Which shows the data better: the graph or the tally chart?

______

Why? ______

______

______

______

______

Challenge!

Show the information on a column graph.

Unit 10 Birthdays pictograph

Use the graph to answer the following questions.

Birthdays in Year 4

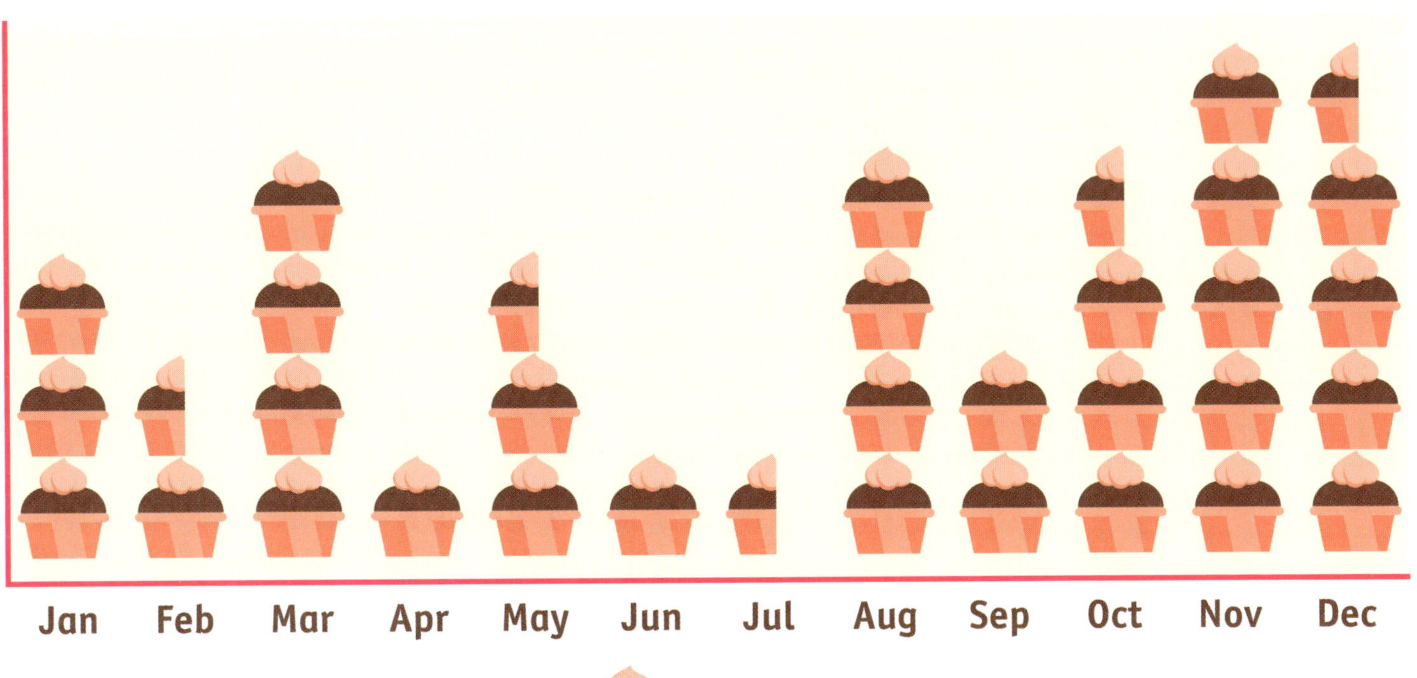

Key [cupcake] = 2 birthdays

1 How many students are in Year 4? ______

2 Which month has the same number of birthdays as March? ______

3 How many students have a birthday in these months?

a July ______ b December ______

c January ______ d November ______

4 Which month has the most birthdays? ______

5 What is the difference in the number of birthdays in these months?

a January and April ______ b September and October ______

c May and February ______ d June and July ______

6 How many students have a birthday in:

a summer? ______ b winter? ______ c autumn? ______ d spring? ______

7 Eight new students joined the class, and they all have birthdays in April.
Draw cupcakes to show their birthdays.

Unit 10 Draw a pictograph

Graphs

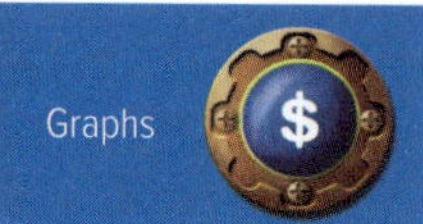

1 Complete the Total column in the tally chart. Then present the data as a pictograph.

Lunch orders at Boorloo Primary

Day	Tally	Total
Monday	卌 卌 ‖	12
Tuesday	卌 卌 卌 ‖	17
Wednesday	卌 卌 卌	
Thursday	卌 卌 |	
Friday	卌 卌 卌 卌	

Lunch orders at Boorloo Primary

Monday Tuesday Wednesday Thursday Friday

Key 🍏 = 2

2 Write two questions you could ask about the graph.

a ______________________________

b ______________________________

Mastery Checklist I can:
- ☐ gather data
- ☐ record information in a table
- ☐ interpret a pictograph
- ☐ construct a pictograph.

 AC9M4ST01 Statistics **MA2-DATA-02** Data A • Collect discrete data • Organise and display data using tables and graphs • Data B • Construct and interpret data displays with many-to-one scales

Unit 11 Chance experiment

chance experiment

1 If you were to roll a die 20 times, predict:

a the number that would occur most often. ___________

b the number that would occur least often. ___________

c how many times the number three would occur. ___________

2 Work in a group of 4. You need a die. Stop after 20 rolls.

Take turns to roll the die. Use tally marks to record the results.

Number	Tally marks	Total
1		
2		
3		
4		
5		
6		

Which number:

a occurred most often? ___________ b occurred least often? ___________

c How many times did the number three occur? ___________

d Were your predictions accurate? ___________

3 Repeat the exercise, rolling the die 30 times.

Number	Tally marks	Total
1		
2		
3		
4		
5		
6		

a Were the results the same? ___________

b Write about the two sets of results.

____

____

____

Unit 11 Graphing an experiment

1 Look at question 2 on page 41.

Draw a column graph to show the results.

a Write a title.

b Write labels for the axes.

Chance words
outcome, likely, equally, occur, chance

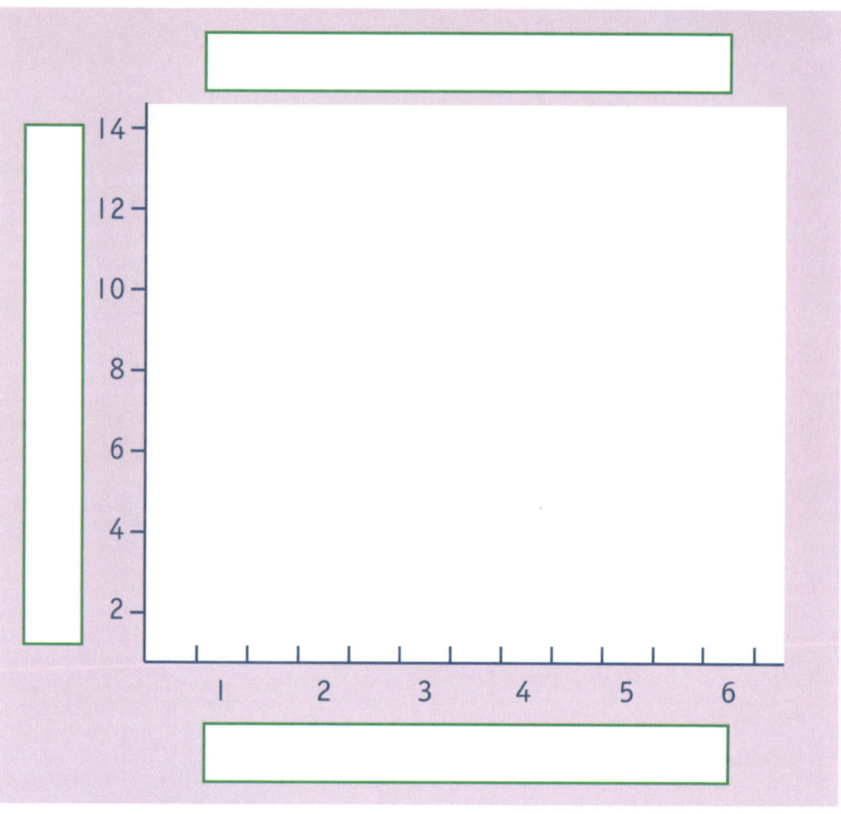

2 **To throw a six, there is a one in six chance.**

Explain what this means. ______________________________

____

____

3 What is the chance you would throw:

a a 2? ______________ b a 5? ______________

c a number less than 4? ______________

d a number more than 2? ______________

4 Does your experiment show these results? ______________

Why? ______________________________

5 If you did the experiment again, would the results be the same? ______________

Why? ______________________________

Challenge!

Work with a friend. Roll 2 dice 20 times. Write your results in a table. Draw a graph of the information.

Mastery Checklist

I can:
- ☐ make predictions about a chance experiment
- ☐ conduct repeated chance experiments and compare the results
- ☐ record results in a table
- ☐ draw a column graph using collected data.

Problem solving

What's the chance?

Work with a partner. Use the information you found in the **Challenge!** on page 42.

Which total was thrown most? __________ Which total was thrown least? __________

How can you use this information to make a mini board game also using two dice?

Instructions:

When you throw a total of	move ahead this number
eg 2, 3 or 4	eg 2 spaces

43	44	45	46	47	48	49
42	41	40	39	38	37	36
29	30	31	32	33	34	35
28	27	26	25	24	23	22
15	16	17	18	19	20	21
14	13	12	11	10	9	8
1	2	3	4	5	6	7

Play the game with your partner. What improvements can you make?

I can solve problems by:

☐ using information to describe the chance of something happening

☐ conducting repeated chance experiments.

Revision Term 1

1 **4798 2450 6090 6005** p 2

a Write in order from smallest to largest.

______ ______ ______ ______

b Write the largest number in words. p 3

____

____

c Write the smallest number as p 3

_____ thousands, _____ tens and _____ ones.

d **7789** Circle the hundreds number and underline the ones number.

2 Match the words to the numbers. p 4

a six thousand and forty six	6006
b six thousand and six	6140
c 60 hundreds and 14 tens	6·46
d 6 ones and 46 hundredths	6046

3 Write the number: p 4

a 1000 more than 962. ______

b 1000 less than 6048. ______

c halfway between 4000 and 5000.

______

4 Use the jump strategy. p 5

a 46 + 17 = ______

b 173 + 26 = ______

5 Use the split strategy. p 5

a 62 + 39 = ______

b 138 + 75 = ______

6 Use the compensation strategy. p 5

a 29 + 59 = ______

b 416 + 38 = ______

7 Double. p 5

a 12 ______ b 17 ______ c 23 ______

8 Use the number line. p 6

153 + 88 = ______

9 There are 326 grapes in one basket and 273 in another. How many altogether? p 6

```
  □□□
+ □□□
-----
```

______ grapes

10 p 7

a
```
  5 3 2
+ 1 1 7
-------
```

b
```
  4 6 9
+ 2 5 3
-------
```

11 p 8

a
```
  7 9
- 2 4
-----
```

b
```
  8 5
- 5 2
-----
```

c
```
  6 7
- 2 4
-----
```

12 Use subtraction strategies. p 9

a 62 − 29 = ______

b 83 − 54 = ______

13 Use the number line. p 10

61 − 38 = ______

61

Revision Term 1

14 Find the change from . p 11

a ☐ b ☐

15 Write in centimetres. p 15

a 20 mm ______ b 6 m ______

c 1·25 m ______

16 Write as metres. p 15

a 400 cm ______ b 2000 mm______

17 Find the perimeter. p 15

a

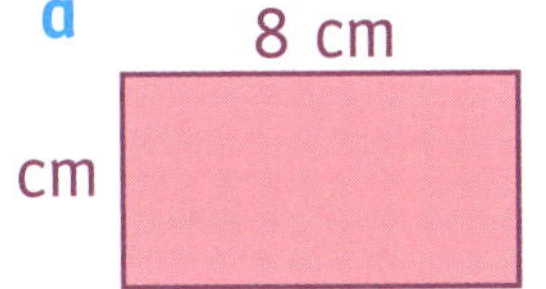

P = ______

b

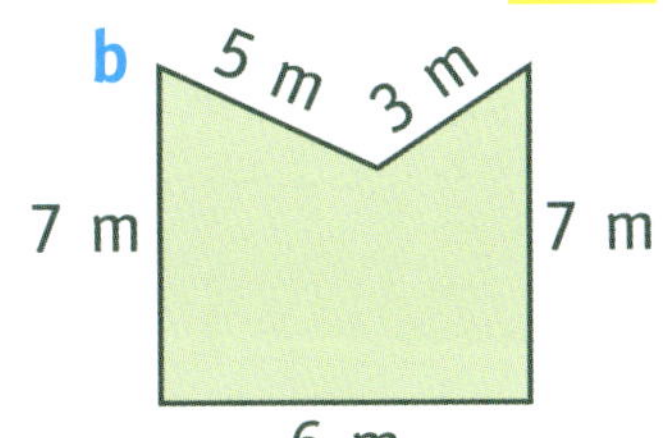

P = ______

18 Name the fraction. p 17

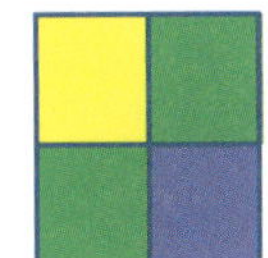

a blue = ______ b green = ______

c red = ______

19 Write the tenths and the hundredths and the decimal. p 19

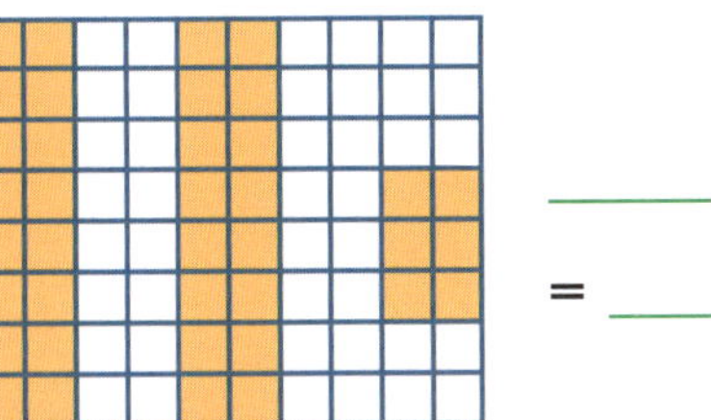

______ + ______

= ______

20 Tick the largest, circle the smallest. p 19

0·25 0·09 0·41 0·39

21 Odd or even? p 26

a odd + odd = ______

b even + even = ______

c odd + even = ______

d odd − odd = ______

e even − even = ______

f odd − even = ______

g even − odd = ______

22 Complete and write the rule. p 29

a 4, 9, 14, ______, ______, ______

Rule ☐

b 1·3, 1·5, 1·7, ______, ______

Rule ☐

23 Name each object. p 36

a

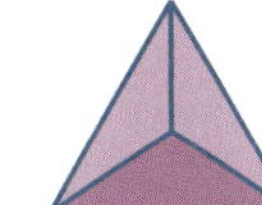

b

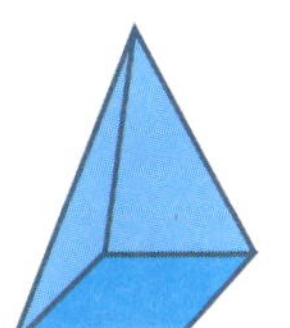

______ ______

24 This table lists books read by some friends in the holidays. Underline the questions that this table does not answer. p 38

John	10	**Tilly**	8
Jodi	9	**Terry**	5

A What do you like to do in the holidays?

B How many books did you read in the holidays?

C Did you enjoy the books you read?

D Who read the most books in the holidays?

NAPLAN* practice

This is a test to see how well you understand what you have learnt.

Instructions

Read each question carefully. There are three different ways to show your answer:

- Shade the bubble next to the correct answer.
- Write a word in a box.
- Write a number in a box.

Use a pencil. DO NOT use a pen. If you make a mistake, rub it out and try again.

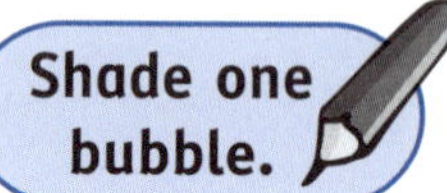

1 Henry has about 2400 old magazines.
How many magazines might he have?

2040 ◯ 2140 ◯ 2375 ◯ 2480 ◯

2 October, September and ____________ .
Which Spring month is missing?

February ◯ November ◯ December ◯ August ◯

3 Which container is holding a litre of water?

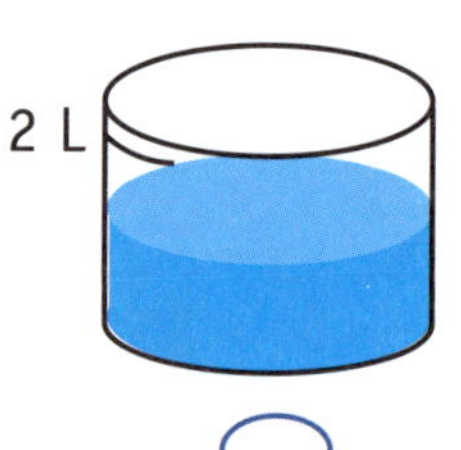

1 L

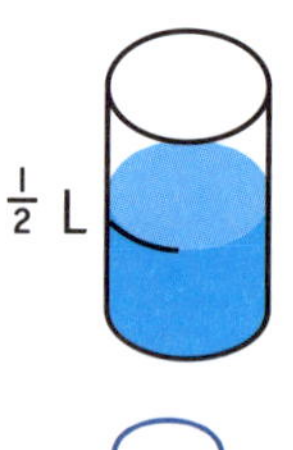

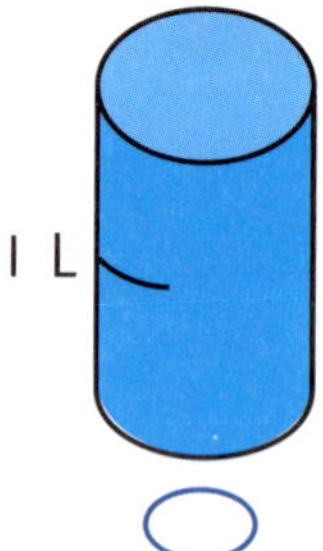

◯ ◯ ◯ ◯

4 Four children tried to make pyramids with cardboard.

Alex used 3 triangles. Danny used 1 triangle.
Ned used 4 triangles. Toby used 2 triangles.

Who made a square pyramid?

Danny ◯ Ned ◯ Alex ◯ Toby ◯

* This is not an officially endorsed publication of the NAPLAN program and is produced independently of Australian governments.

Test practice

5 What number will replace the question mark?

Favourite Cereal	Number of people
Weety Bites	12
Oat Floats	7
Magic Moosli	?
Crunchy Crisps	5
Total	**30**

6 ◯ 7 ◯ 5 ◯ 8 ◯

6 If I buy a red frog for 15 cents and a chocolate frog for 95 cents, what change do I receive from $2?

90c ◯ $1 ◯ $1.10 ◯ 95c ◯

7 Which expression is the same as **84 + 36**?

80 + 30 + 40 + 6 ◯ 84 + 30 + 6 ◯ 80 + 34 + 10 ◯ 34 + 84 + 6 ◯

8 Tallies for runs in cricket.

Sam 卌 卌 || Lily ||| Hana 卌 卌 ||||

Who scored 12 runs?

Jade ◯ Sam ◯ Lily ◯ Hana ◯

9 How much is coloured?

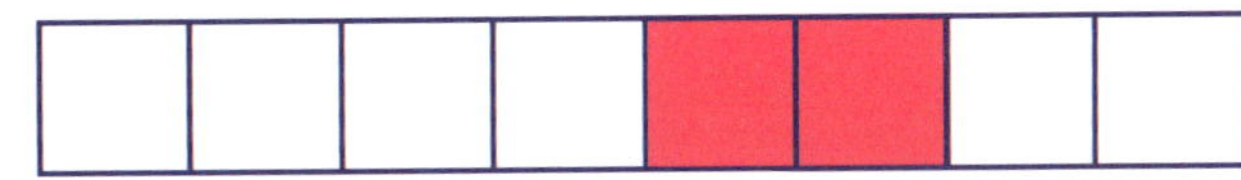

$\frac{1}{4}$ ◯ $\frac{1}{3}$ ◯ $\frac{1}{2}$ ◯ $\frac{4}{2}$ ◯

Test practice

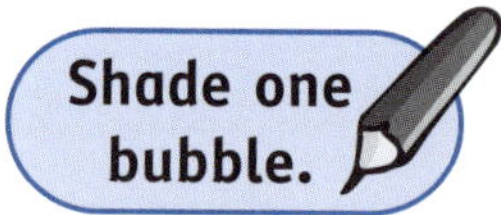

10 Friends shared 45 jelly beans and they each received 9.
How many friends shared the jelly beans?

9 ◯ 7 ◯ 4 ◯ 5 ◯

11 Which decimal number will complete this pattern?

0·79, ______ , 0·81, 0·82, 0·83 

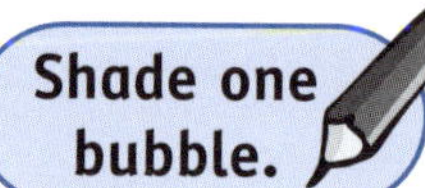

12 Win bought a pen, Val bought a book, Fred bought highlighters and Tarry bought gum. Everyone used a $5 note to pay.

Who received change of $1.60?

Win ◯ Val ◯ Fred ◯ Tarry ◯

13 Which expression matches 15 × 7?

10 × 7 + 5 × 7 ◯ 10 × 5 + 10 × 7 ◯ 7 × 15 + 7 × 10 ◯ 7 × 5 + 7 × 15 ◯

14 What number would come out of this machine if the number 9 went in?

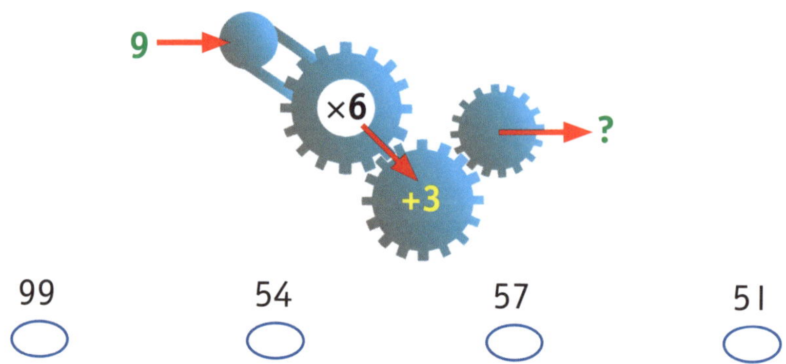

99 ◯ 54 ◯ 57 ◯ 51 ◯

Test practice

15 There is a one in three chance of this spinner landing on red.
How many sections are red?

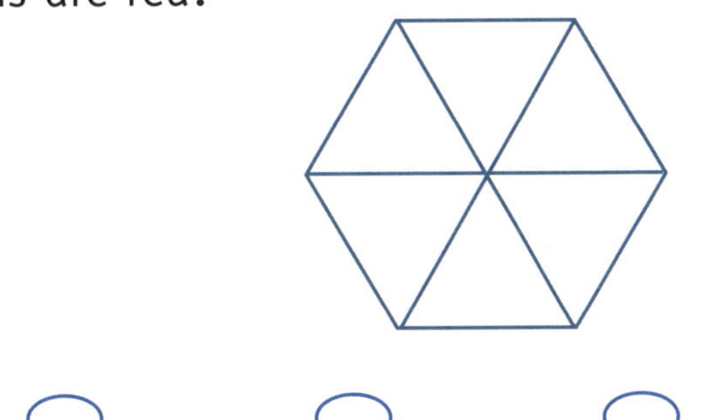

◯ 1 ◯ 2 ◯ 3 ◯ 4

16 This object is cut in two places.

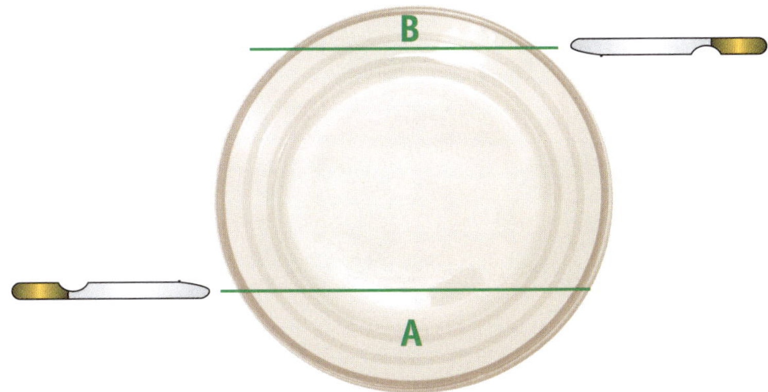

Which statement about the sections is true?

◯ B is larger than A
◯ B is the same as A
◯ A is larger than B
◯ A is smaller than B

17 The perimeter of this rectangle is 26 cm.
What is the length of the short side?

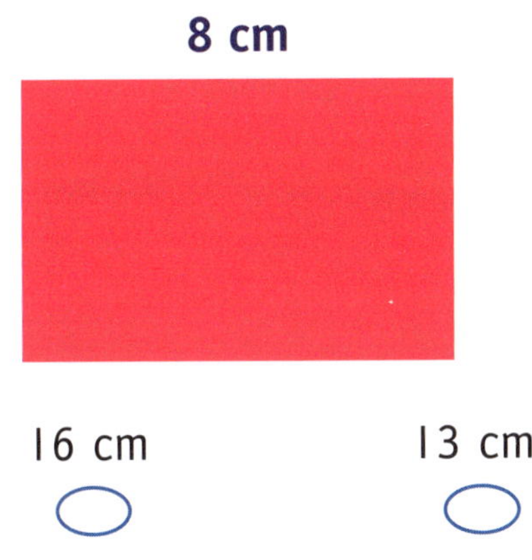

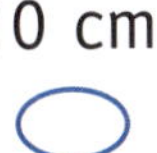

◯ 5 cm ◯ 10 cm ◯ 16 cm ◯ 13 cm

Test practice

Shade one bubble.

18 Which number is missing from this statement?

The yellow 5 is ________ times greater than the pink 5 on the abacus.

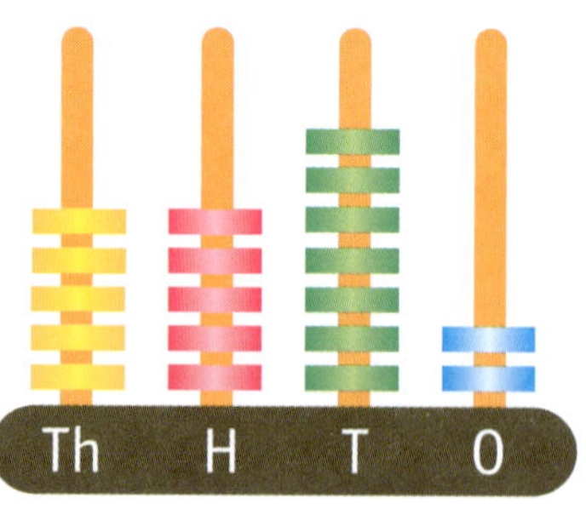

10 ◯ 100 ◯ 1000 ◯ 1 ◯

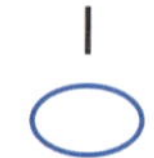

19 This pattern is made with beads in octagons.

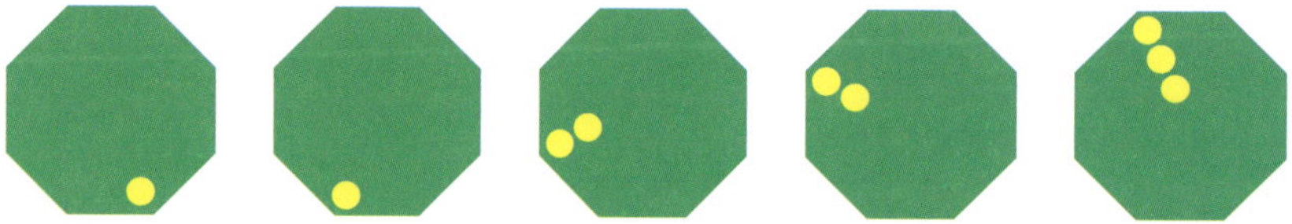

What will be the seventh term of this pattern?

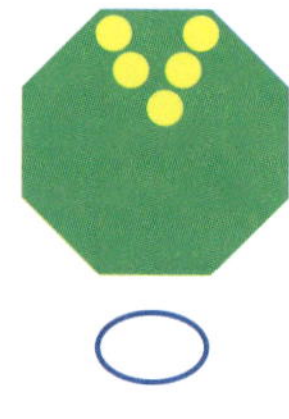 ◯ 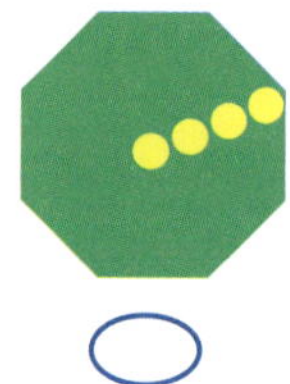 ◯  ◯ 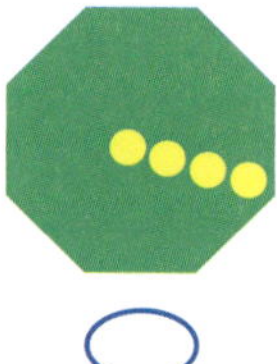 ◯

20 Which shape contains obtuse angles only?

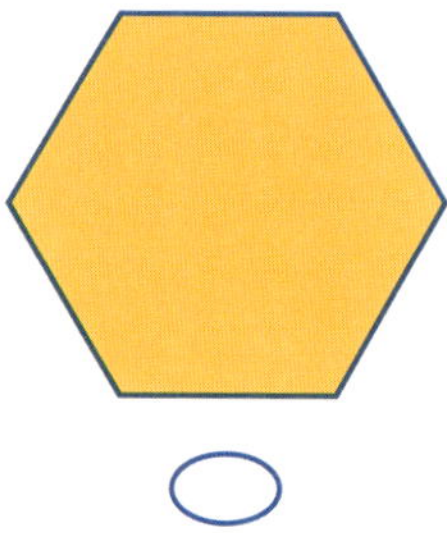 ◯  ◯ 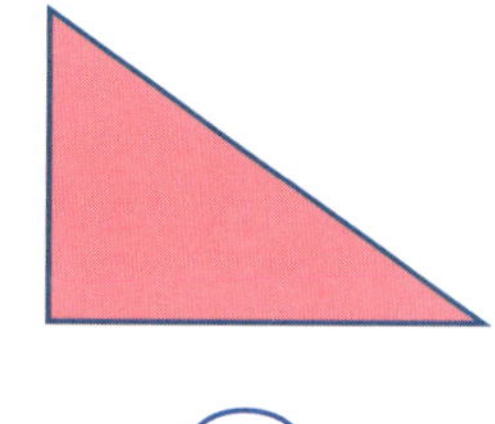 ◯  ◯

21 How many millimetres long is this twig?

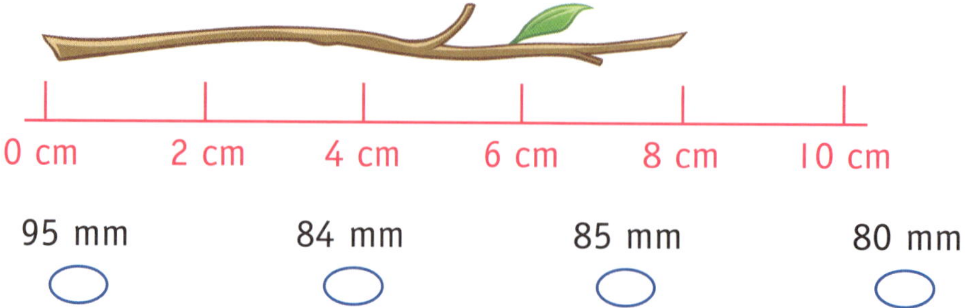

95 mm ◯ 84 mm ◯ 85 mm ◯ 80 mm ◯

Test practice

Shade one bubble.

22 How much more is needed to make 1 kilogram?

450 g

500 g

750 g

600 g

23 Dan is leaving at 6:30 am to drive his car to a meeting. He says he will take 1 hour and 20 minutes. At what time will he arrive at the meeting?

24 Study these scales.

How many apples weigh the same as the mango?

1

2

3

4

25
$$\begin{array}{r} 3\ 8\ 4 \\ +\ 2\ 1\ 7 \\ \hline \blacktriangle\ \bullet\ \blacksquare \end{array}$$

What number would replace the ▲?

5

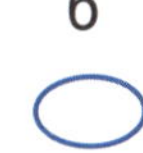

6

2

1

Test practice

Shade one bubble.

26 20 children walk 500 metres to school.
12 children walk 1 kilometre to school.
15 children walk 1·5 kilometres to school.
10 children walk 1·7 kilometres to school.

This is a graph of the information.

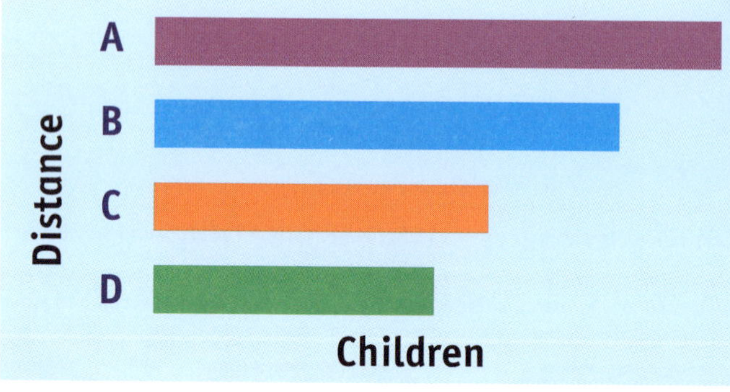

What label belongs at **C**?

1 km ◯ 1·7 km ◯ 500 m ◯ 1·5 km ◯

27 Which piece is missing from this symmetrical design?

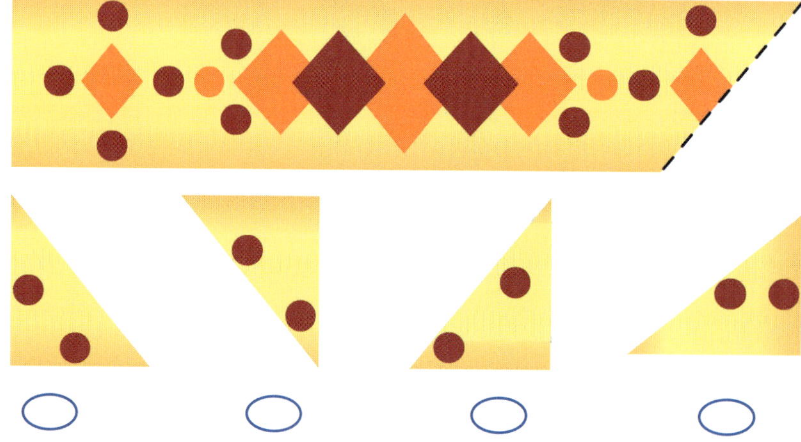

◯ ◯ ◯ ◯

28 Erin has 15 jelly babies and Tony has 11.
How many jelly babies should Erin give Tony so that they have an equal number?

5 ◯ 4 ◯ 3 ◯ 2 ◯

Test practice

Shade one bubble.

29 You pay for this teddy with a $20 note.

How much change do you get?

- ◯ $11.70
- ◯ $10.30
- ◯ $9.70
- ◯ $10.70

30 You are buying this pumpkin.

You give the shopkeeper $2 + $1 + 50c + 10c + 5c.

What coin is missing?

◯

◯

◯

◯

Write your answer in the box.

31 How many bananas weigh the same as the pineapple?

☐

32 Jan, Todd and Milly measured their heights. They were 148 cm, 156 cm and 163 cm tall. What is their combined height in metres?

Write it in decimal form. 

Unit 12 Ten thousands

These children each have 5 numeral cards.

1 a Write the smallest number each child can make using all 5 cards.

Sue ________________ Karl ________________

b Who wrote the smallest? ____________

2 a Write the largest number each child can make.

Sue ________________ Karl ________________

b Who wrote the largest? ____________

3 Write all the 5-digit numbers Sue can make smaller than 15 000.

____

____

4 Write all the 5-digit numbers Karl can make between 24 000 and 25 000.

____

____

5 a Who can write the number closest to 10 000? ________________

b What is it? ________________

6 a Who can write the number closest to 15 000? ________________

b What is it? ________________

Unit 12 Numbers in words

Look at page 54.

Zero
Remember: Whole numbers do not start with zero.

1 a Make the second largest 5-digit number each child can make.

Sue ____________ Karl ____________

b Make the second smallest 5-digit number each child can make.

Sue ____________ Karl ____________

2 Write the answers to question 1a in words.

a Sue ________________________________

b Karl ________________________________

3 Write these using numerals.

a fifty-three thousand, two hundred and seventy-one ____________

b twenty-five thousand, seven hundred and four ____________

c twenty-four thousand and fifty-seven ____________

d seventy-thousand, four hundred and fifty-two ____________

e fifty-seven thousand, three hundred and twelve ____________

4 Who can make the numbers in question 3?

a ________ b ________ c ________ d ________ e ________

5 Sue used the numerals on her cards to make some 5-digit numbers on an abacus.

a b c

Write the numbers she made in words.

a ________________________________

b ________________________________

c ________________________________

Challenge!

Write all the numbers Karl can make.

Hint: They can have 1, 2, 3 or 4 digits. How many numbers did you write?

Unit 12 Ten thousands

96 314

Ten thousands	thousands	hundreds	tens	ones
9	6	3	1	4

90 000 + 6000 + 300 + 10 + 4

1 Write the numbers under each abacus.

a 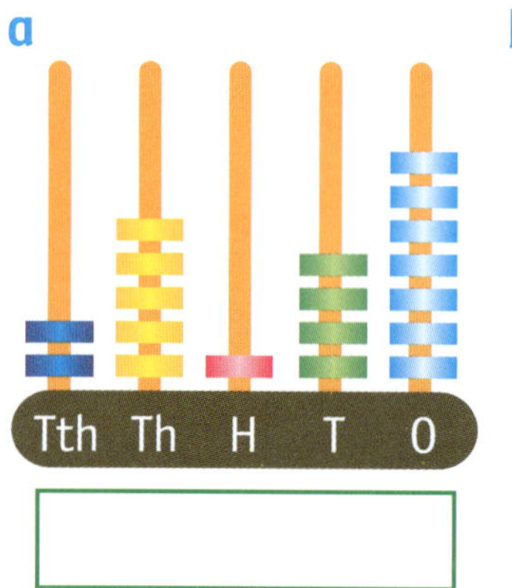

b 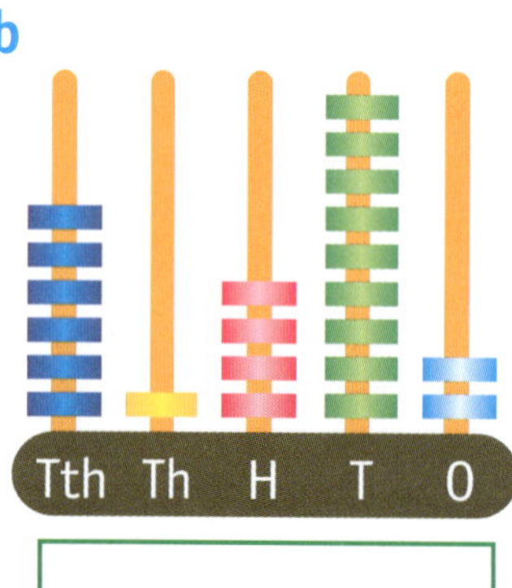

c 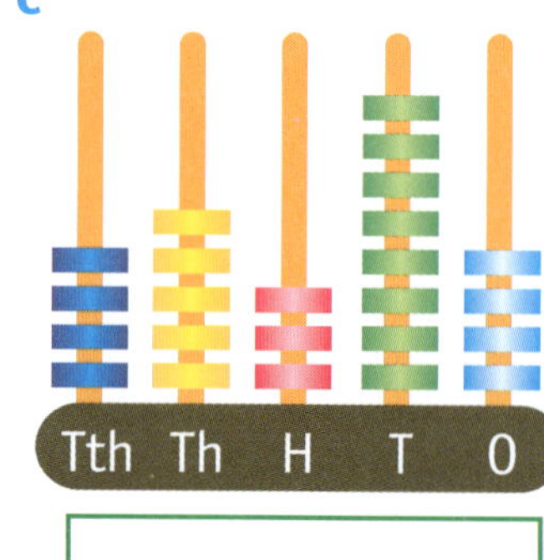

d 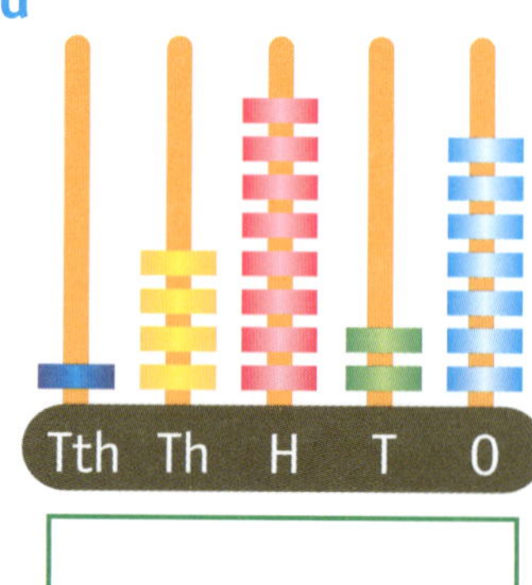

2 Draw each number on the abacus.

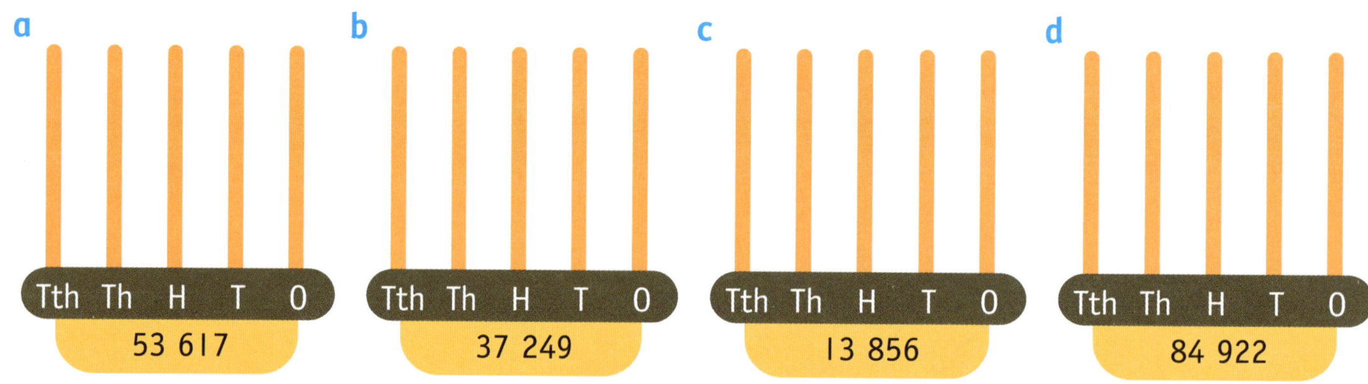

3 Write each number in numerals on the place-value chart.

a forty-one thousand, two hundred and fifty-nine
b seventy-three thousand, five hundred and twenty-seven
c eighty-four thousand, one hundred and sixty-five
d thirty-nine thousand, six hundred and thirty-six
e sixty-seven thousand, four hundred and eighteen

Tth	Th	H	T	O

4 Write these numbers in ascending order.

a 23 749 19 651 30 543

____

b 93 065 79 872 60 157

____

c 51 230 50 947 51 803

____

Remember to leave a space after the thousands!
23 614
small space

Unit 12 Place value

60 000 | 7000 | 4 | 300 | 30 | 9 | 4000 | 50 | 600 | 40 000 | 900 | 7 | 3000 | 5 | 6000 | 70 000 | 50 000 | 500 | 90 | 40

a 67 394 b 46 539 c 73 645 d 54 957

1 Colour the parts to match their number.

2 Write each number in words.

a ______________________________

b ______________________________

c ______________________________

d ______________________________

3 Order the numbers from largest to smallest.

____

4 Write four numbers between 54 000 and 55 000.

a ____________ b ____________ c ____________ d ____________

5 a What is the smallest 5-digit number you can write? ____________

b What is the largest 5-digit number you can write? ____________

Challenge! I have the digits 0, 3, 5, 7, 9 in my name.
3 is in tens place, 9 has the smallest value, and 5 has the second highest value. Who am I? [ ]

Mastery Checklist I can:
- ☐ write numbers in the ten thousands
- ☐ show numbers on an abacus
- ☐ compare and order 5-digit numbers
- ☐ understand place value to 5 digits.

Unit 13 Number facts 7x, 8x, 9x

1 a b c

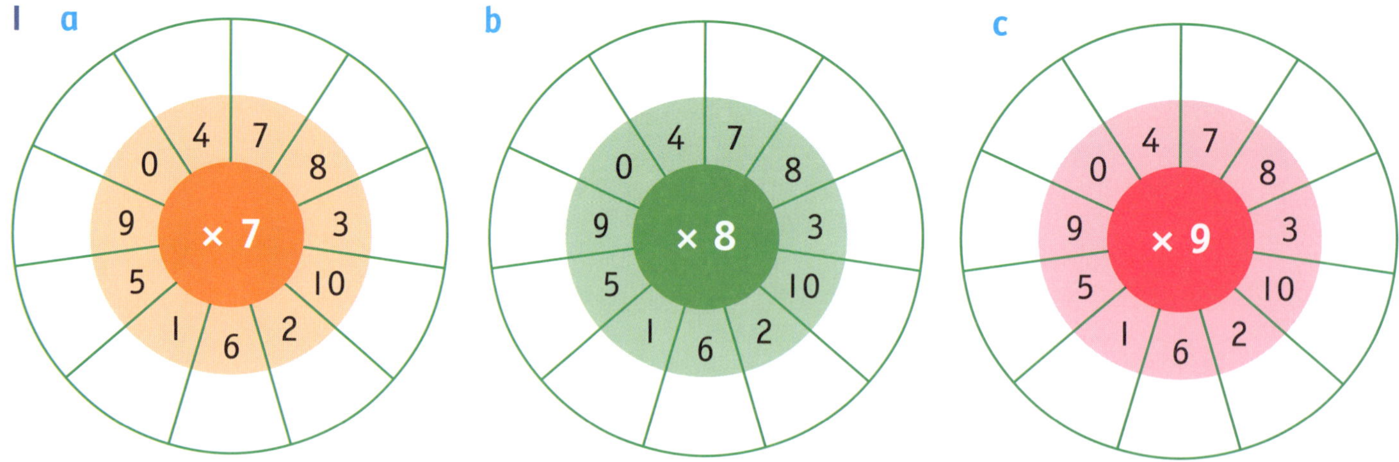

2 Cross the river by stepping only on multiples of 7. Colour the numbers as you cross.

3 Count in eights.

4 Circle the items that cost a multiple of 9c or $9.

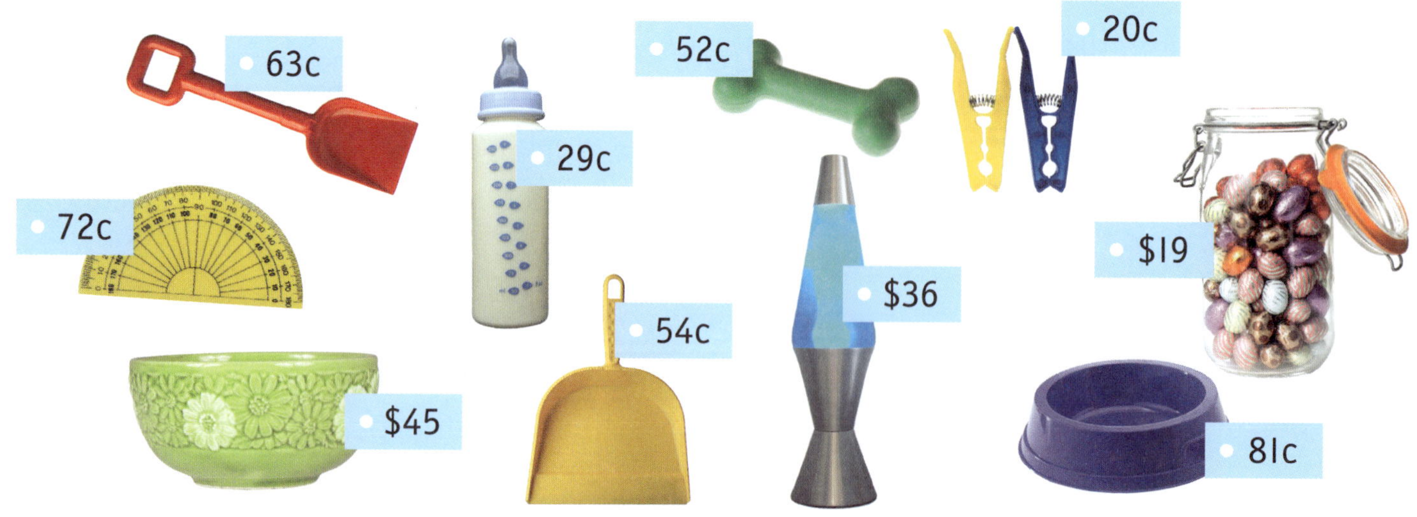

Unit 13 Number facts puzzle

This shows a mixed-up multiplication square. Use the clues to fill in the rest of the table.

×	6					5				
4	24								16	
						5		7		
				24	72					
										60
			16					14		
				21					28	
		6			27					
						45				90
		10								

Draw a diagram

Use an 11 × 11 square and design your own mixed-up multiplication square.

Make sure you can solve it.

Mastery Checklist

I can:
- ☐ use 7×, 8× and 9× tables
- ☐ identify multiples
- ☐ use mental strategies to solve multiplication problems.

Unit 14 Multiplication warehouse

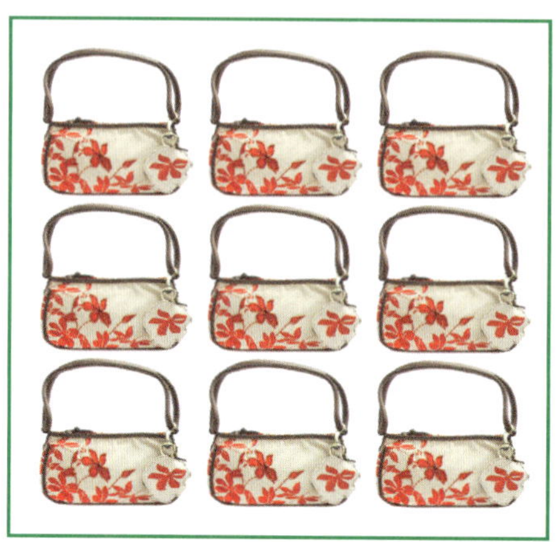

At the warehouse, goods are sold only in whole boxes.

1 In one box how many:

a shoes? ________ b handbags? ________ c necklaces? ________

d dresses? ________ e belts? ________ f skirts? ________

2 Mr Short ordered 5 boxes of each item, Mrs Hall ordered 8 boxes of each item and Miss Fellow ordered 6 boxes of each item. How many did they receive?

	dresses	handbags	belts	skirts	necklaces	shoes
a Mr Short						
b Mrs Hall						
c Miss Fellow						

3 How many in:

a 9 boxes of necklaces? ________ b 3 boxes of belts? ________

c 7 boxes of skirts? ________ d 7 boxes of dresses? ________

e 4 boxes of shoes? ________ f 9 boxes of handbags? ________

Unit 14 Multiples

1, 16, 2, 8, 4 are all **factors** of 16.

16 is a **multiple** of 1, 16, 2, 8, 4.

a 

b 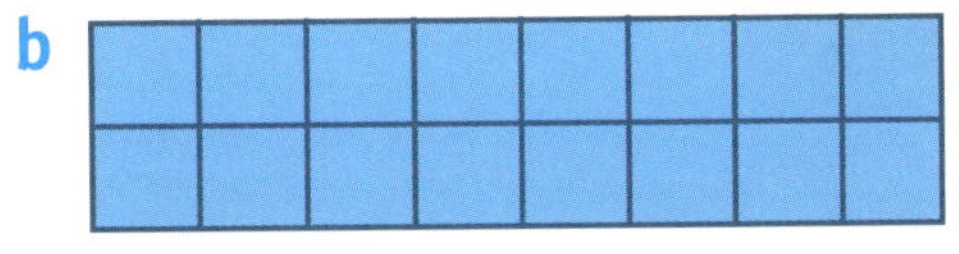

c 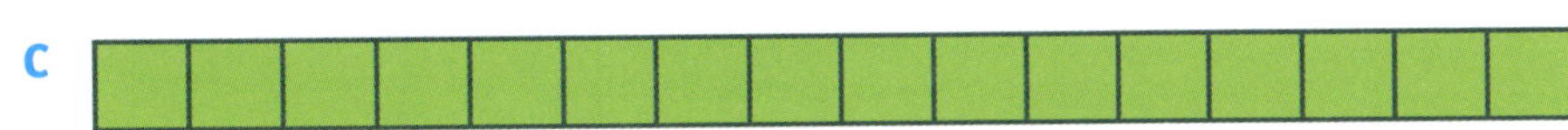

1 How many squares?

a $4 \times 4 =$ ______ b $2 \times 8 =$ ______ c $16 \times 1 =$ ______

2 Use the diagrams to answer the questions.

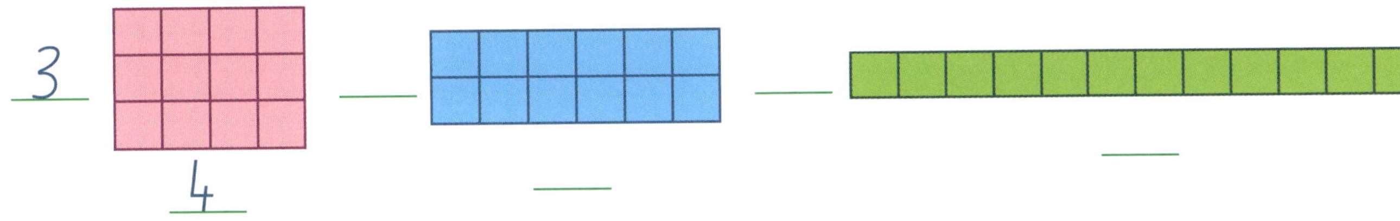

a How many squares in each diagram? ______

b 12 is a multiple of ______ ______ ______ ______ ______ ______

3

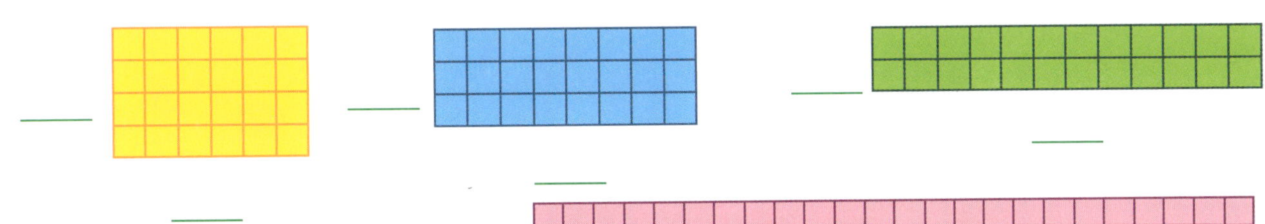

a How many squares in each diagram? ______

b 24 is a multiple of ______ ______ ______ ______ ______ ______ ______ ______

4 True or false?

a 12 is a multiple of 5. ______

b 27 is a multiple of 9. ______

c 32 is a multiple of 8. ______

d 27 is a multiple of 7. ______

e 21 is a multiple of 1. ______

f 54 is a multiple of 6. ______

g 1 is a multiple of 3. ______

h 14 is a multiple of 4. ______

i 25 is a multiple of 5. ______

j 16 is a multiple of 4. ______

k 21 is a multiple of 2. ______

l 18 is a multiple of 5. ______

m 36 is a multiple of 5. ______

n 72 is a multiple of 10. ______

o 24 is a multiple of 3. ______

p 34 is a multiple of 10. ______

Unit 14 Multiplication algorithm

1

a

3 lots of 5 = ______

$$\begin{array}{r} 5 \\ \times\ 3 \\ \hline \\ \hline \end{array}$$

b

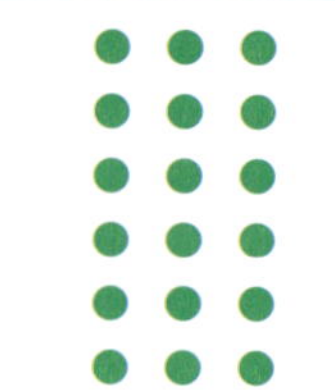

6 lots of 3 = ______

$$\begin{array}{r} 3 \\ \times\ 6 \\ \hline \\ \hline \end{array}$$

c

4 lots of 8 = ______

$$\begin{array}{r} 8 \\ \times\ 4 \\ \hline \\ \hline \end{array}$$

d

6 lots of ______ = ______

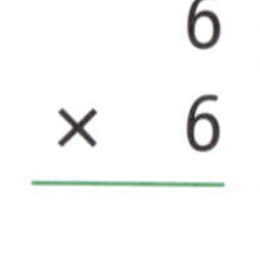

$$\begin{array}{r} 6 \\ \times\ 6 \\ \hline \\ \hline \end{array}$$

e

5 lots of ______ = ______

$$\begin{array}{r} \square \\ \times\ \square \\ \hline \\ \hline \end{array}$$

f

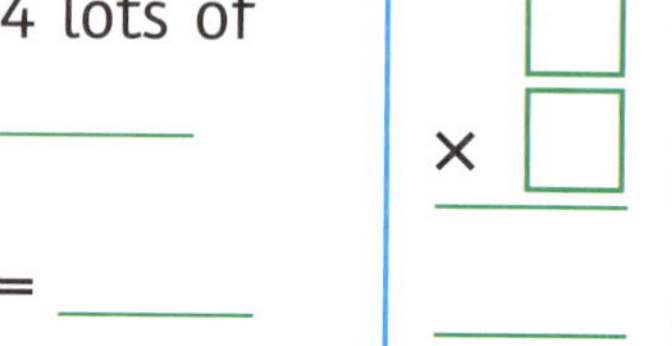

4 lots of ______ = ______

$$\begin{array}{r} \square \\ \times\ \square \\ \hline \\ \hline \end{array}$$

2 Write an algorithm for each.

a hands on 7 clocks

$$\begin{array}{r} 7 \\ \times\ 2 \\ \hline \\ \hline \end{array}$$

b legs on 9 dogs

$$\begin{array}{r} 9 \\ \times\ 4 \\ \hline \\ \hline \end{array}$$

c toes on 8 feet

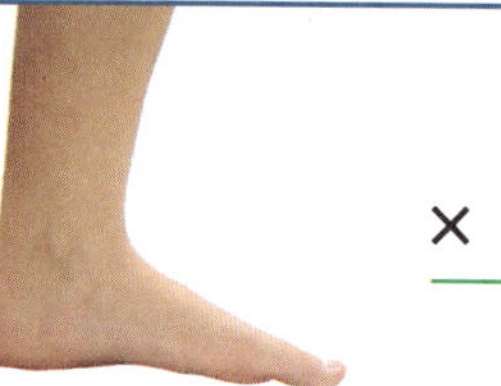

$$\begin{array}{r} \square \\ \times\ \square \\ \hline \\ \hline \end{array}$$

d days in 7 weeks

$$\begin{array}{r} \square \\ \times\ \square \\ \hline \\ \hline \end{array}$$

e corners on 9 triangles

$$\begin{array}{r} \square \\ \times\ \square \\ \hline \\ \hline \end{array}$$

f eyes on 10 owls

$$\begin{array}{r} \square\square \\ \times\ \square \\ \hline \\ \hline \end{array}$$

3

a $\begin{array}{r} 9 \\ \times\ 5 \\ \hline \\ \hline \end{array}$ **b** $\begin{array}{r} 7 \\ \times\ 1 \\ \hline \\ \hline \end{array}$ **c** $\begin{array}{r} 6 \\ \times\ 2 \\ \hline \\ \hline \end{array}$ **d** $\begin{array}{r} 5 \\ \times\ 0 \\ \hline \\ \hline \end{array}$ **e** $\begin{array}{r} 7 \\ \times\ 8 \\ \hline \\ \hline \end{array}$ **f** $\begin{array}{r} 8 \\ \times\ 6 \\ \hline \\ \hline \end{array}$

Mastery Checklist I can:

- ☐ use multiplication facts to solve problems
- ☐ identify multiples
- ☐ complete multiplication algorithms
- ☐ use arrays to multiply.

Problem solving

Use arrays

Divide your class into teams for different activities.
Illustrate the number of children in your class, using arrays.

eg This array shows a class of 18 in rows of 6.

X X X X X X
X X X X X X
X X X X X X

$3 \times 6 = 18$

My class has ______ children.

Show how your class can be arranged in:

Some rows may be only part full.

eg
X X X
X X X
X

$7 = 2 \times 3 + 1$

Teams of 3

Teams of 4

Teams of 5

Teams of 6

Teams of 7

Any other number?

What size were the teams that had no children left over? ______

How can you use the information from these arrays? ______

______

I can solve problems by:

☐ using different arrays to multiply ☐ writing equations and drawing arrays.

Unit 15 Division in the cake shop

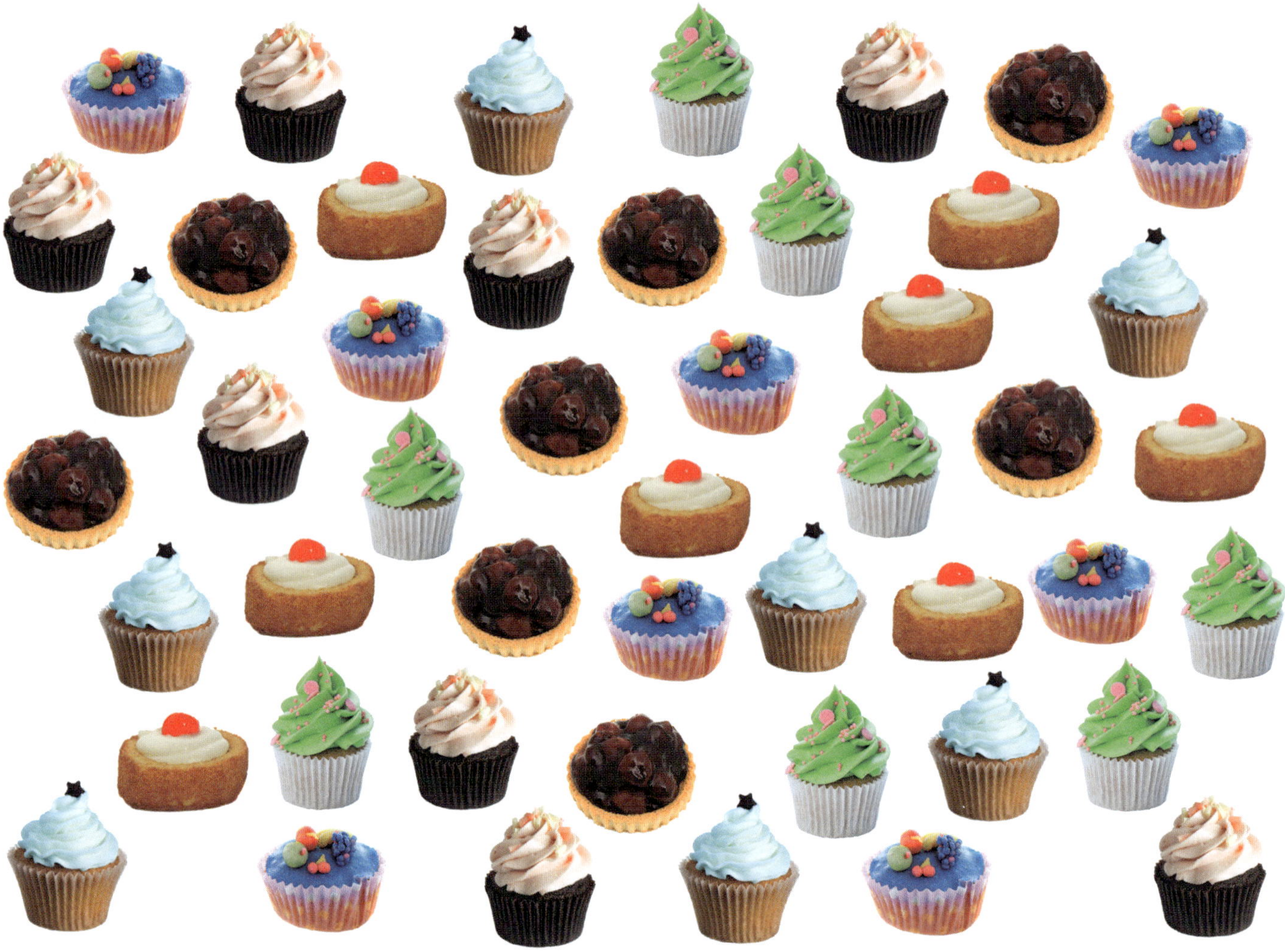

Mr Dough, the cake shop owner, has 7 different ways to package his cakes.

1 How can he pack mixed boxes of cakes without having any left over? eg 3 boxes of 16.

a ________ b ________ c ________

d ________ e ________ f ________

g ________ h ________ i ________

2 How many bags will there be if:

a each flavour of cake is put into a separate bag? ________

b two bags are used for each flavour of cake? ________

c one of each flavour of cake is put into a bag? ________

d two of each flavour of cake are put into a bag? ________

3 Write the division and multiplication number sentences to prove your answers to question 2.

a ________ b ________

c ________ d ________

Unit 15 How many?

1 How many cages?

a 16 birds, 2 in each cage ______

b 24 birds, 6 in each cage ______

c 36 cats, 6 in each cage ______

d 16 rats, 4 in each cage ______

e 49 lizards, 7 in each cage ______

f 54 mice, 9 in each cage ______

g 60 rabbits, 10 in each cage ______

h 72 chooks, 8 in each cage ______

i 42 parrots, 7 in each cage ______

j 40 rabbits, 5 in each cage ______

2

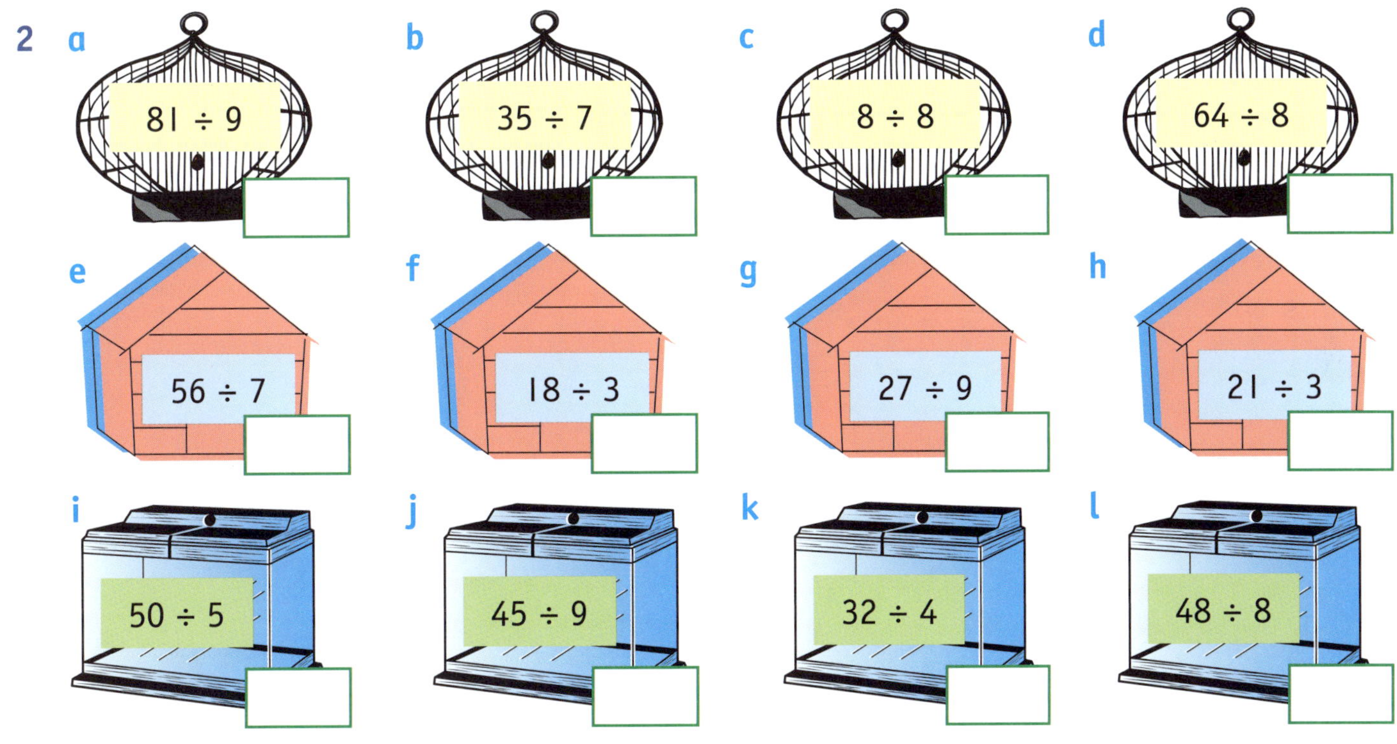

3 a ☐ ÷ 6 = 9 b 14 ÷ ☐ = 2 c ☐ ÷ 5 = 5 d 21 ÷ ☐ = 3

e 9 ÷ 9 = ☐ f ☐ ÷ 10 = 4 g 10 ÷ ☐ = 1 h ☐ ÷ 10 = 10

Challenge!

How many different ways can you put 100 fish into tanks?

Unit 15 Division and multiplication

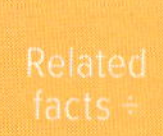

$\overline{)}$ is another division sign. $2\overline{)8}$ means 8 ÷ 2.

The answer 4 is written on top. $\begin{array}{r}4\\2\overline{)8}\end{array}$

1 Write × and ÷ facts for each.

a	b	c	d	e	f
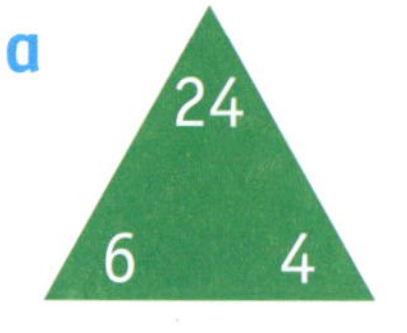	27 3 9	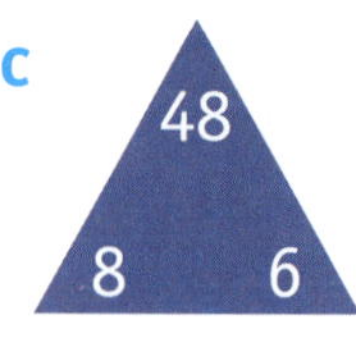		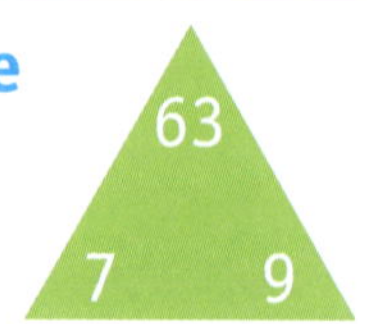	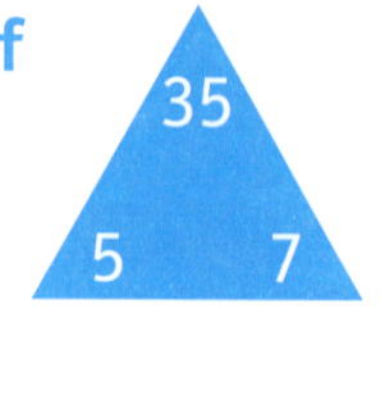
4 × 6 = ____	____	____	____	____	____
6 × 4 = ____	____	____	____	____	____
24 ÷ 6 = ____	____	____	____ 	____ 	____
24 ÷ 4 = ____	____	____	____	____	____

2

a	b	c	d	e	f
$4\overline{)8}$	$2\overline{)4}$	$3\overline{)21}$	$3\overline{)9}$	$2\overline{)6}$	$8\overline{)32}$

g	h	i	j	k	l
$5\overline{)15}$	$3\overline{)6}$	$4\overline{)4}$	$2\overline{)8}$	$5\overline{)10}$	$6\overline{)42}$

3 Check your answers to question 2 by multiplying.

a 4 × 2 = 8 **b** 2 × ____ = ____ **c** 3 × ____ = ____

d 3 × ____ = ____ **e** 2 × ____ = ____ **f** 8 × ____ = ____

g 5 × ____ = ____ **h** 3 × ____ = ____ **i** 4 × ____ = ____

j 2 × ____ = ____ **k** 5 × ____ = ____ **l** 6 × ____ = ____

4 What operation will you use? Write a number sentence and the answer.

a Jim ate 4 apples every day. How many did he eat in 1 week?

____

b Kylie ate 56 cherries last week. How many was that each day?

____

c Farmer Hay had 36 sheep to put into 4 paddocks. How many sheep in each?

____

d Farmer Oats had 5 paddocks with 8 horses in each. How many horses altogether?

____

AC9M4N06 Number **MA2-MR-01** • **MA2-MR-02** Multiplicative relations B • Use number properties to find related multiplication facts • Represent and solve word problems with number sentences involving multiplication or division

Unit 15 Remainders

Remainders
When we divide, the number left over is the remainder.
11 ÷ 5 = 2 r1

1 Write the number sentence and the answer.

a 12 oranges shared by 5 people. ___ ÷ ___ = ___ r ___	b 14 bananas eaten by 3 monkeys. ___ ÷ ___ = ___ r ___	c 55 nuts eaten by 9 squirrels. ___ ÷ ___ = ___ r ___
d 29 sweets shared by 3 children. ___ ÷ ___ = ___ r ___	e 65 snails eaten by 9 lizards. ___ ÷ ___ = ___ r ___	f 40 days. How many weeks? ___ ÷ ___ = ___ r ___
g 30 giraffes for 4 zoos.   ___ ÷ ___ = ___ r ___	h 42 bones for 6 dogs. 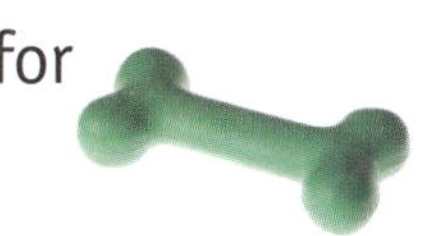 ___ ÷ ___ = ___ r ___	i 70 candles for 8 cakes.  ___ ÷ ___ = ___ r ___
j 70 books put into 7 boxes.  ___ ÷ ___ = ___ r ___	k 82 beads for 9 necklaces.  ___ ÷ ___ = ___ r ___	l 18 eggs for 6 cakes.  ___ ÷ ___ = ___ r ___

2 Follow the pattern.

a	b	c
8 ÷ 2 = ___	9 ÷ 3 = ___	12 ÷ 6 = ___
80 ÷ 2 = 40	90 ÷ 3 = ___	___ ÷ 6 = ___
800 ÷ 2 = 400	900 ÷ 3 = ___	___ ÷ 6 = ___

d	e	f
28 ÷ 7 = ___	48 ÷ ___ = 8	___ ÷ 5 = 7
___ ÷ 7 = ___	480 ÷ 6 = ___	___ ÷ ___ = 70
___ ÷ ___ = ___	___ ÷ 6 = 800	___ ÷ 5 = ___

Challenge! Complete the path by following instructions.

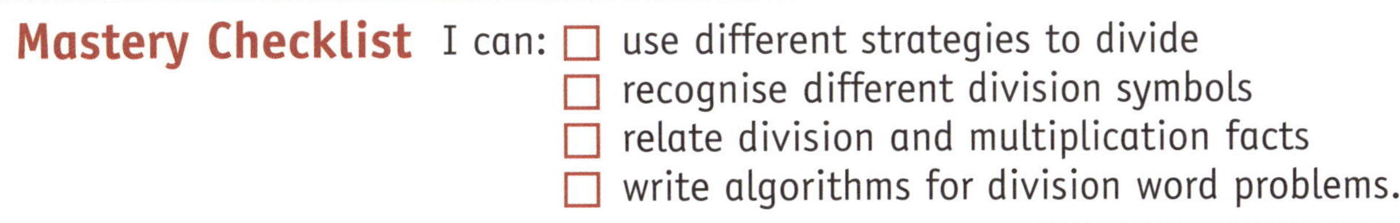

Mastery Checklist I can:
- ☐ use different strategies to divide
- ☐ recognise different division symbols
- ☐ relate division and multiplication facts
- ☐ write algorithms for division word problems.

Unit 16 Writing tenths and decimals

10ths and 100ths

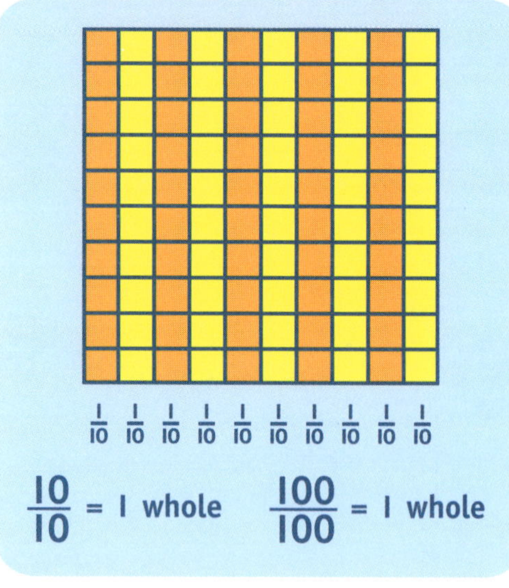

Place values

Ones		Tenths	Hundredths
3	•	5	7
1	•	8	

1 How many tenths are coloured? Write the decimal.

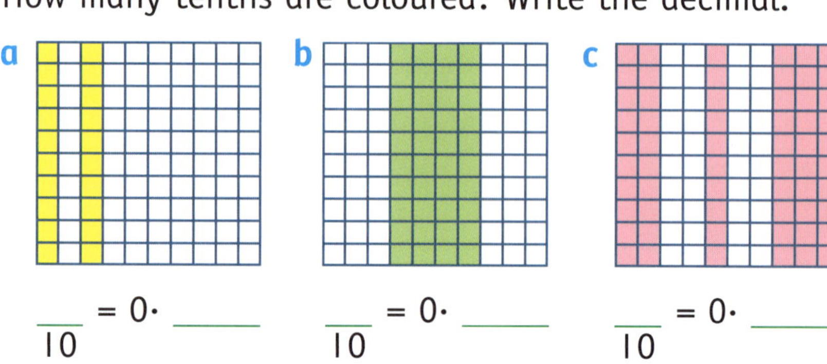

a $\frac{\_\_\_}{10}$ = 0· ______

b $\frac{\_\_\_}{10}$ = 0· ______

c $\frac{\_\_\_}{10}$ = 0· ______

2 In question 1, how many hundredths?

a $\frac{\_\_\_}{100}$ = 0· ______

b $\frac{\_\_\_}{100}$ = 0· ______

c $\frac{\_\_\_}{100}$ = 0· ______

3 Colour to show tenths.

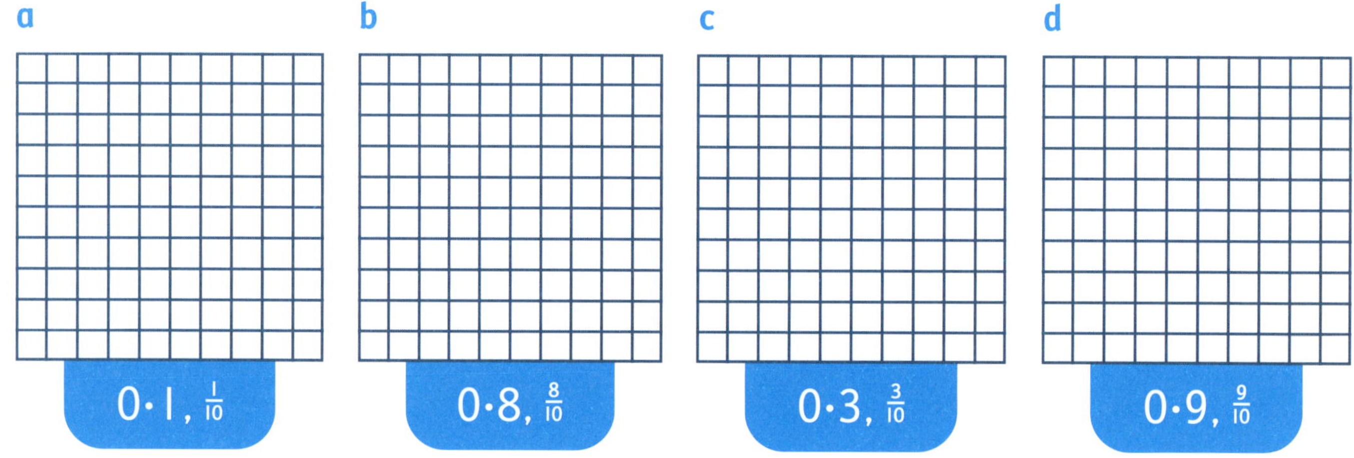

4 In question 3, how many hundredths?

a $\frac{\_\_\_}{100}$ = 0· ______

b $\frac{\_\_\_}{100}$ = 0· ______

c $\frac{\_\_\_}{100}$ = 0· ______

5 Write these on the number line. **0·6 0·1 0·8 0·5**

AC9M4N01 • AC9M4N04 Number **MA2-RN-02** Representing numbers using place value B • Decimals: Extend the application of the place value system from whole numbers to tenths and hundredths • Make connections between fractions and decimal notation

Unit 16 Tenths and hundredths

1 Write **equals**, **is more than** or **is less than** to make the statements true.

a 0·3 ________________ 0·7 b 0·6 ________________ 0·60

c 0·5 ________________ 0·6 d 0·6 ________________ 0·2

e 0·9 ________________ 0·5 f 0·3 ________________ 0·30

$\frac{2}{10}$ = 0·2

$\frac{20}{100}$ = 0·20

0·2 = 0·20

2 Write the decimal.

a $\frac{1}{10}$ _____ b $\frac{7}{10}$ _____ c $\frac{3}{10}$ _____

d $\frac{9}{10}$ _____ e $\frac{4}{10}$ _____ f $\frac{2}{10}$ _____

3 Write as tenths and hundredths.

a 0·5 = $\frac{\quad}{10}$, $\frac{\quad}{100}$ b 0·8 = $\frac{\quad}{10}$, $\frac{\quad}{100}$ c 0·6 = $\frac{\quad}{10}$, $\frac{\quad}{100}$

d 0·1 = $\frac{\quad}{10}$, $\frac{\quad}{100}$ e 0·7 = $\frac{\quad}{10}$, $\frac{\quad}{100}$ f 0·4 = $\frac{\quad}{10}$, $\frac{\quad}{100}$

g 0·2 = $\frac{\quad}{10}$, $\frac{\quad}{100}$ h 0·9 = $\frac{\quad}{10}$, $\frac{\quad}{100}$ i 0·3 = $\frac{\quad}{10}$, $\frac{\quad}{100}$

4 Tick the correct statements and cross the incorrect statements.

a 1·6 equals 1·60 _____ b 0·9 is more than 0·29 _____ c 3·2 equals 2·80 _____

d 5·34 is less than 5·5 _____ e 2·70 equals 2·7 _____ f 4·18 is less than 4·3 _____

g 0·9 is more than 1·1 _____ h 7·10 equals 7·01 _____ i 9·3 is less than 9·25 _____

5

	a		b		c		d	
	$	c	$	c	$	c	$	c
	0 .	10	3 .	40	1 .	15	3 .	25
+	2 .	50	+ 2 .	30	+ 2 .	25	+ 4 .	25
	____		____		____		____	

6 Now use a calculator to work out question 5.
Write what the calculator shows.

a ____________ b ____________ c ____________ d ____________

e What is missing? ______________________________

f Why? ____

A calculator is showing these dollar amounts.
Write them using a $ sign.

a 3·4 [ ] b 1·8 [ ] c 2·9 [ ] d 14·5 [ ]

Unit 16 Adding and subtracting decimals

Working with money 1

When working with decimals, don't forget the decimal point in the answer.

1 Find the cost of:

a one folder and abacus.

$	c
1	.35
+ 7	.58

b calculator and magnifying glass.

c bell and one folder.

d calculator and bell.

2 What is the difference in price between:

a magnifying glass and a folder?

$	c
2	.45
− 1	.35

b abacus and magnifying glass?

c bell and abacus?

d calculator and bell?

3 a $6 \cdot 21 + 4 \cdot 38$ b $4 \cdot 93 + 6 \cdot 08$ c $8 \cdot 02 + 1 \cdot 94$ d $3 \cdot 89 + 1 \cdot 01$ e $5 \cdot 14 + 4 \cdot 63$

f $0 \cdot 72 + 6 \cdot 19$ g $8 \cdot 35 + 0 \cdot 27$ h $3 \cdot 54 + 4 \cdot 37$ i $1 \cdot 29 + 5 \cdot 08$ j $9 \cdot 06 + 0 \cdot 57$

4 a $6 \cdot 34 - 1 \cdot 21$ b $7 \cdot 95 - 2 \cdot 64$ c $5 \cdot 87 - 0 \cdot 35$ d $2 \cdot 46 - 2 \cdot 41$ e $9 \cdot 78 - 5 \cdot 26$

Unit 16 Decimals in order

1 Trace three paths across the stepping stones.
Path 1: from 2·6 to 2·99. **Path 2:** from 1·2 to 1·99. **Path 3:** from 3·5 to 3·99.
Your decimals should be in ascending order.

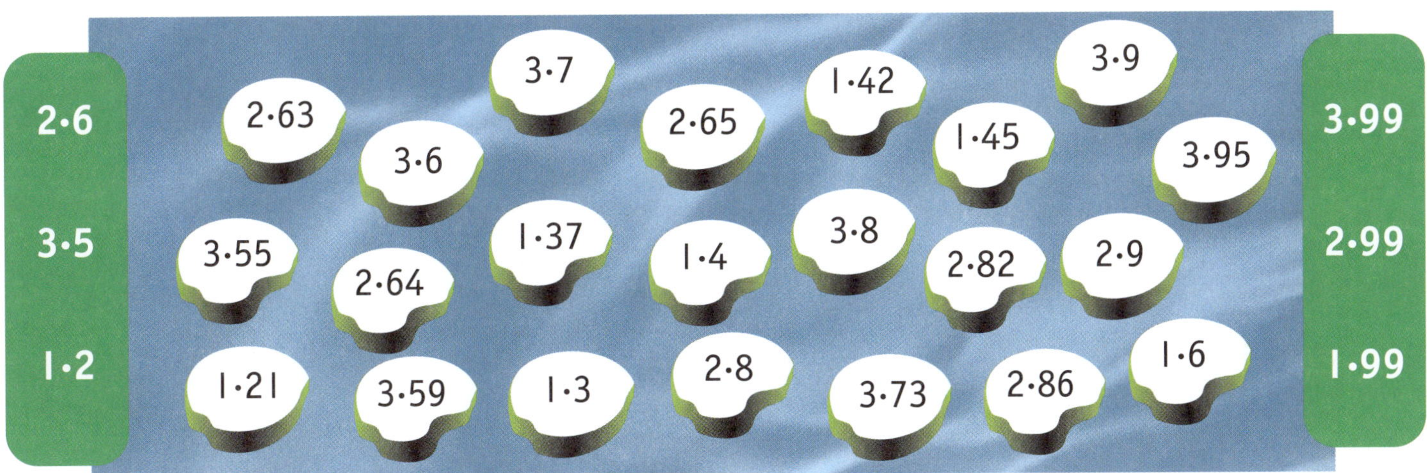

2 Climb the ladders with decimals getting larger by the number given at the top of the ladder. Starting at the bottom.

a **0·1**
3·0
2·4

b **0·01**
2·4
2·35

c **0·1**
2·3
1·8

d **0·1**
2·35
1·75

3 Join the matching decimals and fractions. Use a ruler and coloured pencils. Each set makes a triangle. Colour your design.

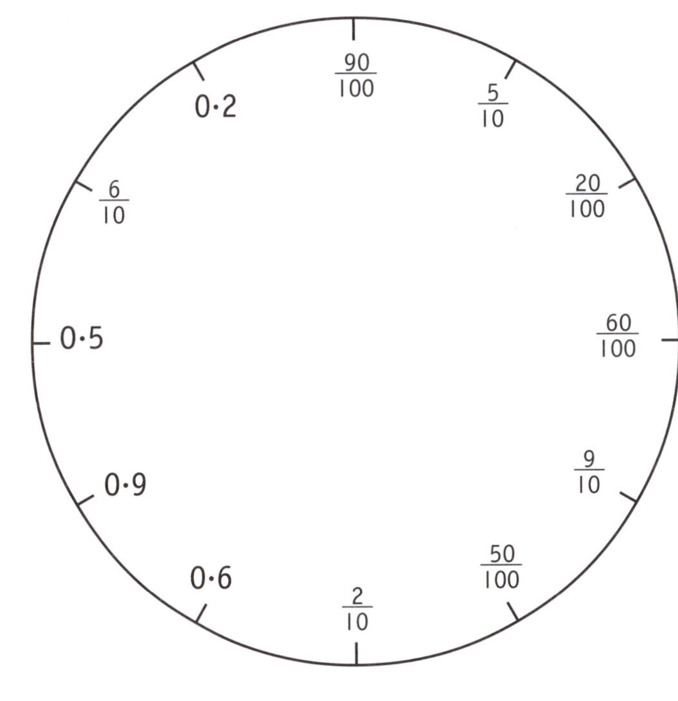

Mastery Checklist

I can:
- ☐ identify place value including tenths and hundredths
- ☐ compare decimals
- ☐ add and subtract decimals
- ☐ write decimals in ascending order.

Year 4 Cooks

Investigation 2

Fifty children from another school are visiting next week.
You will be making morning tea for them.

These ingredients make a batch of 20 Choc-raisin Biscuits.

Ingredients:

- 125 g caster sugar
- 125 g butter, melted
- 1 cup plain flour
- 1 cup self-raising flour
- 1 egg, lightly beaten
- 125 g chocolate pieces
- 125 g raisins

1 How many biscuits will you need for the visitors and yourselves? How many batches?

2 Look up supermarket prices online for these ingredients.
What is the cost for 20 biscuits?

3 Cost for the total number of biscuits:

4 How will you divide the biscuits up to serve them? Explain and draw.

Year 4 Cooks

Investigation 2

It's Pizza Party time in Year 4! How can you make enough for everyone?

This recipe makes 1 pizza.

Ingredients:

- 1 pizza base
- 3 tablespoons pizza sauce
- 1 cup mixed toppings such as pineapple, sliced meat, sun-dried tomatoes, olives
- $\frac{1}{3}$ cup grated cheese

Method:

- Preheat oven to 200 °C.
- Spread base with pizza sauce.
- Add toppings.
- Add grated cheese.
- Cook for 10–15 minutes.

How many pizzas would you need for your whole class? ________

Write the ingredients you'll buy here.	Costs
Total cost	

How would you cut the pizzas so that everyone gets 2 slices?

____

How could you make money from baking pizza?

____

____

To carry out these tasks, I need to:

- [ ] use doubling or adding to multiply ingredients, including fractions
- [ ] calculate the cost of a project
- [ ] calculate how to serve biscuits and pizza
- [ ] draw a diagram and work backwards
- [ ] explain how I solved a fractions problem
- [ ] think about how to make money from an activity.

I enjoyed this task! ☆☆☆☆☆

Revision

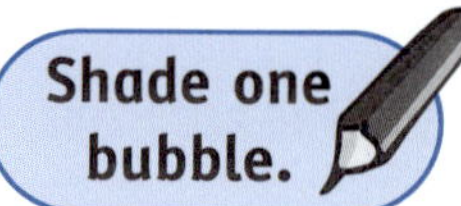

1 What is the place value of the underlined number?

16 852 (the 1 is underlined)

thousandths	tens	ten thousands	hundreds
◯	◯	◯	◯

Write your answer in the box.

2 Each box holds 6 pencils.
Josie bought 9 boxes.
How many pencils did Josie buy?

6 × ☐ **=** ☐

Shade one bubble.

3 Which box shows multiples of 8?

36, 6, 18, 30, 12	28, 14, 7, 35, 21	32, 16, 24, 8, 40	45, 27, 9, 36, 18
◯	◯	◯	◯

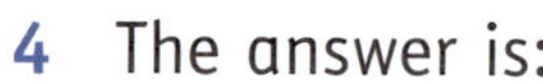

4 The answer is:

$$7\overline{)42}$$?

16	6	60	600
◯	◯	◯	◯

---

5 How many pears in eight boxes?

17	72	720	170
◯	◯	◯	◯

Revision

6 Which statement is true?

12 is a multiple of 5.	8 is a multiple of 18.	24 is a multiple of 8.	4 is a multiple of 14.

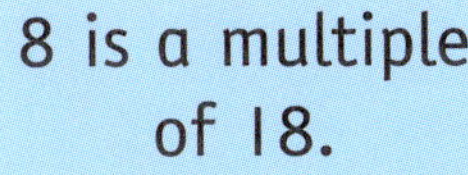

7 I picked 54 strawberries.
I gave 7 friends 7 strawberries each.
How many were left for me?

7 6 5 4

8

$$\begin{array}{r} 1.51 \\ +\ 5.89 \\ \hline \\ \hline \end{array}$$

Write your answer in the box.

9 Which multiple does not belong?

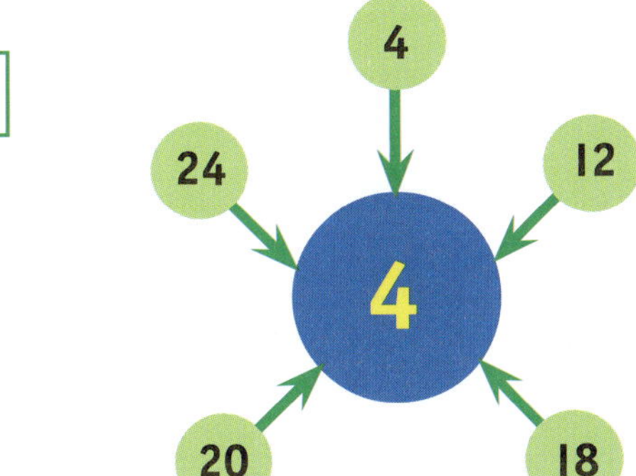

10 Write the number sentence.

81 beetles shared by 9 magpies.

Unit 17 Shopping and change

1 Terri has a $10 note. What change will she get if she buys:

a the book? ____________ b the teddy? ____________ c the truck? ____________

2 List three items she couldn't buy if she only had a $20 note.

____

3 What change from $50 would she get if she bought:

a the skateboard? ____________ b the board game? ____________

4 What notes and coins could she get in the change from:

a the skateboard? ________________________

b the board game? ________________________

5 What notes and coins would she use if she had the exact money to buy:

a the phone and the board game? ________________________

b the robot and the book? ________________________

6 Write the number sentence and the answer. Find the difference in cost between:

a the truck and the teddy. ________________________

b the scooter and the robot. ________________________

Challenge! I'm having a sale. Slash all the above prices in half.

Truck =		Robot =		Board game =		Scooter =	
Skateboard =		Phone =		Teddy =		Book =	

Unit 17 Money amounts

1 Circle the ones in the cents.

a $4.65 b $8.34 c $15.98 d $7.90 e $52.15

2 Underline the tens in the cents.

a $9.45 b $11.56 c $94.80 d $27.35 e $102.75

3 Circle the ones in the dollars.

a $7.81 b $18.65 c $38.90 d $56.20 e $55.50

4 Underline the tens in the dollars.

a $46.70 b $29.80 c $72.85 d $926.15 e $718.25

5 What money amount is shown on these calculator screens?

a 

b 

c 62.9

d 

e 

f 

g 

h 

6 What is the best way to round off? eg $8.50 rounds to $9.

a $38.75 ____________

b $1.20 ____________

7 Look at page 76. Estimate the total cost of these items. Write how you estimated:

a the teddy, the robot and the truck to the nearest dollar. ____________

____

b the skateboard, the board game and the phone to the nearest $10. ____________

____

c the board game, the book and the skateboard to the nearest $10. ____________

____

8 What three items have a total cost of $28.50? ____________

____

9 I need to pay for the skateboard with cash. I have given the cashier a $20 note and a $5 note. I only have coins left. What is the least number of coins I must give to pay the full amount for the skateboard? ____________

Unit 17 Notes and coins

1 Round these to the nearest 5c.

a 67c ______ b 58c ______ c 82c ______
d 17c ______ e 24c ______ f 36c ______
g 41c ______ h 19c ______ i 73c ______

Rounding to the nearest 5c
1c, 2c → 0
3c, 4c, 5c, 6c, 7c → 5
8c, 9c → 10

2 Round these to the nearest whole dollar.

a $1.28 ______ b $4.69 ______ c $8.37 ______ d $2.12 ______ e $6.52 ______
f $5.70 ______ g $7.89 ______ h $3.26 ______ i $5.95 ______ j $9.45 ______

3 Match the front and back of each note and write its value.

a 

A 

b 

B 

c 

C 

d 

D 

e 

E 

4 State the value of each coin.

a 
b 
c 
d 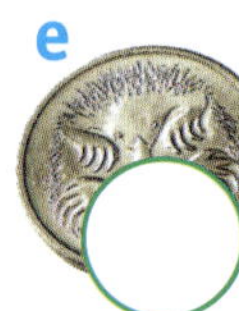
e 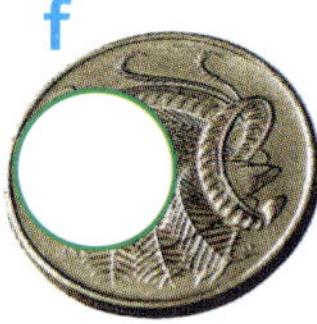
f

5 List the smallest number of coins needed to make:

a 65c. ______________________ b $3.85. ______________________
c $10.20. ______________________ d $7.35. ______________________

Mastery Checklist I can:
- ☐ work out change
- ☐ round to the nearest 5 cents
- ☐ round to the nearest dollar
- ☐ identify Australian notes and coins and their values.

Problem solving

Money counts

1 The Hirmiz family of parents, grandparents and children are off to the Summer Fair. Jeremy Hirmiz made this list of expenses.

	Bus	Entry to the Fair
Seniors	$2.50	$6
Adults	$4.00	$10.50
Children	$3.50	$4.50

There are 2 seniors, 4 adults and 8 children in the whole family. How much will it cost for them all to travel by bus and go to the Fair? *Hint:* use doubling.

Seniors	Adults	Children	Total

2

Charity Collection

Class	Mon	Tues	Wed	Thurs	Fri
4X	$3.50	$3.65	$4.65	$2.25	$2.80
4Y	$4.75	$2.30	$2.80	$3.15	$3.60
4Z	$1.95	$3.15	$5.40	$2.35	$4.05

The Principal wants to give awards for great effort. Make up 5 awards she can give, eg best two-day total. Which classes will get the awards and why?

Challenge!

How much was collected altogether for charity by Year 4?

I can solve problems by:

☐ adding different amounts of money ☐ writing algorithms.

Unit 18 Patterns with 10

A

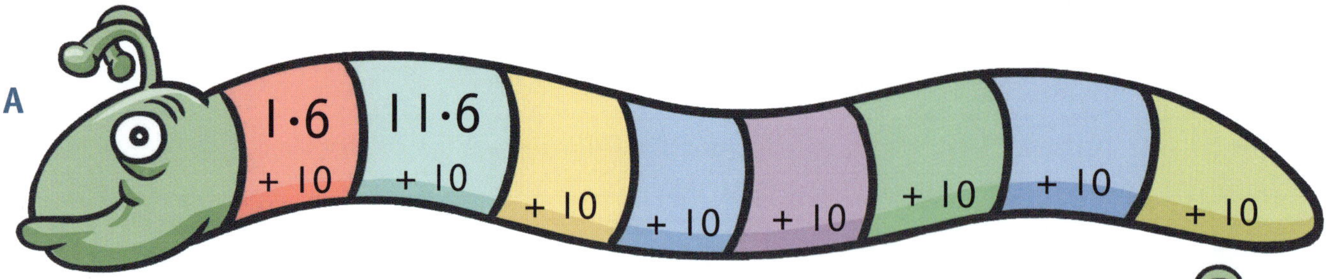

1·6	11·6						
+ 10	+ 10	+ 10	+ 10	+ 10	+ 10	+ 10	+ 10

B

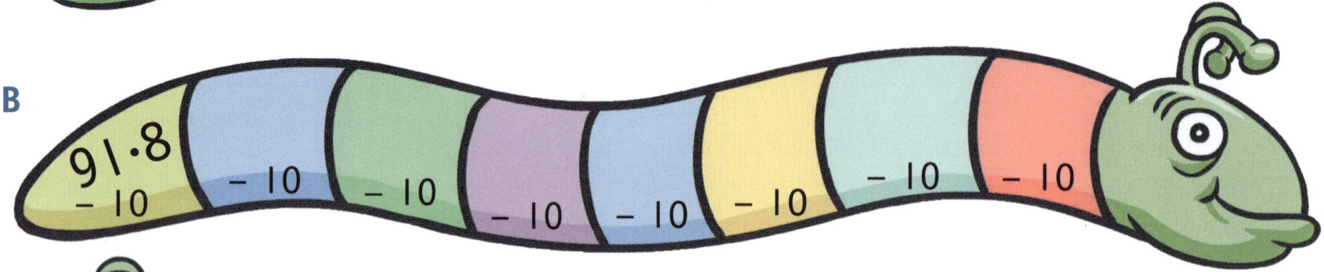

91·8							
− 10	− 10	− 10	− 10	− 10	− 10	− 10	− 10

C

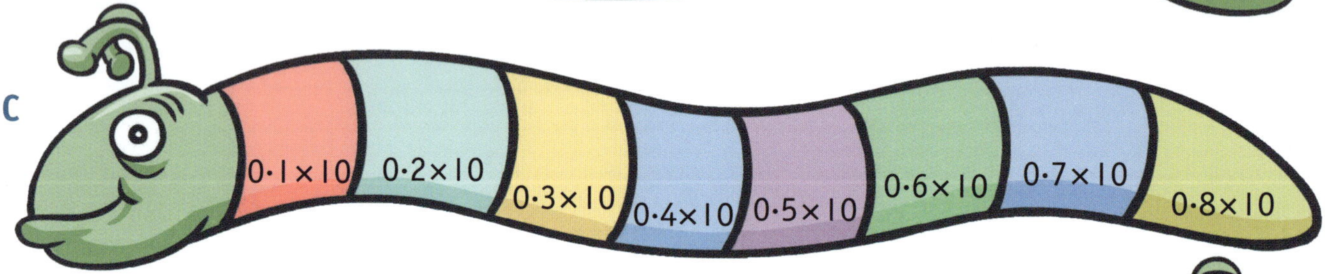

0·1 × 10	0·2 × 10	0·3 × 10	0·4 × 10	0·5 × 10	0·6 × 10	0·7 × 10	0·8 × 10

D

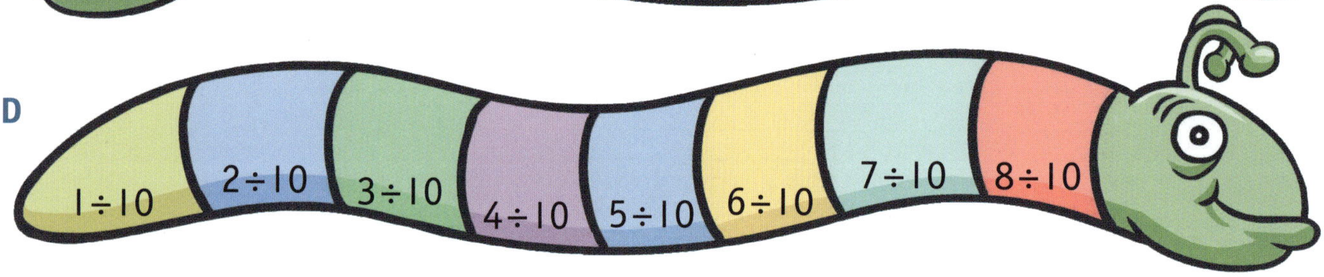

1 ÷ 10	2 ÷ 10	3 ÷ 10	4 ÷ 10	5 ÷ 10	6 ÷ 10	7 ÷ 10	8 ÷ 10

1 Use a calculator to complete each pattern.

2 Write what happens each time.

A ________________________________

B ________________________________

C ________________________________

D ________________________________

3 Now make up another pattern using whole numbers and decimals and × 10 or ÷ 10 . Write what happens.

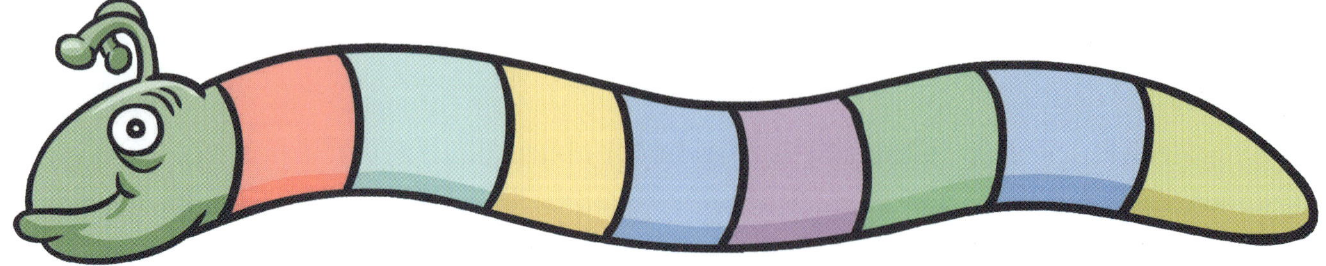

____

Unit 18 More patterns with 10

1 Use what you found out on page 80 to complete the following patterns and state the rule.

a 0·2, ____, 20·2, ____, ____, 50·2, ____, 70·2 Rule: ____

b 1·9, 11·9, ____, ____, ____, ____ Rule: ____

c ____, 113·5, ____, 93·5, ____, ____ Rule: ____

d 0·6, 6·0, ____, ____, ____, ____ Rule: ____

e 0·12, ____, 12·0, ____, ____, ____ Rule: ____

f 1 000 000, ____, ____, ____, 100 Rule: ____

g 83·4, ____, ____, 53·4, ____, ____ Rule: ____

h 0·1, 0·2, ____, ____, 0·5, ____, ____ Rule: ____

2 Complete each pattern following the given rule.

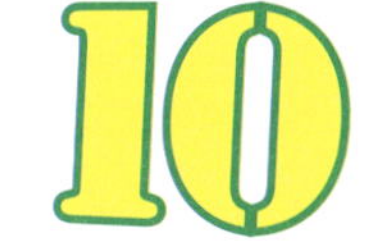

a Add 10·1 3·4, ____, ____, ____, ____

b Subtract 10·1 99·9, ____, ____, ____, ____

c Multiply by 10 0·3, ____, ____, ____, ____

d Multiply by 100 0·8, ____, ____, ____, ____

e Divide by 10 32 000, ____, ____, ____, ____

3 Describe how you can calculate the next term in each pattern.

a 10·6, 106, 1060, 10 600, ____ ____

b 3·5, 4·5, 5·5, 6·5, ____ ____

c 22·3, 22·4, 22·5, 22·6, ____ ____

d 124·5, 114·5, 104·5, 94·5, ____ ____

e 16 000, 1600, 160, 16, ____ ____

f 23·9, 123·9, 223·9, 323·9, ____ ____

4 Find the rest of each pattern and join them in order with a line.

a 2·4, 12·4, 22·4, — 60 600, 6000, 60 000

b 0·06, 0·6, 6, — 75, 7·5, 0·75, 0·075

c 75 000, 7500, 750, — 32·4, 42·4, 52·4, 62·4

Unit 18 Number sentence patterns

We can make equivalent number sentences to help solve problems.

eg Henri keeps 8 chickens and 2 roosters. His mother has the same number of fowls, but she has 6 chickens. How many roosters does she have?

Working: 8 + 2 is the same as 6 + **?**

8 + 2 is 10 which is the same as 6 + 4, so Henri's mother has 4 roosters.

1 Make three number sentences which have the same total as:

a 4 + 7 ________ ________ ________

b 5 + 8 ________ ________ ________

c 11 + 6 ________ ________ ________

d 16 + 9 ________ ________ ________

e 18 + 6 ________ ________ ________

2 Match the equivalent number sentences and write them showing equivalence.

eg 17 + 2 → 15 + 4   17 + 2 = 15 + 4

a 17 + 9   12 + 13 ________

b 23 + 6   18 + 8 ________

c 15 + 10   26 + 5 ________

d 18 + 7   16 + 13 ________

e 22 + 5   19 + 6 ________

f 19 + 12   16 + 11 ________

3 Show how to use equivalent number sentences to answer the questions.

a I saved $15 one week and then another $20 the next week.
Jenni saved $13 the first week and wants to equal my savings in the next week.

How much more does she have to save?

________ = ________

b There are 28 boys and 12 girls in one bus on the excursion.
16 girls get into the other bus and 24 boys follow.

Do the buses have equal loads?

________ = ________

Make a table Annie has ten pets – some dogs and some cats. Make a table to show the possible numbers of dogs and cats she could have.

Unit 18 Missing numbers

1 Find the missing numbers for these number sentences.

a $7 \times$ _____ $= 21$ b $9 \times$ _____ $= 18$ c $5 \times$ _____ $= 25$

d _____ $\times 4 = 24$ e _____ $\times 6 = 30$ f _____ $\times 5 = 35$

2 a $50 =$ _____ $\times 10$ b $35 =$ _____ $\times 7$ c $42 =$ _____ $\times 6$

d $36 = 6 \times$ _____ e $45 = 9 \times$ _____ f $28 = 4 \times$ _____

3 Match the number sentences that have the same answer.

a

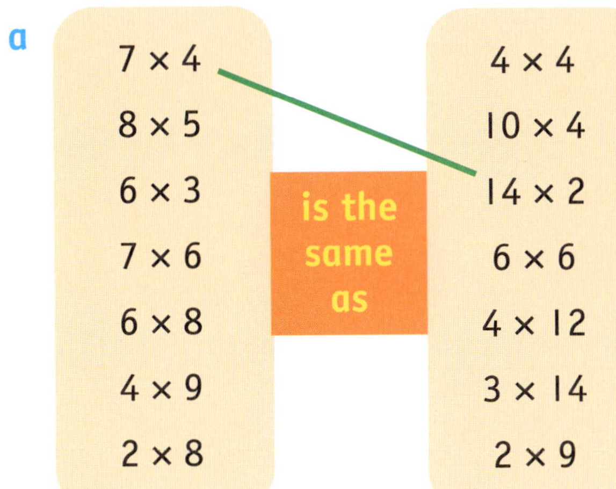

b

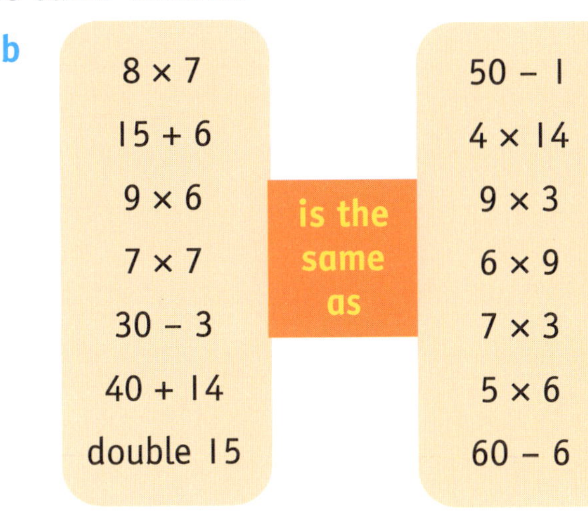

4 Match the story to two number sentences. Complete the number sentences.

a I bought 5 cards for 95c.
How much was each card? _____

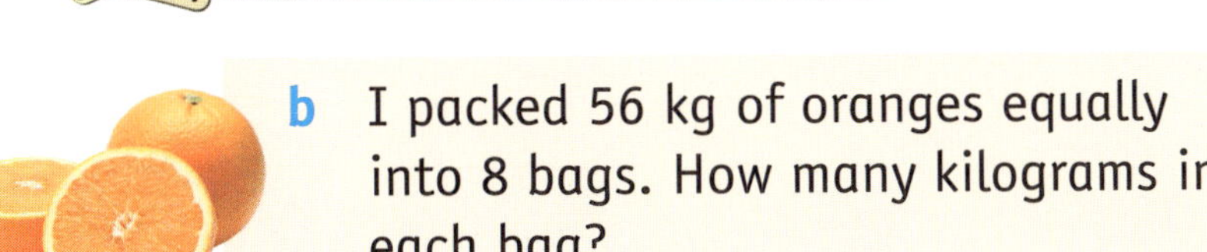

b I packed 56 kg of oranges equally into 8 bags. How many kilograms in each bag? _____

c The fisherman found a muddle of 64 octopus legs on the beach. How many octopuses were in the muddle? _____

d I rode my bike for 120 km over 10 days. How many km did I average each day? _____

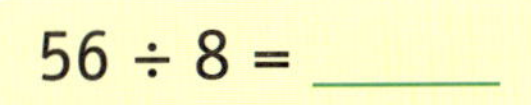

$8 \times$ _____ $= 64$

$10 \times$ _____ $= 120$

$5 \times$ _____ $= 95$

_____ $\times 8 = 56$

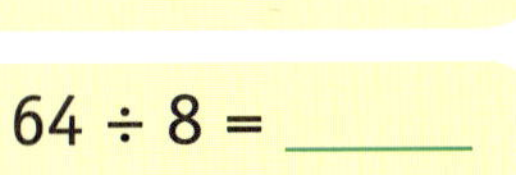

$95 \div 5 =$ _____

$120 \div 10 =$ _____

Mastery Checklist I can:
- ☐ continue patterns using all four operations
- ☐ make equivalent number sentences
- ☐ find missing numbers in number sentences
- ☐ match word problems to number sentences.

Unit 19 Lines and shapes

Parallel lines never meet.

Perpendicular lines meet at right angles.

1 Circle the parallel lines. Tick the perpendicular lines.

a
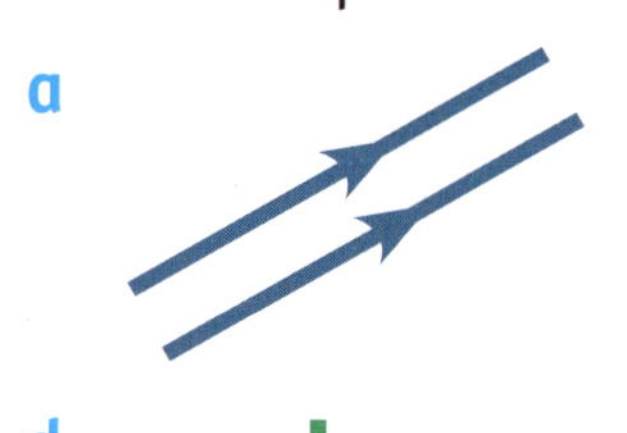

b

c
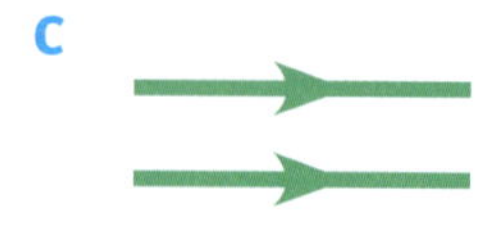

d
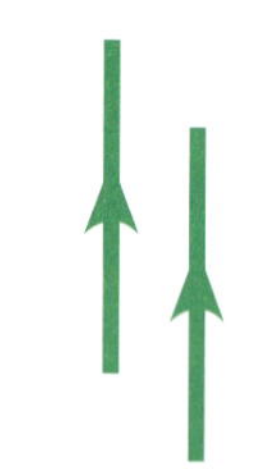

e

f
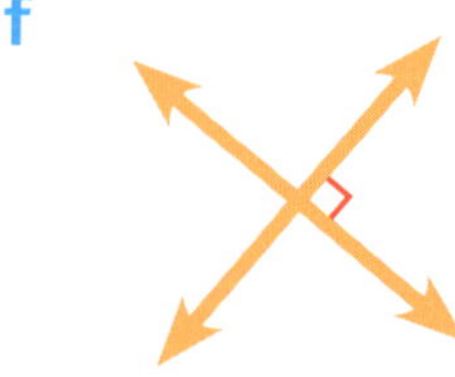

g
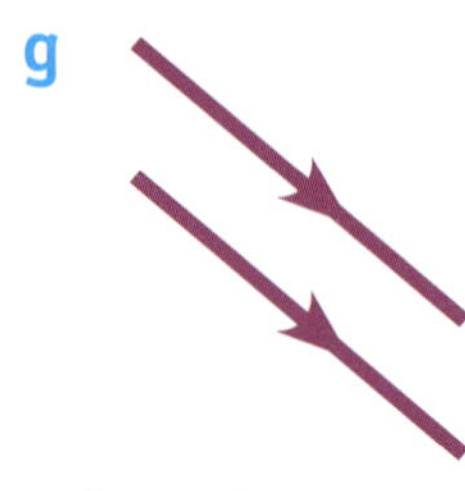

2 Measure each side. Complete the statement with facts about the shape's lines and sides.

a

A rectangle ______________________________
____
____

b

A square ______________________________
____
____

c

A parallelogram ______________________________
____
____

3 Draw three different trapeziums.

Challenge! Draw a picture of a house and garden using only triangles, rectangles, trapeziums, circles and pentagons.

Unit 19 2D shapes

1 Match each shape to its name.

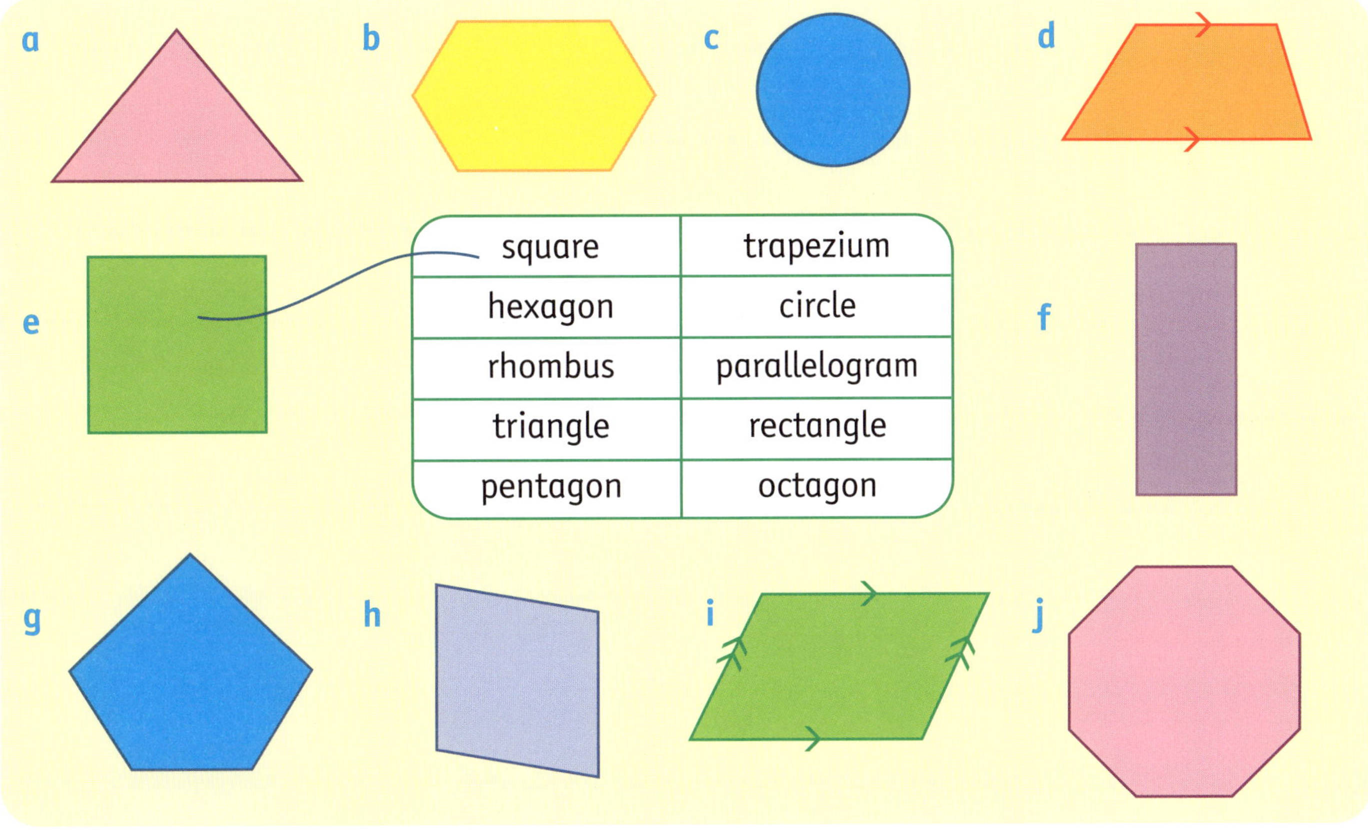

square	trapezium
hexagon	circle
rhombus	parallelogram
triangle	rectangle
pentagon	octagon

2 a Why is this [triangle] a triangle? ______________________________

____

b Why is this [parallelogram] a parallelogram? ______________________________

____

3

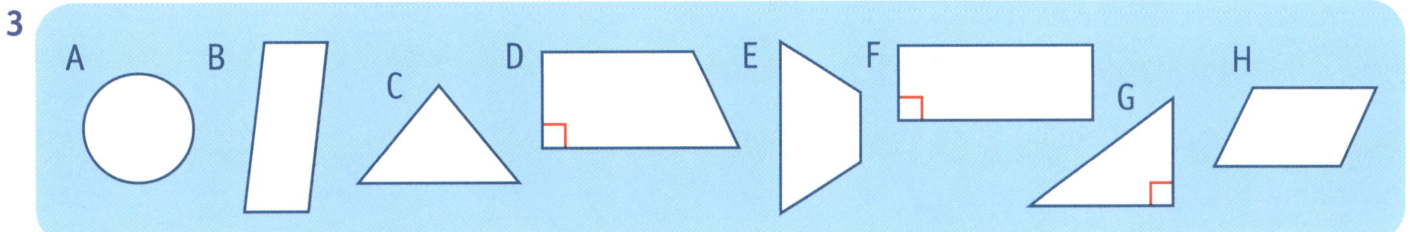

a Tick the shapes that have parallel sides. b Circle the shapes that have a right angle.

Draw a diagram

Draw diagrams of:

a 3 shapes that have acute angles.

b 3 shapes that have more than four sides.

c Name your shapes.

Unit 19 Symmetry

1 Using a pencil and ruler draw in lines of symmetry.

2 a Use a mirror to check your lines.

b How many did you get right? __________

3 Which shapes are not symmetrical? ____________________

4 Name the shapes. a D ________________ b H ________________

c Do all trapeziums have a line of symmetry? __________

5 Which shape has more than 1 line of symmetry? __________

6 Name the 2 shapes you could use to make:

A ______________ and ______________

B 2 __________________________

C ______________ and ______________

F __________________________

G __________________________

H __________________________

Unit 19 Logos

A logo is a picture, drawing or symbol that identifies a brand or business.

This Ford logo has two ovals.

1 Trace the 2D shapes that make up these logos, and label them.

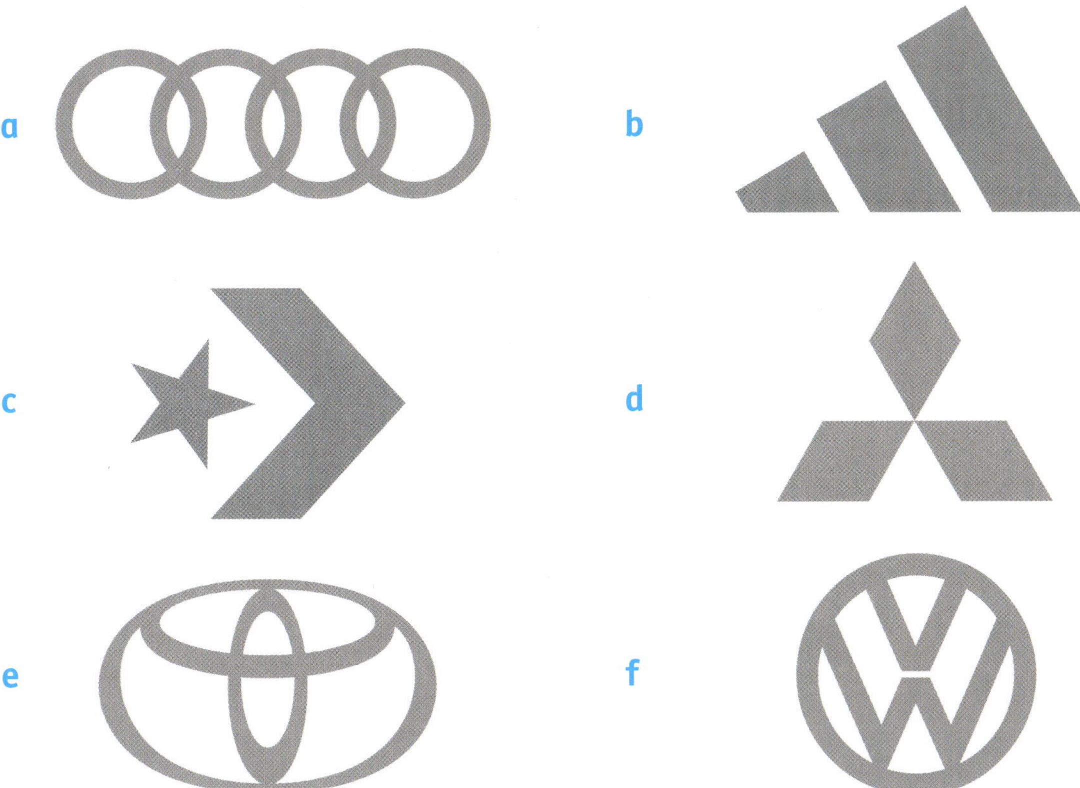

2 Find three more logos that are made up of 2D shapes. Draw and label them.

3 Design a logo for yourself that uses 2D shapes.

Unit 19 Changing shapes

Position 

1 Copy each of the following shapes using computer drawing tools. Draw each shape again and carry out the change given here. What shape do the two make together? Copy it here.

eg triangle, reflected square	**a** triangle, rotated half a turn
b parallelogram, translated	**c** rhombus, translated
d trapezium, rotated half a turn	**e** square, reflected

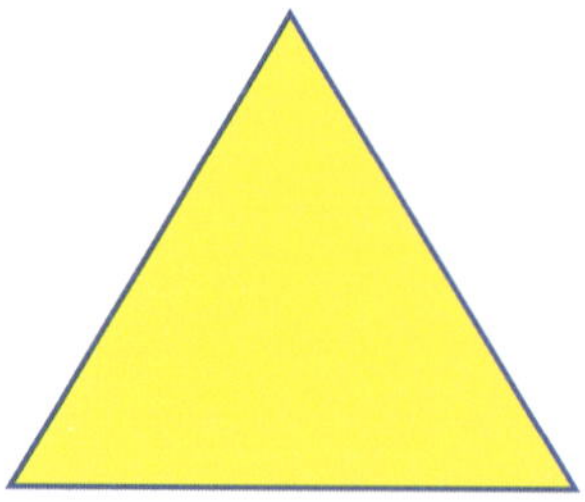

Challenge!

Make a pattern by rotating, reflecting and translating one shape, eg draw a house using just a triangle.

Mastery Checklist

I can:
- ☐ identify parallel and perpendicular lines
- ☐ name and draw 2D shapes
- ☐ draw lines of symmetry
- ☐ identify shapes in logos
- ☐ combine 2D shapes to form a new shape.

Unit 20 Capacity

Volume and capacity

baby's bottle

bottle

bucket

bath

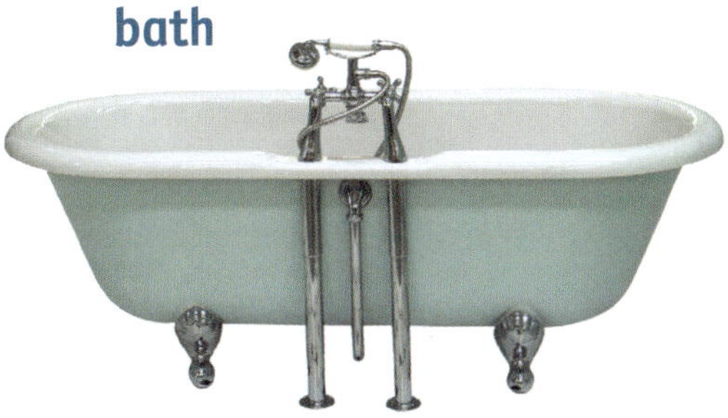

milk barrel

cup

glass

soup can

petrol can

flask

oil can

thimble

1 Fill a large, clear, plastic bottle with one litre of water to see how much space it takes up.

2 Circle the containers above which hold more than 10 litres.

3 Name two of the containers that:

a hold more than 20 litres. ____________________

b hold about half a litre. ____________________

c hold less than half a litre. ____________________

4 Tick the object that holds the least. Cross the object that holds the most.

5 Write three things that are measured in litres.

a ____________ b ____________ c ____________

Unit 20 Millilitres

L = litre
mL = millilitre
1 L = 1000 mL

1 Write as litres.

a 2000 mL ______ b 7000 mL ______ c 5000 mL ______ d 9000 mL ______

2 Write as millilitres.

a 3 L ______ b 6 L ______ c 8 L ______ d 10 L ______ e 4 L ______

3 Write as litres and millilitres.

a 2500 mL 2 L 500 mL b 3200 mL ______

c 1700 mL ______ d 5850 mL ______

e 6120 mL ______ f 8225 mL ______

4

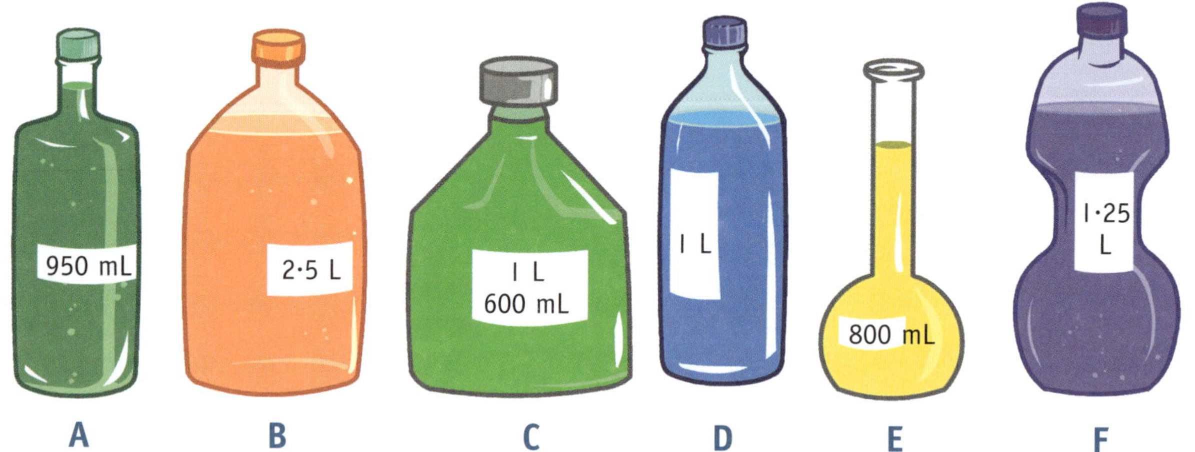

a Which bottle holds the most? ______ b Which bottle holds the least? ______

c How much more to make 1 litre? Bottle A ______ Bottle E ______

5 How many mL in:

a 1·5 L? ______ b 7·5 L? ______ c 2·25 L? ______ d 4·25 L? ______

Activity • Make a measure

You need an empty, large, plastic bottle, a 100 mL measure and a permanent marker pen.

Using the small measure, pour 100 mL of water into the bottle.

Mark the level with the pen. Write 100 mL next to the mark.

Keep adding 100 mL at a time and mark each new level (200 mL, 300 mL etc.) until you reach 1000 mL.

Use your bottle to measure quantities up to 1 L.

Unit 20 Measuring capacity

1 Would you use litres or millilitres to measure:

a a cup of tea? ______________ b water in a pool? ______________

c a dose of medicine? ______________ d milk in a baby's bottle? ______________

e ice-cream in a large tub? ______________ f petrol in a tank? ______________

2 Draw a line and colour to show the amount given.

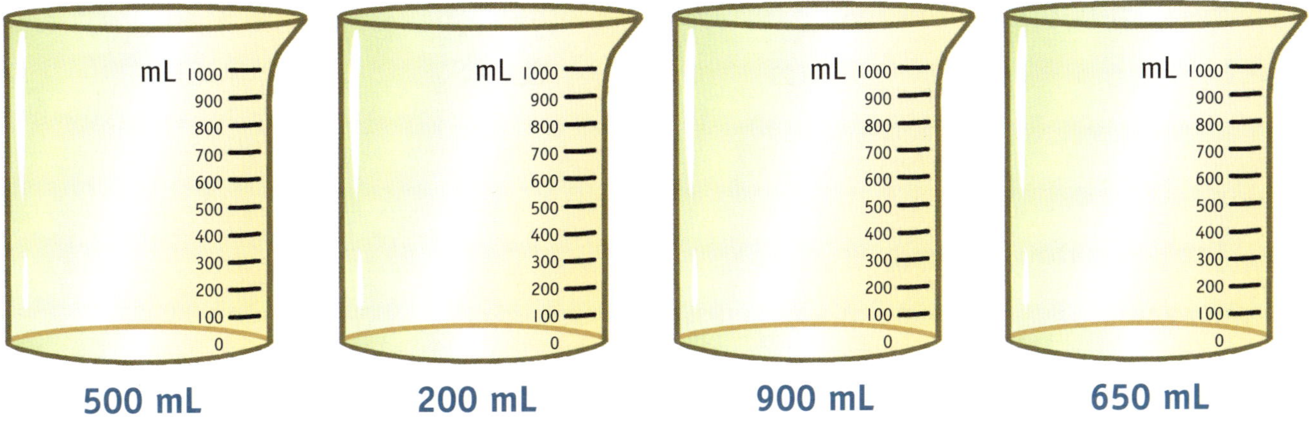

500 mL 200 mL 900 mL 650 mL

3 Fill an ice-cream container to the brim with water. Place it in a larger bowl. Choose an object (eg a large stone) and place it in the ice-cream container. Measure how much water overflowed. Repeat with two different objects.

Objects	Overflow in mL
a	
b	
c	

d Which object had: most overflow? ______________ least overflow? ______________

4 Half fill a clear container with water. Use the three objects from question 3. Place them one at a time into the container. Mark the level of water each time. Which object increased the level:

a most? ______________ b least? ______________

5 Comment about your results. ______________________________

____

____

In the laboratory

1 Professor Dinkum Thinkum has just mixed her favourite potion, which she will only give to special friends and family. She has exactly one litre (1 L). She wants to give her son twice as much as her daughter, but only half as much as she has herself. Three of her friends will share the rest.

How much potion will everyone receive? Use millilitres.

	Guess 1	Guess 2	Guess 3
Clever Son	________	________	________
Bright Daughter	________	________	________
Prof. Dinkum Thinkum	________	________	________
Friend 1	________	________	________
Friend 2	________	________	________
Friend 3	________	________	________
	Total = ______	Total = ______	Total = ______

2 Clever Son has to take 1 L of his famous jelly juice to school, but he only has a 3 L jug and a 5 L bucket. How can he measure exactly 1 L using these two containers?

____

____

____

____

____

3 Bright Daughter made 2 L of Grow-Up-Fast drink and 3 L of Shrinking Milk. She sells 200 mL bottles of Grow-Up-Fast drink for $3 each and 250 mL bottles of Shrinking Milk for $2 a bottle. Which one will make her the most money?

____

____

____

____

____

I can solve problems by:

☐ understanding capacity ☐ measuring and using logical thinking.

Unit 20 Volume

build with blocks

A cubic unit has length, breadth and height.

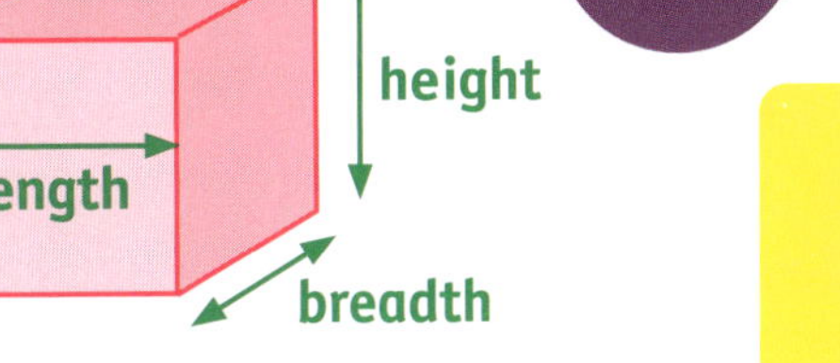

1 Build these models. Find the volume for each one.

a

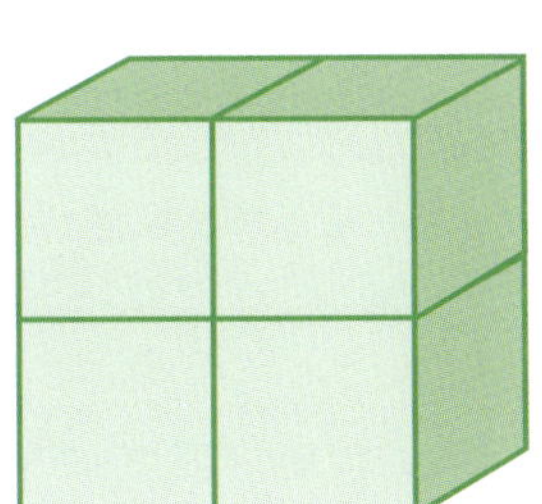

$2 \times 1 \times 2 =$ ______

b

cm^3

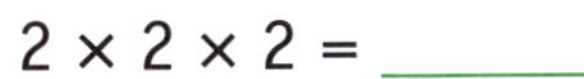

c

cm^3

$4 \times 1 \times 2 =$ ______

d

cm^3

$3 \times 2 \times 2 =$ ______

e

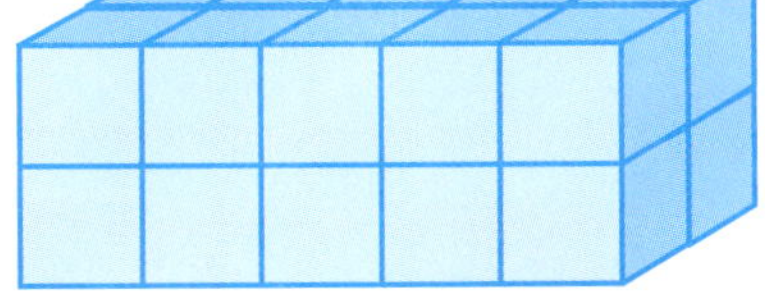

cm^3

$5 \times 2 \times 2 =$ ______

f

cm^3

$4 \times 2 \times 4 =$ ______

2 Make a model that is 2 cubes long, 3 cubes wide and 2 cubes high.

What is the volume of this model? ______

Mastery Checklist I can:
- ☐ compare capacities in litres
- ☐ use mL and L
- ☐ measure and record capacity
- ☐ measure volume using cubic centimetres.

Unit 21 Language of chance

A fifty-fifty

B one chance in six

C one chance in four

D one out of three

E one in five

F equal chances

1 The above are all outcomes.

eg Toss a coin. There are two outcomes — head or tail.

The outcome  *(tail) is one chance in two.*

Write a different experiment for each of the outcomes above.

a ______

b ______

c ______

d ______

e ______

f ______

2 What are the chances of:

a being born in May? ______

b the puppy being female? ______

c throwing an even number on a die? ______

3 Each spinner has only red or green.

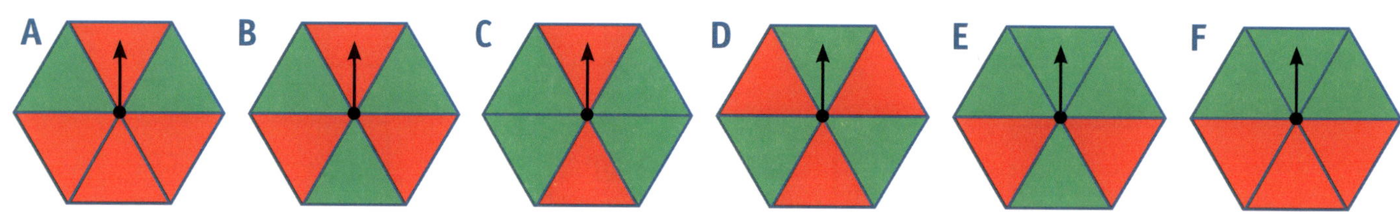

On which spinners is the arrow:

a equally likely to land on red or green? ______

b more likely to land on red? ______

c Which spinners are fair spinners? ______

Challenge!

In my pencil case I have four pens — blue, black, green and red. I take out two of them without looking.

What are the chances that I picked out blue or red? ______

Why? ______

______

AC9M4P01 Probability MA2-CHAN-01 Chance B • Describe the likelihood of outcomes of chance events

Unit 21 Travel graph

Six friends recorded the distances they travel to school each day.

Name	Distance (km)
Samad	4
Demeter	9
Patrice	14
Peta	10
Suellen	6
Lila	10

1 Complete these graphs.

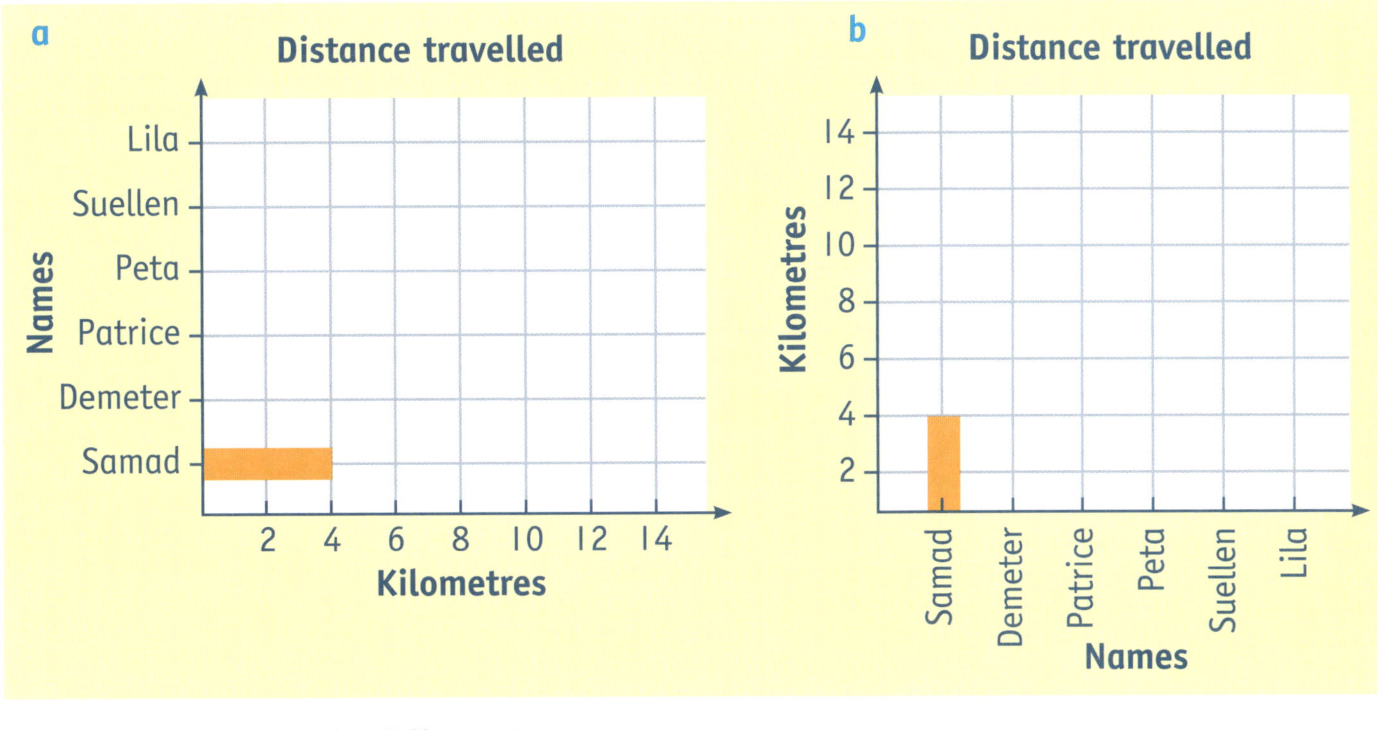

2 a Why are the graphs different? ______________________________

____

b Do they tell us the same information? ____________

3 a Who lives closest to school?____________

b Which two friends live the same distance from school? ____________ ____________

c Does this mean they live near each other? ____________ Why? ____________

____

4 Write a new title that tells exactly what the graph is about.

____

Mastery Checklist I can:
- ☐ describe chances and outcomes
- ☐ identify experiments that use chance
- ☐ draw a horizontal and vertical column graph
- ☐ answer questions about data displays.

Revision Term 2

1 **6 5 0 9 3** p 54

Use these five digits to make:

a the largest number ____________

b the smallest number ____________

2 Write using numerals. p 56

a eighty-seven thousand, six hundred and thirteen

____

b nine hundred and ninety-nine thousand and nine

____

3 Circle the number with the most ten thousands. p 56

35 876, 15 986, 19 897

4 Complete. p 58

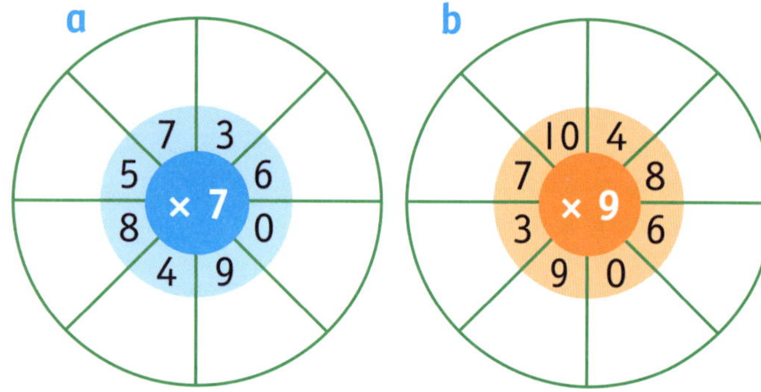

5 True or false? p 61

a 12 is a multiple of 4. ________

b 49 is a multiple of 9. ________

c 56 is a multiple of 7. ________

6 p 62

a 7×3 = ____ b 8×6 = ____ c 4×8 = ____ d 9×7 = ____

7 Complete. p 65

a ☐ ÷ 3 = 1 b 42 ÷ ☐ = 7

c 90 ÷ 9 = ☐ d ☐ ÷ 5 = 9

8 Write the × and ÷ facts. p 66

a 80, 8, 10

____ × ____ = ____

____ × ____ = ____

____ ÷ ____ = ____

____ ÷ ____ = ____

b 42, 6, 7

____ × ____ = ____

____ × ____ = ____

____ ÷ ____ = ____

____ ÷ ____ = ____

9 Write **equals**, **is more than** or **is less than** to make the statements true. p 68

a 0·7 ____________ 0·2

b 0·9 ____________ 0·90

c 0·30 ____________ 0·6

10 Colour to show the equivalent fraction and then write the tenths and hundredths. p 68

a

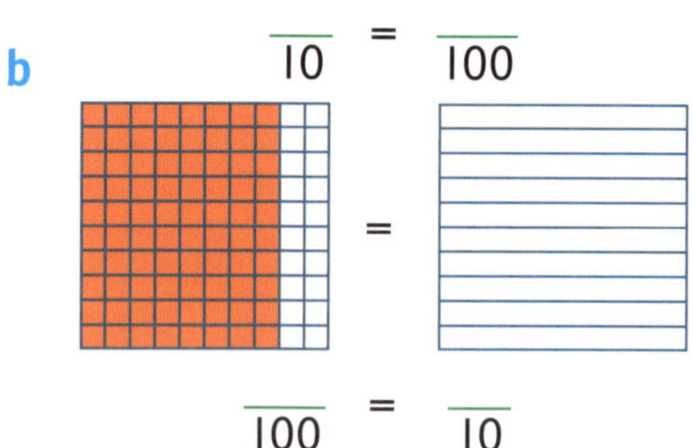

$\frac{\quad}{10}$ = $\frac{\quad}{100}$

b

$\frac{\quad}{100}$ = $\frac{\quad}{10}$

11 Follow the rule: p 71

a +0·1; 0·7, ____, ____, ____, ____

b +0·1; 1·2, ____, ____, ____, ____

c +1·0; 2·4, ____, ____, ____, ____

Revision Term 2

12 Change from $5. p 76

a

b

13 Round to the nearest 5c. p 78

a 36c ________

b 41c ________

c 68c ________

14 Name the smallest number of coins needed to make: p 78

a 95c ________

b $3.75 ________

15 Make two number sentences to equal each of the following. p 82

a 17 + 9 = ________ ________

b 6 × 9 = ________ ________

16 Find the missing number. p 83

a 7 + ______ = 12 + 9

b 35 ÷ 5 = 49 ÷ ______

17 Draw: p 84

a parallel lines.

b perpendicular lines.

c a trapezium.

d a parallelogram.

18 a Reflect the shape. p 88

b Translate the shape.

c Rotate the shape.

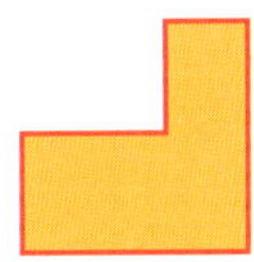

19 Write as millilitres (mL). p 90

a 7 L ________

b 12 L ________

20 Write as litres. (L) p 90

a 2000 mL ________

b 8000 mL ________

21 Would you use L or mL to measure the capacity of: p 91

a a teapot? ______ b a bath? ______

22 Find the volume. p 93

______ cm^3

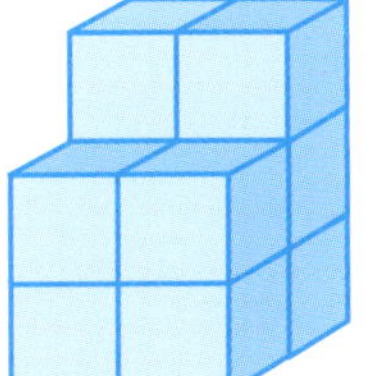

23 Draw all the possible outcomes if you toss 2 coins. Use **H** for heads and **T** for tails. p 94

Unit 22 Rounding thousands

3694 3718 3467
3554 3499
3640 3748 3549
3639 3619
3507 3732

When rounding: Remember
0, 1, 2, 3, 4 — leave
5, 6, 7, 8, 9 — + 1
eg 7650 → 8000
4399 → 4000

When rounding to hundreds, look at the tens place.

When rounding to thousands, look at the hundreds place.

1 Round to the nearest hundred.

a 793 ______ b 419 ______ c 854 ______
d 278 ______ e 647 ______ f 338 ______
g 35 124 ______ h 56 602 ______
i 90 848 ______ j 63 169 ______

2 Colour the numbers that round to 3700 red, 3600 blue, 3500 yellow.

3 Round to the nearest thousand.

a 5284 ______ b 7307 ______ c 3784 ______ d 8074 ______
e 1514 ______ f 9436 ______ g 24 480 ______ h 56 503 ______
i 85 991 ______ j 62 564 ______ k 30 827 ______ l 91 733 ______

Used cars	Colour	Price in '000s
Honda	Blue	19
Mercedes	Silver	47·5
Renault	Red	7
BMW	Green	38·5
Rolls Royce	Yellow	22
Suzuki	Black	12·5

4 a What does the **Price in '000s** mean?

______

______

b Write the real price of each car.

Honda ______ Mercedes ______
Renault ______ BMW ______
Rolls Royce ______
Suzuki ______

c The dealer rounds the price to the nearest five hundred. What will he charge for these cars?

Ford $9825 ______ Holden $17 460 ______
Pulsar $12 690 ______ Subaru $26 195 ______

Unit 22 Comparing numbers

1 On this number line, which card would have the value of:

a 6500? _____ b 6098? _____ c 6567? _____ d 6250? _____ e 6921? _____

2 Draw cards on the number line with the value of: a 6800. F b 6450. G

3 Circle the larger number.

a 17 065 16 750 b 92 108 92 180 c 60 547 56 740

d 80 416 80 604 e 29 743 29 751 f 4968 40 009

g 28 011 20 118 h 19 999 91 111 i 70 006 69 074

4 Write **is more than**, **is less than** or **equals** to make the statements true.

a 3840 ______________________________ 3000 + 800 + 4

b 9000 + 200 + 6 ______________________________ 9206

c 80 + 8000 ______________________________ 8088

d 3 + 30 + 5000 ______________________________ 5333

e 70 + 6 + 900 + 1000 ______________________________ 1976

f 5075 ______________________________ 50 + 7 + 5000

5 Add 1000.

a 8468 _________ b 3156 _________ c 19 803 _________ d 24 065 _________

6 Subtract 1000.

a 7850 _________ b 5206 _________ c 36 168 _________ d 99 999 _________

7 Add 10 000.

a 3020 _________ b 7951 _________ c 54 687 _________ d 30 156 _________

Draw a table

Take five different numerals from 0 to 9. Use this table to help you find every possible number that can be made using these five digits.

1 digit	2 digits	3 digits	4 digits	5 digits

Unit 22 Addition with trading

43

56

35

69

48

27

72

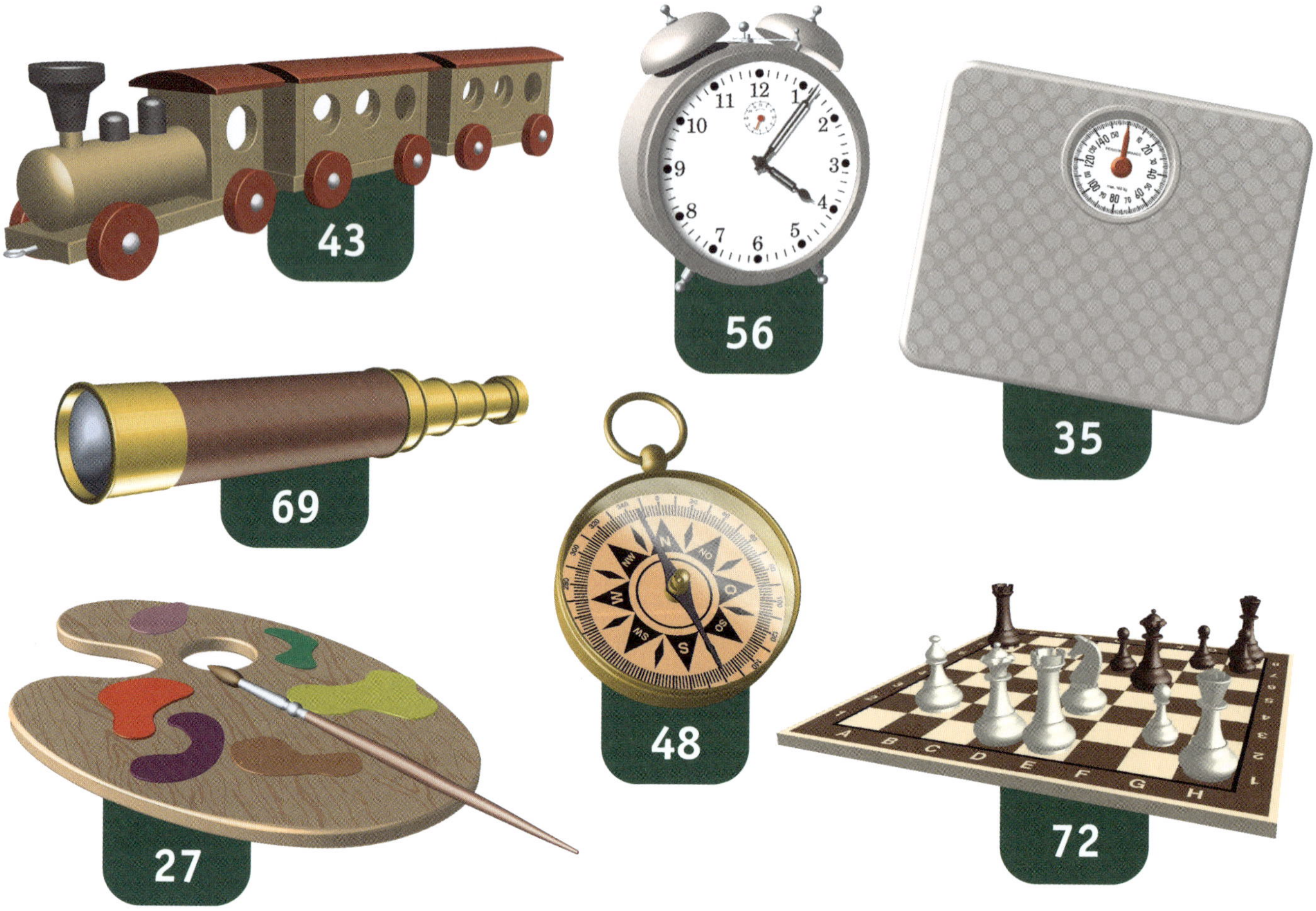

A gift shop owner counted all the items in the shop.

1 Which item was there: a most of? ____________ b least of? ____________

2 Group these items.

a trains + clocks = ________ + ________ = ________

b paints + chess sets = ________ + ________ = ________

c scales + trains = ________ + ________ = ________

3 Set these out as an algorithm.

a telescopes + scales

b compasses + trains

c paints + telescopes

a

Tens	Ones

b

Tens	Ones

c

Tens	Ones

4 Which two items:

a add to 125? ____________________

b total 141? ____________________

Unit 22 Addition algorithms

Setting out

H	T	O
1	1	
1	3	6
4	7	7
6	1	3

1

a

H	T	O
	2	6
	4	3
+	1	7

b

H	T	O
	1	4
	3	5
+	5	2

c

H	T	O
	7	6
	3	4
+	6	9

d

H	T	O
	8	1
	2	9
+	4	3

2

a

H	T	O
1	6	7
+ 3	1	4

b

H	T	O
3	3	8
+ 4	5	9

c

H	T	O
6	7	3
+ 2	1	8

d

H	T	O
1	8	7
+ 7	0	9

e

H	T	O
3	0	5
+ 5	7	7

f

H	T	O
4	6	3
+ 2	5	9

g

H	T	O
5	7	5
+ 1	6	6

h

H	T	O
3	9	8
+ 1	7	1

i

H	T	O
2	8	4
+ 6	4	9

j

H	T	O
4	5	7
+ 3	1	8

k

H	T	O
6	2	8
+ 1	5	1

l

H	T	O
2	5	8
+ 5	5	1

m

H	T	O
4	6	9
+ 2	4	0

n

H	T	O
3	0	2
+ 6	2	8

o

H	T	O
5	3	4
+	7	7

3 Use page 100. Write algorithms to work out answers.

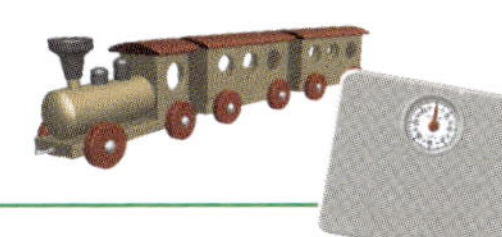

a Which 2 items add to 120? ______

b Which 2 items add to 104? ______

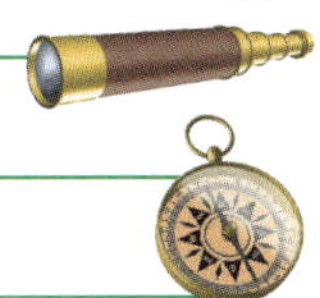

c Which 3 items add to 139? ______

d Which 3 items add to 173? ______

Working

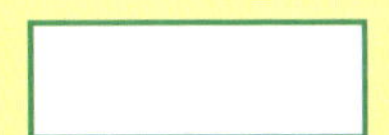

Challenge! What is the total of all the items on page 100? ☐

Unit 22 Estimation with addition

1 Estimate the answer before working.

	Estimate	Answer
a 58 + 64		
b 37 + 99		
c 72 + 63		
d 85 + 38		

	Estimate	Answer
e 124 + 132		
f 268 + 311		
g 406 + 192		
h 385 + 297		

2 a Add these numbers: 16, 38, 24, 73. ______

b How did you add them? ______

______

c Add them another way. ______

d Did you get the same answer? ______

e Which was the best way? ______

f Why? ______

3 Estimate answers first.

a In the treasure chest there were 183 rubies and 378 diamonds. How many jewels altogether?

Est. [ ]

Ans. [ ]

b Jock wrote 252 words on one page and 169 on the next. How long was his story?

Est. [ ]

Ans. [ ]

c Megan poured 95 mL of orange juice into a glass and then 289 mL of lemonade. How much was in the glass?

Est. [ ]

Ans. [ ]

d Write a problem for the answer.

Est. [680]

Ans. [674]

Challenge! Write three four-digit numbers. Estimate their total. Add them using a calculator. Were you close?

[ ]

Unit 22 Addition stories

Word problems

1 Write a story problem for these number sentences using the theme of **Pirates**.
Estimate your answers by rounding numbers appropriately.

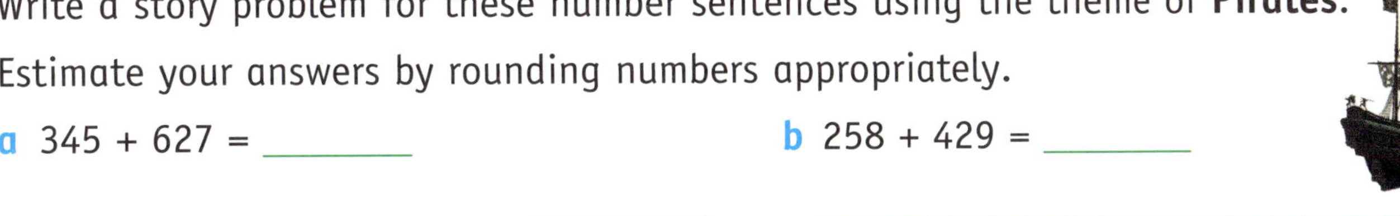

a 345 + 627 = ______

b 258 + 429 = ______

2 Write a story problem for these number sentences using the theme of **Underground**.
Estimate your answers by rounding numbers appropriately.

a 4582 + 334 = ______

b 2729 + 145 = ______

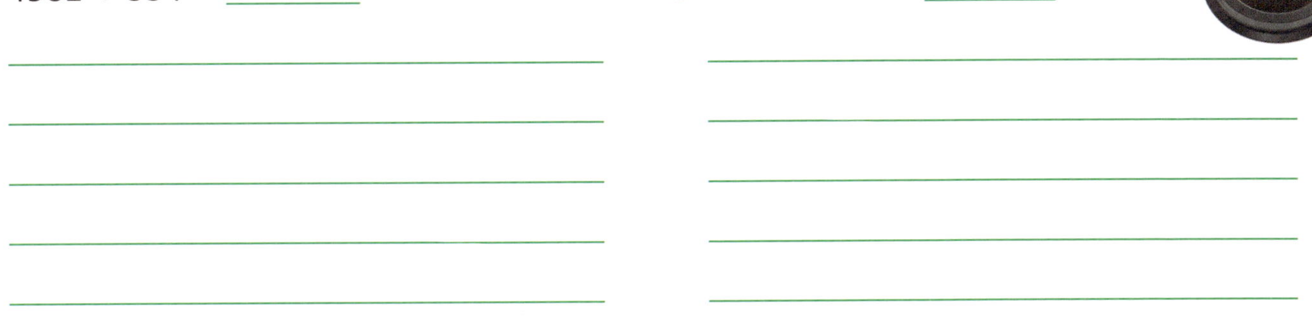

3 Write a story problem for these number sentences using the theme of **Music**.
Estimate your answers by rounding numbers appropriately.

a \$56.25 + \$28.80 = ______

b \$99.20 + \$4.65 = ______

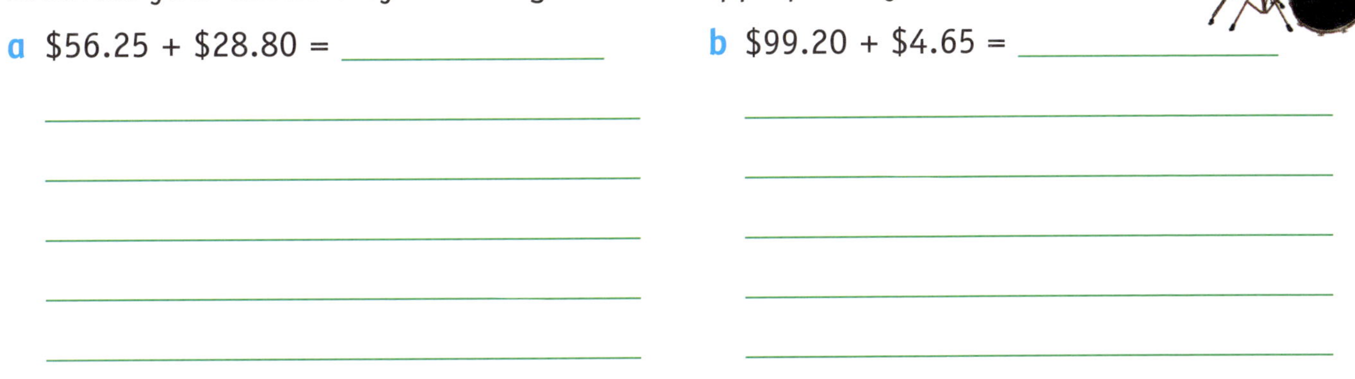

Mastery Checklist

I can:
- ☐ round thousands
- ☐ trade ones for ten to add
- ☐ complete addition algorithms with 3-digit numbers
- ☐ use estimation to solve addition problems
- ☐ write story problems to match a number sentence.

Unit 23 Multiplying two-digit numbers

1 Complete the patterns.

a $3 \times 4 =$ ____
$30 \times 4 =$ 120
$300 \times 4 =$ 1200

b $7 \times 6 =$ ____
$70 \times 6 =$ ____
$700 \times 6 =$ ____

c $9 \times 5 =$ ____
$9 \times 50 =$ ____
$9 \times 500 =$ ____

d $8 \times 8 =$ ____
$8 \times 80 =$ ____
$8 \times 800 =$ ____

2

	H	T	O
a	3	0	0
×			3

	H	T	O
b	4	0	0
×			2

	H	T	O
c	8	0	0
×			1

	H	T	O
d	2	0	0
×			3

	H	T	O
e	2	0	0
×			4

3

	H	T	O	
		3	1	
×			7	
			7	← 7 × 1
	2	1	0	← 7 × 30
	2	1	7	← 7 × 31

a

	H	T	O	
		3	6	
×			2	
				← 6 × 2
				← 30 × 2
				← 36 × 2

b

	H	T	O	
		4	3	
×			5	
				← 3 × 5
				← 40 × 5
				← 43 × 5

c

	H	T	O	
		6	4	
×			6	
				← 4 × 6
				← 60 × 6
				← 64 × 6

d

	H	T	O	
		7	4	
×			3	
				← 4 × 3
				← 70 × 3
				← 74 × 3

e

	H	T	O	
		5	2	
×			7	
				← 2 × 7
				← 50 × 7
				← 52 × 7

	H	T	O
f		4	6
×			8

	H	T	O
g		5	7
×			7

	H	T	O
h		9	4
×			9

	H	T	O
i		6	9
×			5

	H	T	O
j		7	4
×			6

Problem solving

Remember! Give your answer a name – eg metres, kilometres, snakes, years.

Read, Plan, Work, Check

1 An emperor penguin can live for 19 years. Buddy says he has lived 4 times an emperor penguin's life span. How old is Buddy?

What to find? ______________________

Number sentence: ______________________

Answer: ______________

Working

2 An emu's top speed is 45 kilometres per hour. Sir Fly-off's plane can go 5 times as fast. How fast can it fly?

What to find? ______________________

Number sentence: ______________________

Answer: ______________

Working

3 A red-bellied black snake can have up to 42 baby snakes at a time. How many baby black snakes could be born in 6 litters?

What to find? ______________________

Number sentence: ______________________

Answer: ______________

Working

4 A tree kangaroo can leap up to 15 metres to another tree. How many metres could it travel in 8 leaps?

What to find? ______________________

Number sentence: ______________________

Answer: ______________

Working

I can solve problems by:

☐ using multiplication and division ☐ writing algorithms and choosing the best strategy.

Unit 23 Division algorithms

For each question, write an algorithm.

1 The Flying Saucer Ride holds 9 children. How many rides are needed for:

a 18 children? b 54 children? c 27 children? d 72 children? e 45 children?

9) 18

2 The Ghost Train holds 6 children. How many trains are needed for:

a 36 children? b 48 children? c 18 children? d 42 children? e 6 children?

3 The River Cave Ride holds 8 children. How many boats are needed for:

a 56 children? b 24 children? c 64 children? d 32 children? e 40 children?

Unit 23 Estimation

Use the picture on page 106 for questions 1, 2 and 3.

1 How many Ghost Trains would be needed for:

a 15 children? ______ Why? ______________________________

____

b 35 children? ______ Why? ______________________________

____

Estimate

370 ÷ 6

36 ÷ 6 = 6

Est. 60

231 ÷ 8

24 ÷ 8 = 3

Est. 30

Estimate these answers.

2 How many boats would be needed on the River Cave Ride for:

a 160 children? ________ b 250 children? ________ c 629 children? ________

How many Flying Saucer Rides would be needed for:

d 361 children? ________ e 187 children? ________ f 641 children? ________

3 Which ride?

a It took 4 rides for 36 children. ______________________________

b It took 4 rides for 32 children. ______________________________

c It took 4 rides for 24 children. ______________________________

4 a How many groups of 4 in 28? ________ b Divide 70 by 10. ________

c Share 40 equally among 5. ________ d 9 divided by 9. ________

e How many threes make 21? ________ f Divide 54 equally among 6. ________

5 a 42 ÷ 7 = ☐ b ☐ ÷ 3 = 4 c 45 ÷ ☐ = 9

d ☐ ÷ 8 = 7 e 90 ÷ 9 = ☐ f 42 ÷ ☐ = 6

6 Complete each path.

a **80** ÷ 8 → ☐ × 4 → ☐ ÷ 8 → ☐ × 6 → ☐ ÷ 3 → ☐

b **56** ÷ 7 → ☐ × 8 → ☐ ÷ 2 → ☐ ÷ 4 → ☐ × 9 → ☐

Trial and error

Mia bought twice as many Carousel Ride tickets as Manny.

Together their tickets cost $6.30. ☐

How many tickets did each buy? ☐

Unit 23 Division with Remainders

1 Work the division. Check your answer.

a $6\overline{)15}$ = 2 r 3

Check
6 x 2 = 12
12 + 3 = 15

b $7\overline{)30}$

Check

c $5\overline{)23}$

Check

Multiply to check

$7\overline{)25}$ = 3 r 4

Check

3 × 7 = 21

21 + 4 = 25

d $4\overline{)38}$

Check

e $8\overline{)76}$

Check

f $2\overline{)19}$

Check

g $3\overline{)23}$

Check

h $8\overline{)59}$

Check

i $7\overline{)58}$

Check

j $9\overline{)78}$

Check

k $5\overline{)37}$

Check

2 Write an algorithm to answer each of these.

a There were 21 strawberries in the bowl. Six birds ate 3 strawberries each. How many were left in the bowl? ________

b Mrs Lucky had 66 pencils. How many did she have left when she gave her 7 children 9 pencils each? ________

c I had 34 jelly beans and gave 6 friends five each. How many were left for me? ________

Work backwards

Moby had 8 marbles left after he gave his friends 6 each. He had 50 marbles to start with.

How many friends did he have?

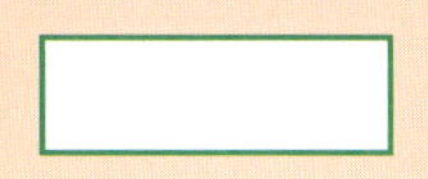

Mastery Checklist

I can:
- ☐ multiply 2-digit numbers
- ☐ solve division algorithms
- ☐ estimate answers to division problems
- ☐ use multiplication to check division answers.

Problem solving

Read, Plan, Think, Do

1 A Great White shark grew 180 cm in 6 years.
How many centimetres did it grow each year?

Plan: What to find? ______________________

Think: Number sentence: ______________________

Answer: ______________

Do: Working

2 Five baby chimps weigh 45 kilograms together.
How many kilograms does each baby chimp weigh?

Plan: What to find? ______________________

Think: Number sentence: ______________________

Answer: ______________

Do: Working

3 Every four years from age 14 to age 50, a female elephant may have a baby.
How many babies could it have in its lifetime?

Plan: What to find? ______________________

Think: Number sentence: ______________________

Answer: ______________

Do: Working

4 Wolf packs are made up of about 6 wolves. If rangers counted 78 wolves from a helicopter, about how many packs would that be?

Plan: What to find? ______________________

Think: Number sentence: ______________________

Answer: ______________

Do: Working

I can solve problems by:

☐ using multiplication or division ☐ writing algorithms and choosing the best strategy.

Unit 24 Denominators

A

B
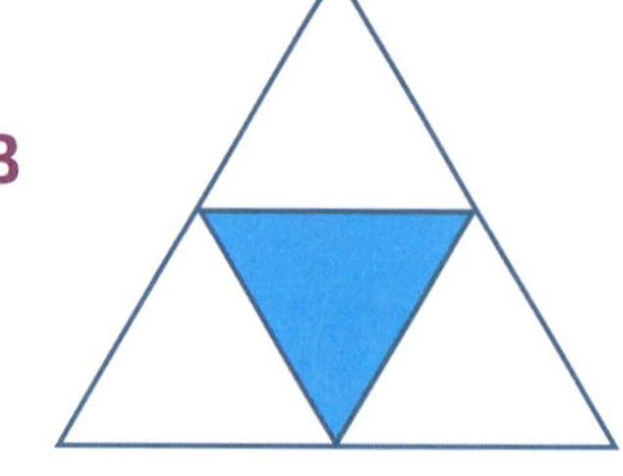

C

D
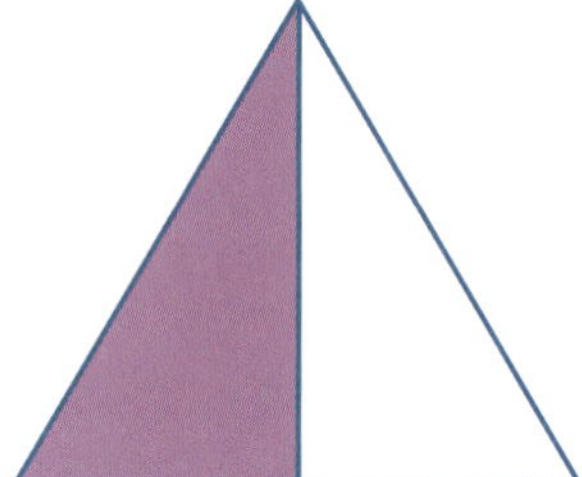

E

F
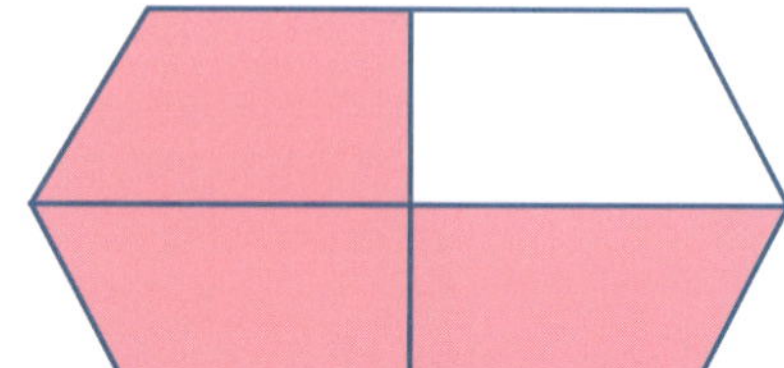

G
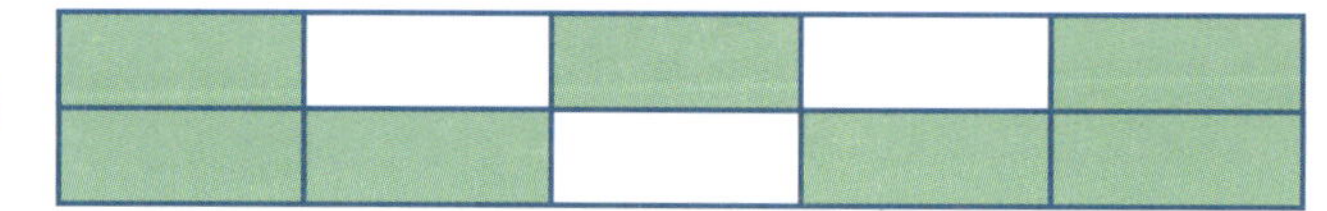

1 What is the denominator for:

A? ______ B? ______ C? ______ D? ______ E? ______ F? ______ G? ______

2 Write the fraction for the coloured section of each.

A ______ B ______ C ______ D ______ E ______ F ______ G ______

3 Write the fraction for the white section of each.

A ______ B ______ C ______ D ______ E ______ F ______ G ______

4 Make 1 whole.

A $\frac{5}{8} + \frac{\square}{8} = 1$ B $\frac{1}{4} + \frac{\square}{4} = 1$ C $\frac{1}{5} + \frac{\square}{\square} = 1$ D $\frac{\square}{2} + \frac{\square}{2} = 1$

E $\frac{\square}{\square} + \frac{\square}{\square} = 1$ F $\frac{\square}{\square} + \frac{\square}{\square} = \square$ G $\frac{\square}{\square} + \frac{\square}{\square} = 1$

5 Draw diagrams to show:

a $1\frac{1}{4}$

b $2\frac{1}{2}$

c $1\frac{4}{5}$

Unit 24 Mixed numerals

1 What fraction is the coloured part?

a 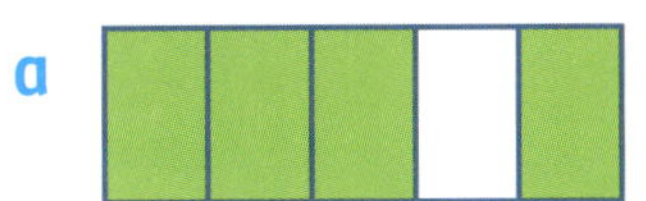 ______

b 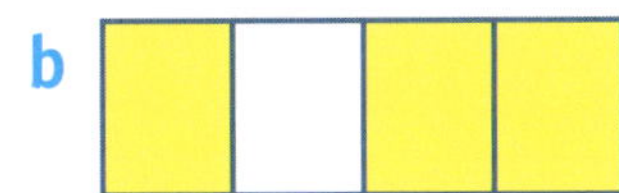 ______

c 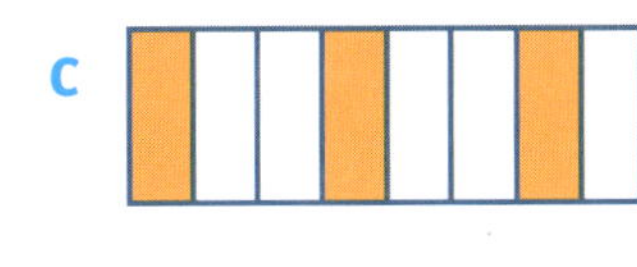 ______

$\frac{2}{3}$ ← numerator, ← denominator

The **denominator** tells us how many parts altogether.

The **numerator** tells us how many parts we have.

2 Draw diagrams to show the fraction.

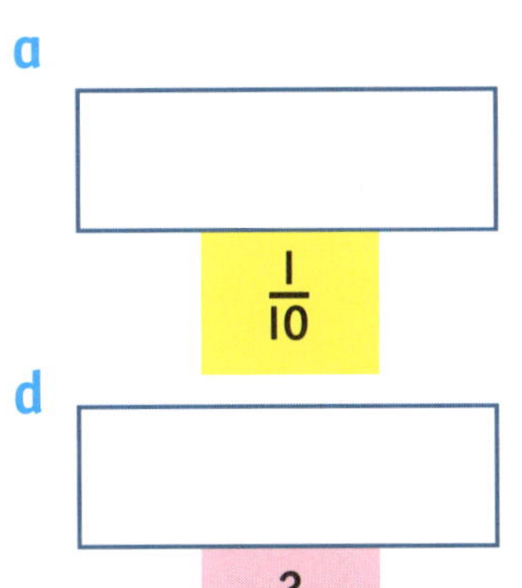

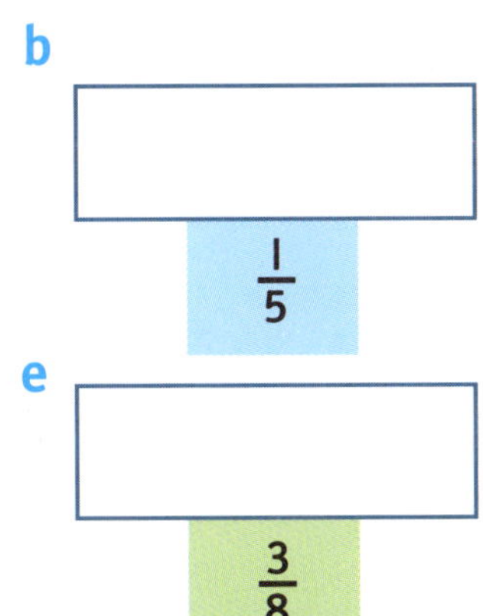

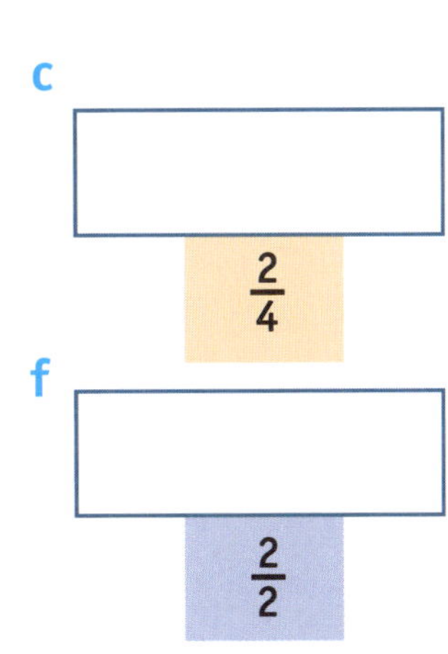

3 Draw lines and colour to show the fraction.

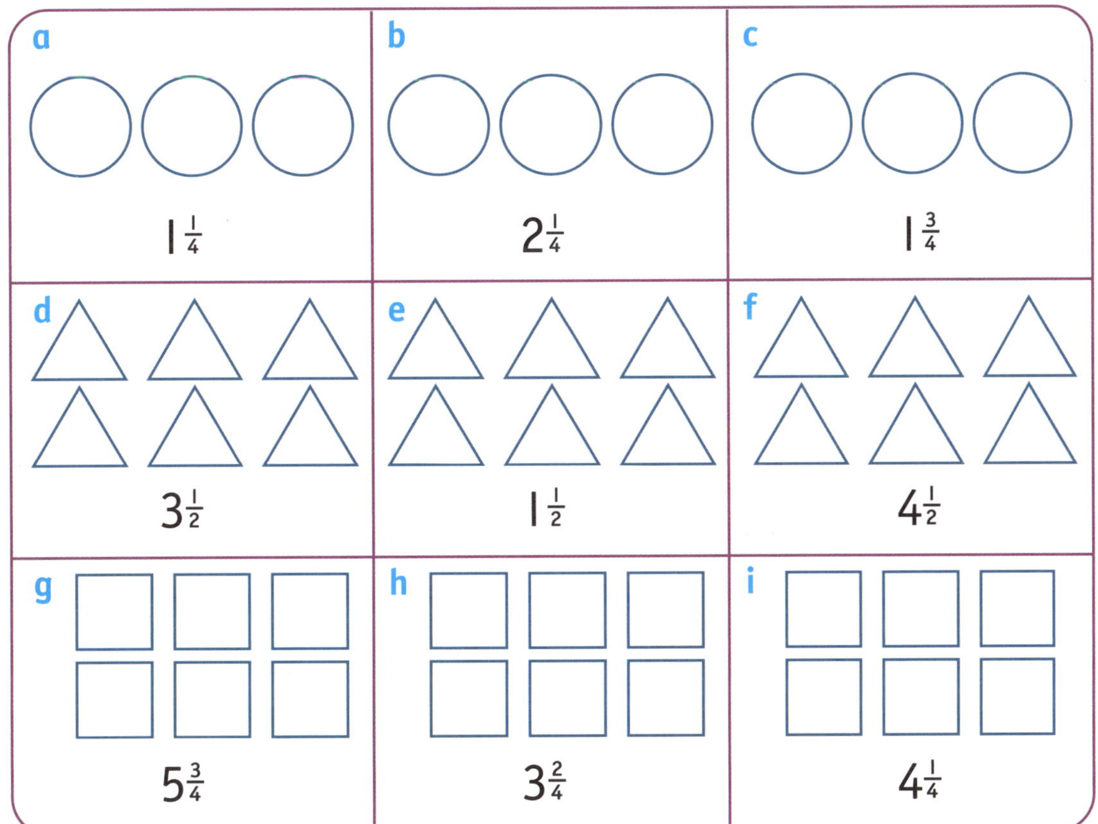

Sometimes we have whole numbers with fractions.

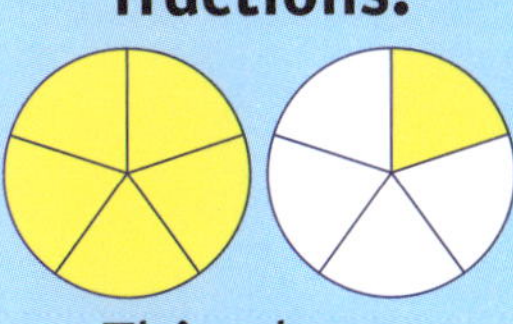

This shows 1 whole and 1 fifth.

$1\frac{1}{5}$

Draw a diagram

Draw a diagram to show $5\frac{3}{8}$. How many eighths altogether?

Unit 24 Equivalent fractions

1 On these number lines show:

a $\frac{1}{2}$ on the top.
0·5 on the bottom.

b $\frac{1}{5}$ on the top.
0·2 on the bottom.

c $\frac{3}{5}$ on the top.
0·6 on the bottom.

d $\frac{2}{5}$ on the top.
0·4 on the bottom.

e $\frac{4}{5}$ on the top.
0·8 on the bottom.

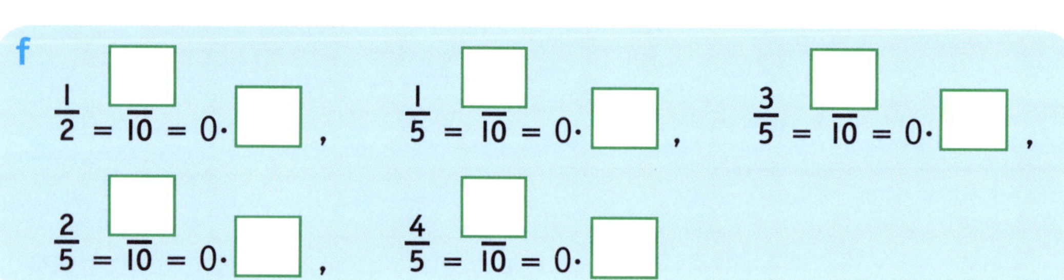

f $\frac{1}{2} = \frac{\square}{10} = 0\cdot\square$, $\frac{1}{5} = \frac{\square}{10} = 0\cdot\square$, $\frac{3}{5} = \frac{\square}{10} = 0\cdot\square$,

$\frac{2}{5} = \frac{\square}{10} = 0\cdot\square$, $\frac{4}{5} = \frac{\square}{10} = 0\cdot\square$

2 True or false?

a $\frac{2}{5} = 0\cdot2$ ______ b $\frac{7}{10} = 0\cdot7$ ______ c $\frac{1}{5} = 0\cdot5$ ______ d $\frac{1}{2} = 0\cdot4$ ______

e $\frac{1}{10} = 0\cdot1$ ______ f $\frac{1}{2} = 0\cdot5$ ______ g $\frac{3}{5} = 0\cdot3$ ______ h $\frac{4}{5} = 0\cdot8$ ______

3 Colour to show these fractions are equal.

a $\frac{1}{2} = \frac{2}{4}$

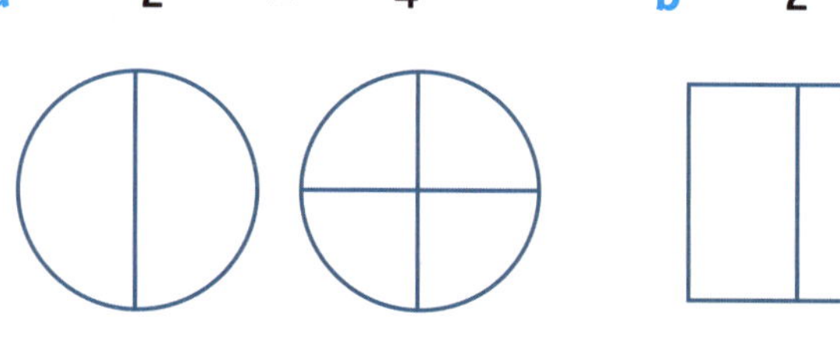

b $\frac{1}{2} = \frac{4}{8}$

c $\frac{3}{4} = \frac{6}{8}$

d $\frac{4}{5} = \frac{8}{10}$

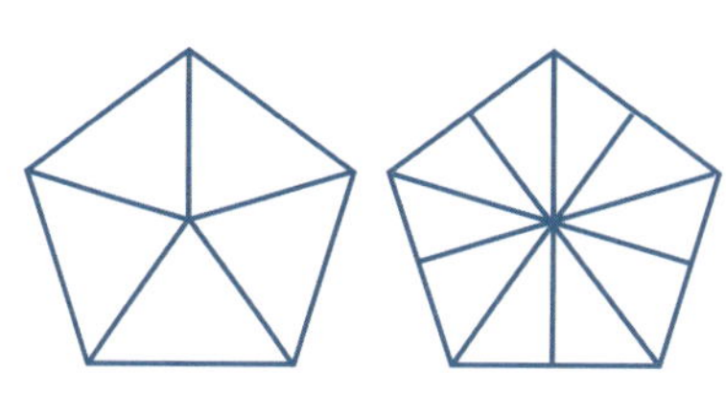

Some fractions have different names but are the same size.

Challenge!

Draw a diagram to show $1\frac{3}{4} = 1\frac{9}{12}$.

Unit 24 Rounding

0 1 2 3 4 5

To the nearest whole number!

If the tenths place is 0, 1, 2, 3, 4, do not change the whole number. eg 1·3 is closer to 1.

If the tenths place is 5, 6, 7, 8, 9, add 1 to the whole number. eg 1·8 is closer to 2.

1 Place these numbers on the number line.

a 0·8 b 2·1 c 4·7 d 1·3 e 3·4

2 Round them off to the nearest whole number.

a ______ b ______ c ______

d ______ e ______

3 Round these off to the nearest whole number.

a 7·4 ______ b 10·1 ______ c 8·6 ______ d 0·8 ______ e 9·2 ______

f 15·5 ______ g 6·7 ______ h 20·9 ______ i 5·3 ______ j 16·5 ______

4 A $11.59 B $15.38 C $9.71 D $19.16 E $24.39 F $16.90

Write the price of each mask to the nearest dollar.

A ______ B ______ C ______ D ______ E ______ F ______

5 Bill had to round these decimals off to the nearest whole number. Tick the ones he has correct and write the correct answers for the ones he has wrong.

Number	Bill's answer	Your answer	Number	Bill's answer	Your answer
a 17·4	17		e 15·9	16	
b 23·09	24		f 2·35	3	
c 5·28	6		g 18·51	18	
d 10·72	11		h 12·64	12	

6 Write 5 numbers that would round off to 6.

Mastery Checklist I can:
- ☐ identify the numerator and denominator in a fraction
- ☐ recognise quarters, halves and thirds
- ☐ show mixed numerals
- ☐ show fractions on a number line
- ☐ make connections between fractions and decimals
- ☐ round decimals.

Holidays!

Investigation 3

You and a friend are to have a special holiday! Find out what the most popular place for holidays is, then plan your holiday.

1 Survey and use tally marks to find the most popular place for holidays.

2 Draw a horizontal column graph to show the most popular places for holidays.

Most Popular Places for a Holiday

	1	2	3	4	5	6	7	8	9	10

3 Choose a time, day and month to leave for your holiday and explain why you chose them.

4 Write down four things that you want to buy on your holiday with $200 spending money. Estimate a cost for each item.

AC9M4ST03 Statistics **MAO-WM-01** Working mathematically • choosing and applying mathematical techniques to solve problems **MA2-DATA-01** Data A • Organise and display data using tables and graphs • **MA2-AR-01** Additive relations B • Apply addition and subtraction to familiar contexts, including money and budgeting

5 How can you organise your clothes?

Decide on 3 main items of clothing you will need and two colours for each item, eg 2 sweaters, blue and green; 2 hats, green and red; 2 pairs of pants, green and brown.

Make a clothing plan for all the ways you can wear your clothes, wearing one of each, each day. For how many days will you be able to wear a different outfit?

_______ days

6 What do holidays cost?

Plan a budget for the number of days of your holiday.

You will need to plan for:

Accommodation	_______ days @ _______	per day	_______
Meals	_______ days @ _______	per day	_______
Entertainment	1. _______		_______
	2. _______		_______
	3. _______		_______
		Total:	_______
		Add your plane fare	_______
		Add your $200 spending money	_______

Grand total cost

To carry out these tasks, I need to:

- ☐ ask survey questions
- ☐ make a tally
- ☐ make a horizontal column graph
- ☐ choose a suitable time for an activity and explain my choice
- ☐ draw a diagram to show choices of clothing
- ☐ calculate costs for activities
- ☐ add to get a total of costs.

I enjoyed this task! ☆☆☆☆☆

Revision

Shade one bubble.

1 Which one is closest to 5000?

5104

2 In the treasure chest there are 207 diamonds and 329 pearls.
How many jewels altogether?

536 

527

636

529

3 What fraction is shaded?

$\frac{1}{4}$ $\frac{1}{2}$ $\frac{2}{2}$ $\frac{4}{4}$

4

	H	T	O
		7	8
×			6

428 84 648 468

5 Which spinner would you use if you wanted to land on green?

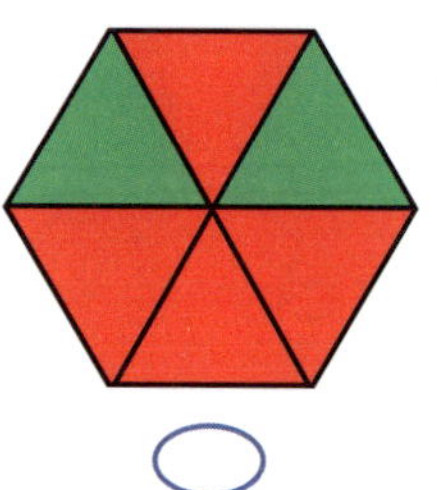

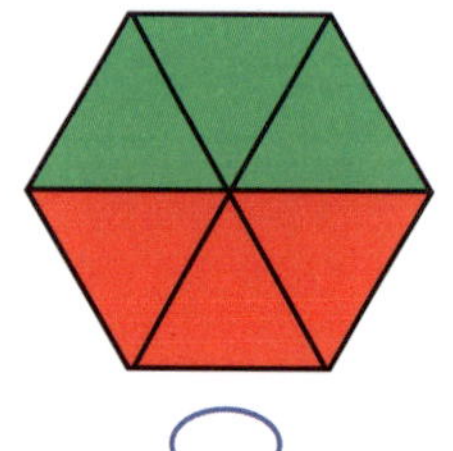

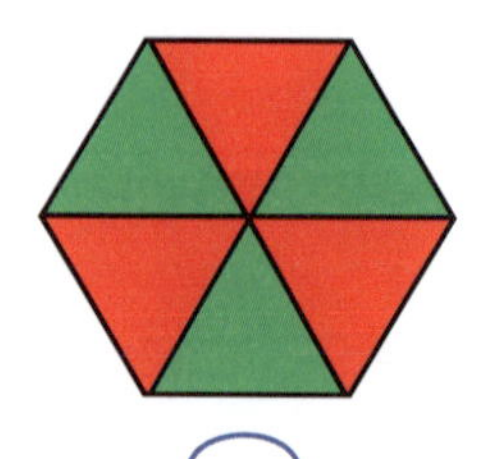

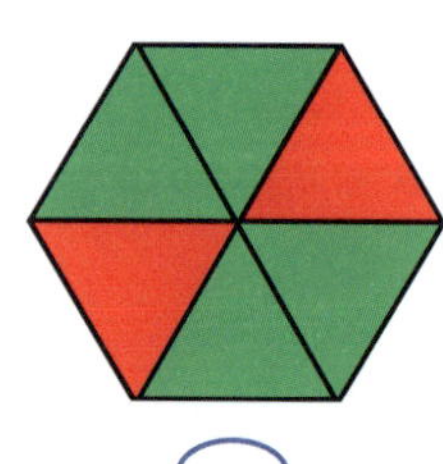

Revision

Shade one bubble.

6 $\square \div 9 = 7$

$\square = 62$  $\square = 16$  $\square = 63$  $\square = 49$

---

7 What are the missing numbers?

$$\frac{3}{5} = \frac{\square}{10} = 0{\cdot}\square$$

3, 3 5, 5 6, 6 10, 10

---

8 What is the price rounded to the nearest 5 cents?

\$16.00 \$16.40 \$16.35 \$16.50

---

9 This diagram is showing:

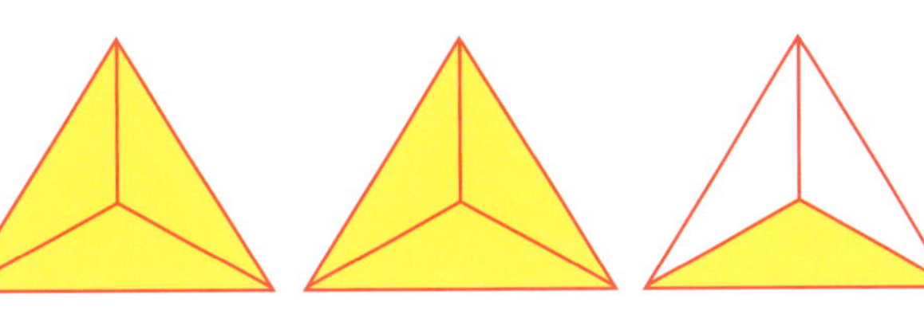

$2\frac{1}{3}$ $3\frac{1}{3}$ $7\frac{1}{3}$ $2\frac{7}{3}$

---

10 Estimate and then work out the answer.

Write your answer in the box.

There were 489 caterpillars and 245 cicadas living in a gum tree. How many insects altogether?

Est. $\square$

Ans. $\square$

Unit 25 Related number sentences

Algebra

4 12 7 6 5 2 1 10 9 3 20 8

1 Complete using the numbers above.

a $7 + 4 = \square + 1$ b $9 - 3 = 5 + \square$ c $8 \times \square = 20 - 4$

d $12 \div 3 = \square - 1$ e $12 \div 6 = \square \times 1$ f $20 + \square = 3 \times \square$

2 Write as many expressions as you can using the numbers.
There must be two numbers and an operations sign (+, −, ÷, ×) on each side of the = (is equal to).

	=	
	=	
	=	
	=	
	=	
	=	
	=	

Unit 25 Missing values

1 Complete these sequences.

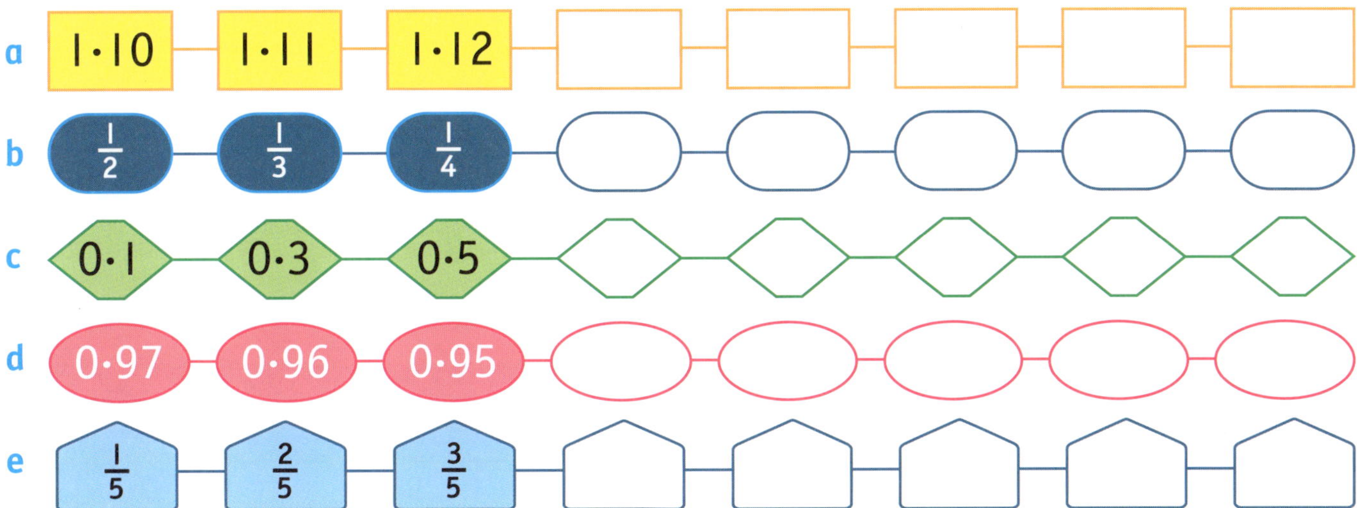

2 True or false?

a 6 + 8 = 8 + 6 ______

b 4 × 9 = 9 × 4 ______

c 12 ÷ 4 = 4 ÷ 12 ______

d 16 − 5 = 5 − 16 ______

e 3 × 2 × 7 = 2 × 7 × 3 ______

f 6 + 8 + 4 = 4 + 7 + 8 ______

g 12 ÷ 6 ÷ 2 = 6 ÷ 2 ÷ 12 ______

h 16 + 7 + 3 = 13 + 17 + 6 ______

i 36 × 10 = 10 × 36 ______

j 3 × 17 × 0 = 6 × 0 × 14 ______

k 27 + 12 + 13 = 12 + 27 + 13 ______

l 3 × 2 + 6 = 3 × 6 + 2 ______

3 a 7 × ★ = 28
★ = ______

b ★ − 6 = 11
★ = ______

c 42 ÷ ★ = 6
★ = ______

d ★ + 18 = 40
★ = ______

e 15 = 30 ÷ ★
★ = ______

f 49 = ★ + 36
★ = ______

g 56 = 4 × ★ × 7
★ = ______

h 71 = ★ − 29
★ = ______

i 2 × ★ = 50
★ = ______

j ★ ÷ 9 = 9
★ = ______

k 100 − ★ = 37
★ = ______

l 72 + 36 = ★
★ = ______

m 4 + 7 + ★ = 16
★ = ______

n ★ − 6 = 14
★ = ______

o 100 ÷ 2 ÷ ★ = 5
★ = ______

p 3 × 7 × 2 = ★
★ = ______

Challenge! Find the value of the star in each.

a 36 + 52 = 100 − 51 + ★ 

b ★ × 4 ÷ 5 = ★ − 2 ☐

Unit 25 Equal terms

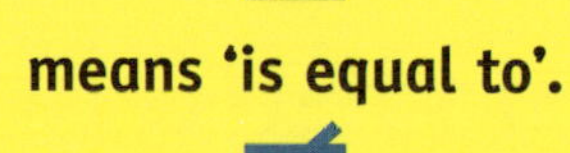

= means 'is equal to'.

≠ means 'is not equal to'.

1 Use = or ≠.

a 4×3 ______ 6×2

b $8 + 7$ ______ $9 + 6$

c 4×6 ______ 3×7

d $16 - 9$ ______ $8 - 1$

e 9×3 ______ 7×4

f $16 \div 4$ ______ $35 \div 7$

g $64 \div 8$ ______ $56 \div 7$

h $100 - 36$ ______ 8×8

i $5 + 17$ ______ $33 - 12$

j $8 + 8$ ______ 8×2

k $7 + 7$ ______ 7×7

l $42 + 14$ ______ 8×7

m $50 - 16$ ______ 7×5

n $72 \div 8$ ______ $12 - 3$

2    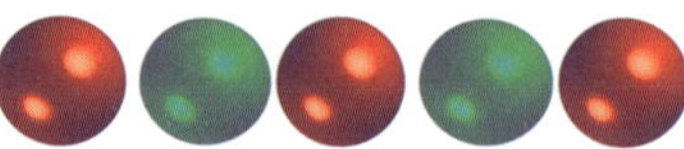 

a Look at the pattern to complete the table.

Order of term	1	2	3	4	5	6	7	8
Term	1	3						

b Draw the 10th term.

c Describe the pattern.

3    

a Look at the pattern to complete the table.

Order of term	1	2	3	4	5	6	7	8
Term	2	4	6					

b Draw the 12th term.

c Describe the pattern.

4 Draw your own pattern, then complete the table.

Order of term	1	2	3	4	5	6	7	8
Term								

AC9M4N09 Number MA2-AR-02 Additive relations B • Complete number sentences involving additive relations to find unknown quantities • MA2-MR-02 Multiplicative relations A • Generate and describe patterns • Multiplicative relations B • Use known number facts and strategies

Unit 25 Patterns + and ×

1 a 2 + 3 + 8 = ____
3 + 2 + 8 = ____
8 + 3 + 2 = ____

b 7 + 4 + 6 = ____
4 + 6 + 7 = ____
6 + 4 + 7 = ____

c 9 + 2 + 5 = ____
5 + 2 + 9 = ____
2 + 9 + 5 = ____

d 8 + 5 + 1 = ____
1 + 8 + 5 = ____
1 + 5 + 8 = ____

e 9 + 7 + 11 = ____
11 + 9 + 7 = ____
7 + 11 + 9 = ____

f 8 + 7 + 13 = ____
13 + 8 + 7 = ____
8 + 13 + 7 = ____

g 16 + 8 + 4 = ____
8 + 16 + 4 = ____
8 + 4 + 16 = ____

h 15 + 7 + 9 = ____
7 + 9 + 15 = ____
9 + 15 + 7 = ____

2 Write the rule about adding numbers.

____

3 a 2 × 3 × 4 = ____
4 × 2 × 3 = ____
3 × 4 × 2 = ____

b 7 × 2 × 3 = ____
2 × 3 × 7 = ____
2 × 7 × 3 = ____

c 5 × 7 × 2 = ____
7 × 5 × 2 = ____
2 × 5 × 7 = ____

d 9 × 4 × 5 = ____
5 × 9 × 4 = ____
4 × 5 × 9 = ____

e 6 × 8 × 5 = ____
5 × 8 × 6 = ____
5 × 6 × 8 = ____

f 9 × 6 × 10 = ____
10 × 6 × 9 = ____
9 × 10 × 6 = ____

g 4 × 8 × 2 = ____
8 × 2 × 4 = ____
2 × 4 × 8 = ____

h 3 × 9 × 7 = ____
9 × 7 × 3 = ____
3 × 7 × 9 = ____

4 Write the rule about multiplying numbers.

____

5 In question 3 circle the easiest multiplication in each group.

6 These numbers have to be added. Circle the numbers you would add first.

a 

b 

c 

d 

e 

f 

g 51 68 49

h 22 18 36

i 43 19 31

j Why did you choose those numbers? ______________________________

7 Work the answers mentally for question 6.

a ____ b ____ c ____ d ____ e ____ f ____ g ____ h ____ i ____

Mastery Checklist I can:
- ☐ find unknown numbers in number sentences
- ☐ identify equivalent number sentences
- ☐ identify terms in a number pattern
- ☐ describe number patterns
- ☐ identify patterns in addition and multiplication.

Unit 26 Values of notes and coins

Currency

A

B

C

D

E

F

G

H

I

J

K

1 What is the value of each bank note?

A ________ B ________ C ________ D ________ E ________

2 What is the value of each coin?

F ________ G ________ H ________ I ________ J ________ K ________

3 How many make $100?

A ________ B ________ C ________ D ________ E ________

4 How many make $10?

F ________ G ________ H ________ I ________ J ________ K ________

5 Make $20 four different ways.

a ________________ b ________________

c ________________ d ________________

6 Make $5 four different ways.

a ________________ b ________________

c ________________ d ________________

Challenge!

If I have one of each note and coin, how much do I have? ________

Unit 26 Equivalent coins

1 Circle the equivalent coins.

a	$3	
b	$2.80	
c	$7.35	
d	$1.95	

2 Which coins would you use to pay for:

a the gnome? ______________________

b the doll? ______________________

c the duck? ______________________

3 What change would you get from $5 for:

a the gnome? ______________________

b the doll? ______________________

c the duck? ______________________

Unit 26 Spending money

1 Round each price to the nearest:

dollar

a tape ☐ b saw ☐
c hammer ☐ d spanner ☐
e screwdriver ☐

five cents

f tape ☐ g saw ☐
h hammer ☐ i spanner ☐
j screwdriver ☐

2 Which single note would you use to buy the:

a tape? ________ b saw? ________ c hammer? ________
d spanner? ________ e screwdriver? ________
f saw and hammer? ________ g tape and screwdriver? ________

3 How much change would you get from $5? (Remember to round to the nearest 5c.)

a tape ________ b screwdriver ________ c spanner ________

4 How much change would you get from $20?

a saw ________ b hammer ________

Challenge!

a How much would it cost to buy one of each item? ☐

b How much change would there be from $50? ☐

Mastery Checklist

I can:
- ☐ identify the values of Australian notes and coins
- ☐ use different combinations to make amounts
- ☐ identify equivalent coins
- ☐ round money
- ☐ work out change.

 AC9M4N07 • AC9M4N08 Number **MA2-AR-01** Additive relations B • Apply addition and subtraction to familiar contexts, including money and budgeting

Problem solving

Healthy Eating

1 a You have $10 for lunch. Choose 3 items that would make a healthy lunch.

b Make 3 sets of choices.

My 1st choices	My 2nd choices	My 3rd choices
______	______	______
______	______	______
______	______	______
Total price ______	Total price ______	Total price ______

c Estimate the cost of each using rounding.

My 1st choice	My 2nd choice	My 3rd choice
______	______	______

d You have this amount of money. What could you buy?

$4	$6	$8
______	______	______
______	______	______
______	______	______

I can solve problems by:

☐ adding different amounts of money ☐ estimating and checking answers.

Unit 27 Kilograms

One kilogram is 1000 grams.

This can be written using a **decimal point:** 1·0 kg

whole kilograms ← → part kilograms

1 kg 200 g = 1200 g = 1·2 kg

1 whole kilogram — 200 grams

1 Write the missing masses.

kg and g	g	kg
a 4 kg 300 g	4300 g	4·3 kg
b	2700 g	
c 5 kg 750 g		
d		2·25 kg
e		7500 g
f 8 kg 400 g		

2 Write the masses as decimal kilograms.

a 5500 g 5.5 kg b 3250 g ______ c 8750 g ______
d 1000 g ______ e 6200 g ______ f 4250 g ______
g 7000 g ______ h 2200 g ______ i 9250 g ______
j 10 750 g ______ k 3300 g ______ l 5800 g ______

3 Write the masses in grams.

a 3·25 kg 3250 g b 10·5 kg ______ c 4·6 kg ______
d 8·75 kg ______ e 9·1 kg ______ f 7·4 kg ______
g 2 kg ______ h 6·4 kg ______ i 9·75 kg ______
j 1·25 kg ______ k 5·73 kg ______ l 2·2 kg ______

4 Write these masses in order from smallest to largest:

3250 g, 1·2 kg, 5 kg, 100 g, 100 kg, 6000 g, 8·75 kg, 1 g

____

Unit 27 Grams and kilograms

1 Change to kilograms.

a 3000 g ________ b 9000 g ________ c 1000 g ________

d 7000 g ________ e 5000 g ________ f 1500 g ________ kg ________ g

g 5200 g ________ kg ________ g h 8125 g ________ kg ________ g

2 Change to grams.

a 4 kg ________ b 6 kg ________ c 2 kg ________ d 5 kg ________

e 2 kg 600 g ________ f 9 kg 150 g ________

g 3 kg 475 g ________ h 6·5 kg ________

i 2·25 kg ________ j 8·75 kg ________ k 1·5 kg ________

kilogram kg
gram g
1000 g = 1 kg

3 Look at page 128. Use a calculator.

Write the total mass in kilograms and grams.

a 1 apple + 1 rockmelon + 1 potato = ________

b 10 strawberries = ________ c 8 oranges = ________

d 6 cucumbers = ________ e 10 mushrooms + 1 onion + 1 capsicum = ________

4 How many more grams must be added to make $\frac{1}{2}$ kg?

a 250 g ________ b 405 g ________ c 110 g ________ d 338 g ________

5 Would you use grams or kilograms to weigh:

a an elephant? ______ b a mouse? ______ c a sparrow? ______ d a horse? ______

e a packet of biscuits? ______ f a big bag of rice? ______

g a tea bag? ______ h a mattress? ______ i a tea towel? ______ j a dishwasher? ______

6 Write the mass of each object.

a b c d

Challenge!

a Use a calculator to find the total mass of all the items on page 128. ________

b How many more grams will make 7 kg? ________

Unit 27 Mass at the market

apple 269 g

pumpkin 2 kg

capsicum 180 g

orange 200 g

pineapple 1 kg

potato 310 g

onion 125 g

mushroom 45 g

tomato 250 g

strawberry 20 g

cucumber 480 g

rockmelon 750 g

1 Which is the heaviest item? ____________

2 Which is the lightest item? ____________

3 Order the items from heaviest to lightest. ____________

____

4 Which two items together weigh 1 kg? ____________

5 How much would 2 weigh?

a strawberries ________ b oranges ________

c pumpkins ________ d onions ________

6 Which items weigh more than 200 g but less than half a kilogram?

____

7 Which item weighs $\frac{1}{4}$ of a kilogram? ____________

8 How many strawberries in 100 g? ________

Unit 27 Using scales

1 You need balance scales, weights and objects from the classroom. Work with a partner. Choose 5 objects of varying weights.

a Estimate the mass of each below.

b Weigh each item using the balance scales and weights.

Object	Estimate			Actual Mass
	Less than $\frac{1}{2}$ kg	About 1 kg	More than 1 kg	
1				
2				
3				
4				
5				

c Order the objects from heaviest to lightest.

____

2 Use your scales. How many:

a pencils weigh about 200 g? ______

b Maths books weigh about 2 kg? ______

c pencil cases weigh about 1 kg? ______

d erasers weigh about 1 kg? ______

3

A

B

C $1\frac{1}{2}$ kg

D
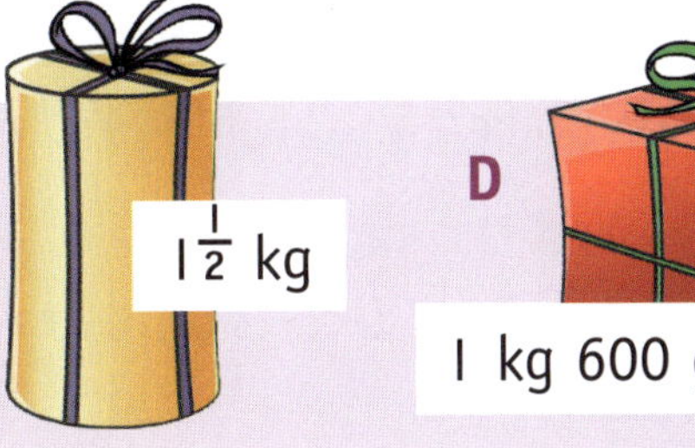

a Write the weights in grams. A ________ B ________ C ________ D ________

b Order them from lightest to heaviest. ______________________________

Trial and error Find an object that has a mass of:

a 100 g [ ] b 2 kg [ ] c 600 g [ ]

Mastery Checklist I can:
- ☐ write masses in kilograms and grams in different ways
- ☐ convert between grams and kilograms
- ☐ identify and combine the masses of objects to make given weights
- ☐ use scales to measure and compare masses.

Problem solving

At the markets

Helping at the markets, Leon, Alfie, Carl and Frank said they carried tonnes of food. Could they be right?

1 5 packets of nuts weigh 500 g and an empty box weighs 200 g. The box can hold 40 packets. What is the mass of a full box? Complete the table.

Box	With 5 packets	With 10 packets	With 15 packets	With 20 packets	With 25 packets	With 30 packets	With 35 packets	With 40 packets
200 g	700 g	1200 g	1700 g					

How many boxes would each boy need to carry to have carried a tonne of food? ______

2 The nut packets were increased in size to 250 g packs. How many will be in a full box weighing the same as in question 1? ______ Use a table to find out.

3 Work backwards and make a table.

The boys picked vegetables to sell.

Leon picked the most, while Alfie picked 2 kg less than Leon. Carl picked 1 kg less than Alfie and 1 kg more than Frank. Frank picked 10 kg of vegetables.

How much did each boy pick? ______

Boys	**kg**
Frank	

I can solve problems by:

☐ understanding mass ☐ measuring and using logical thinking.

AC9M4N08 Number **MAO-WM-01** Working mathematically • choosing and applying mathematical techniques to solve problems • **MA2-MR-01** Multiplicative relations B • Represent and solve word problems with number sentences involving multiplication or division

Unit 28 Reflect, translate, rotate

Shape position

1 Has the artist used reflect, translate or rotate to make these patterns?

A ______________ B ______________ C ______________

2 Use this shape.

a Reflect it.

b Translate it.

c Rotate it.

3 Reflect, translate or rotate?

______________ ______________ ______________

4 Draw your own pattern using reflect, translate or rotate.

Unit 28 Axis of symmetry

An **axis of symmetry** divides a shape into halves that are mirror images of each other.

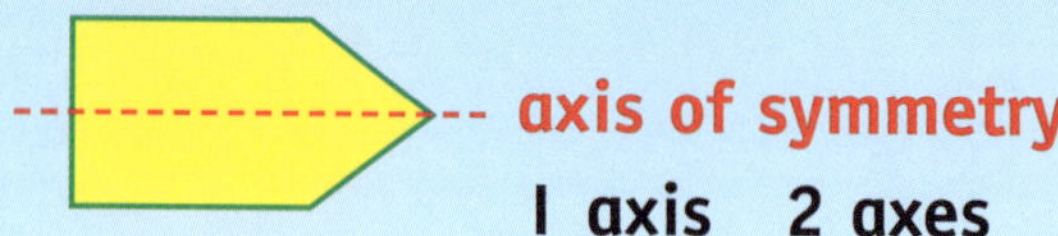

1 axis 2 axes

1 Colour each to make a symmetrical pattern. Use a mirror to help you.

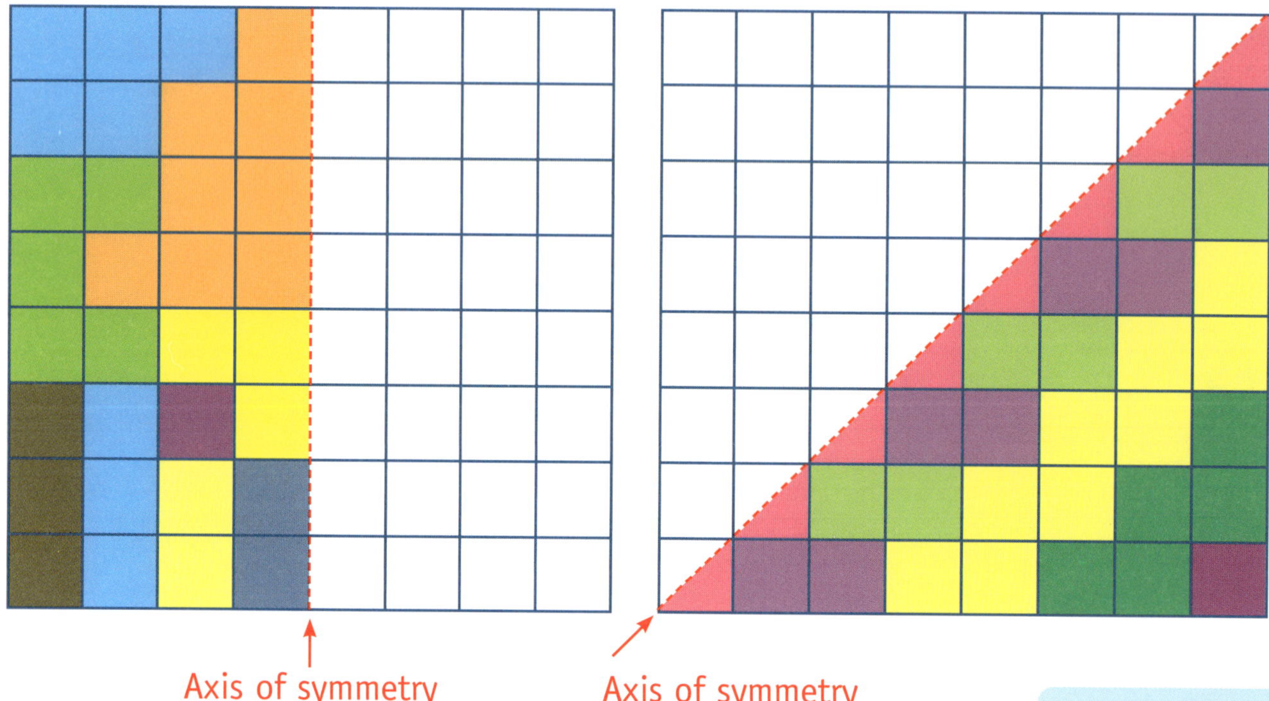

Rotations: full turn, three-quarter turn, half turn, quarter turn.

2 Mark the axis of symmetry, then draw each shape after a clockwise quarter turn is made.

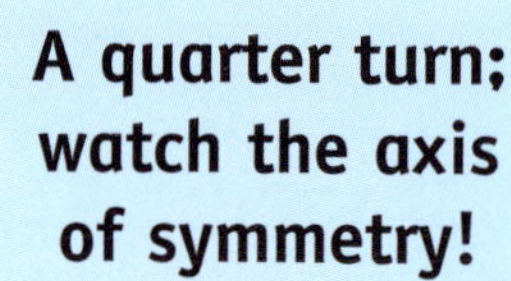

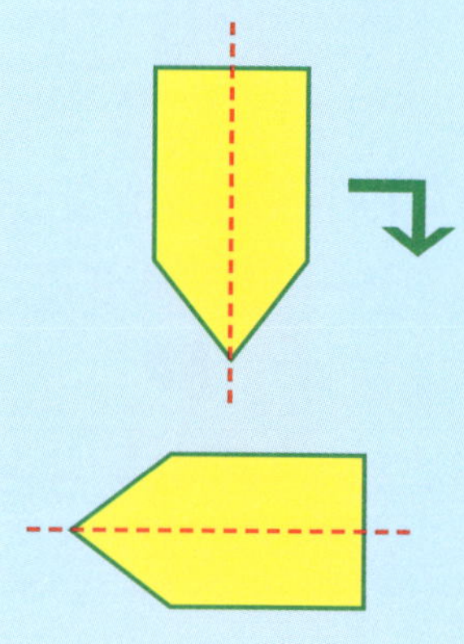

a

b

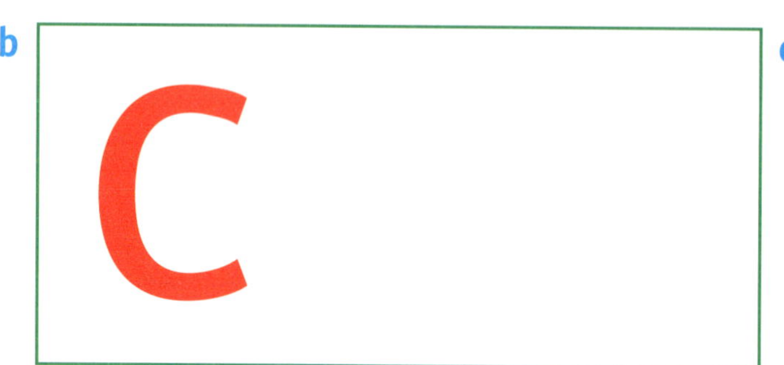

c

Unit 28 Tessellating shapes

Tessellating shapes fit together without any gaps or overlaps.

Squares tessellate.

1 Circle the shapes that will tessellate.

a 

b 

c 

d 

e 

f 

g 

2 Colour the patterns made with tessellating shapes.

a 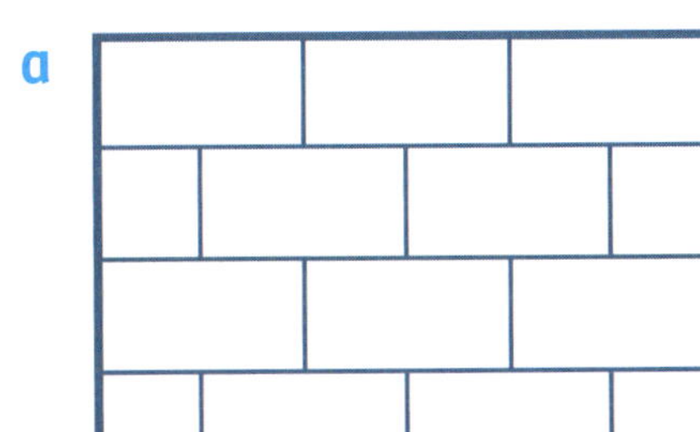

b 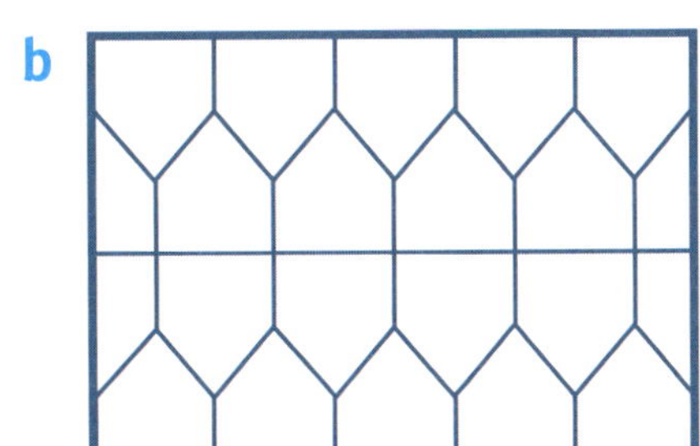

c 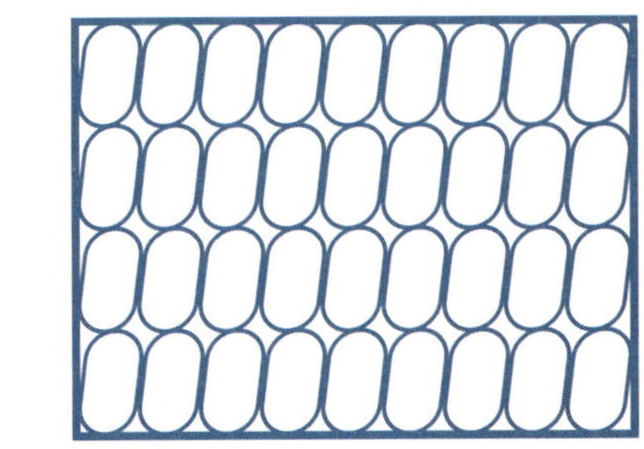

3 Were the above tessellations made using translation, reflection or rotation? ____________

4 Draw your own tessellating patterns using the given shapes. Use reflection and rotation.

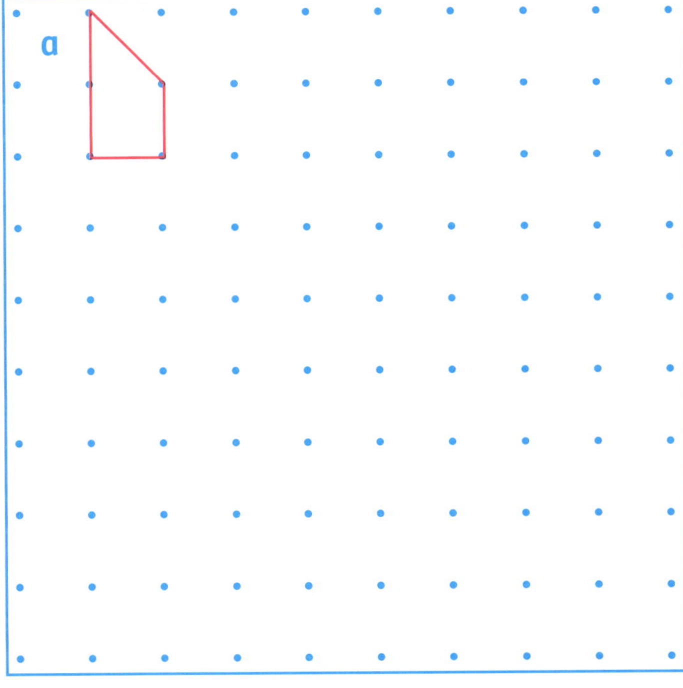

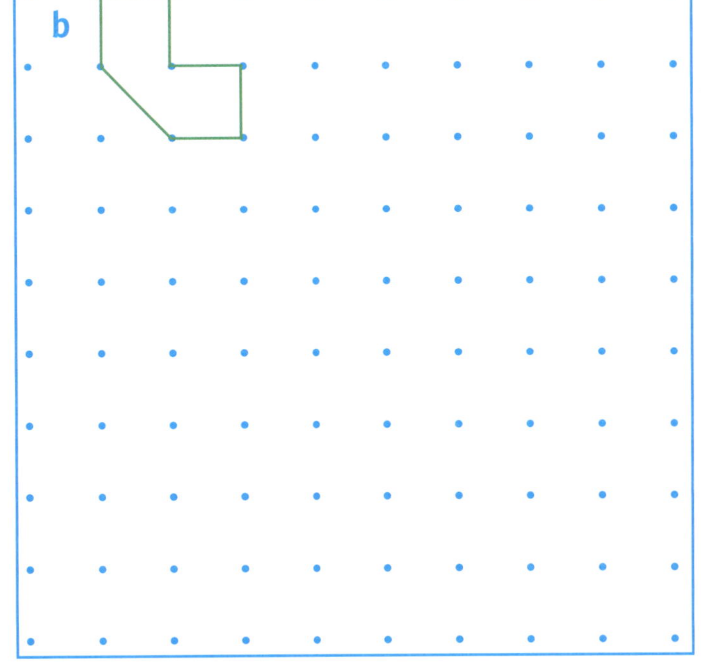

Unit 28 Making a shape

Let's make a tessellating shape.

You need a 4 cm square of cardboard, scissors and sticky tape.

1. Draw a simple shape on one side of your square.
2. Cut it out.
3. Sticky tape it to the opposite side.

Hint. *It is a good idea to sticky tape it front and back.*

You now have a tessellating shape.

(You can start with a simple shape, eg  and then make harder ones.)

1 Trace around your shape to make a colourful tessellating pattern.

Mastery Checklist

I can:
- ☐ identify translations, rotations and reflections
- ☐ create symmetrical patterns, pictures and shapes
- ☐ identify tessellating shapes
- ☐ create a tessellation.

Unit 29 Survey

You have overseas visitors staying. You have a weekend to share a special activity.

1 Survey 30 people to find out their favourite activity. Ask adults as well as children.

Activity	Tally marks	Total
Sailing a boat		
A bushwalk		
Camping		
Surfing at a beach		
Staying on a farm		
Visiting the city		

2 Draw a graph to show the results of your survey.
Remember to label the axes and give your graph a title.

3 a What is the most popular activity? ______

b What is the least popular activity? ______

4 a Are you influenced by your survey? ______

b Where would you take overseas visitors? ______

Unit 29 Mystery graph

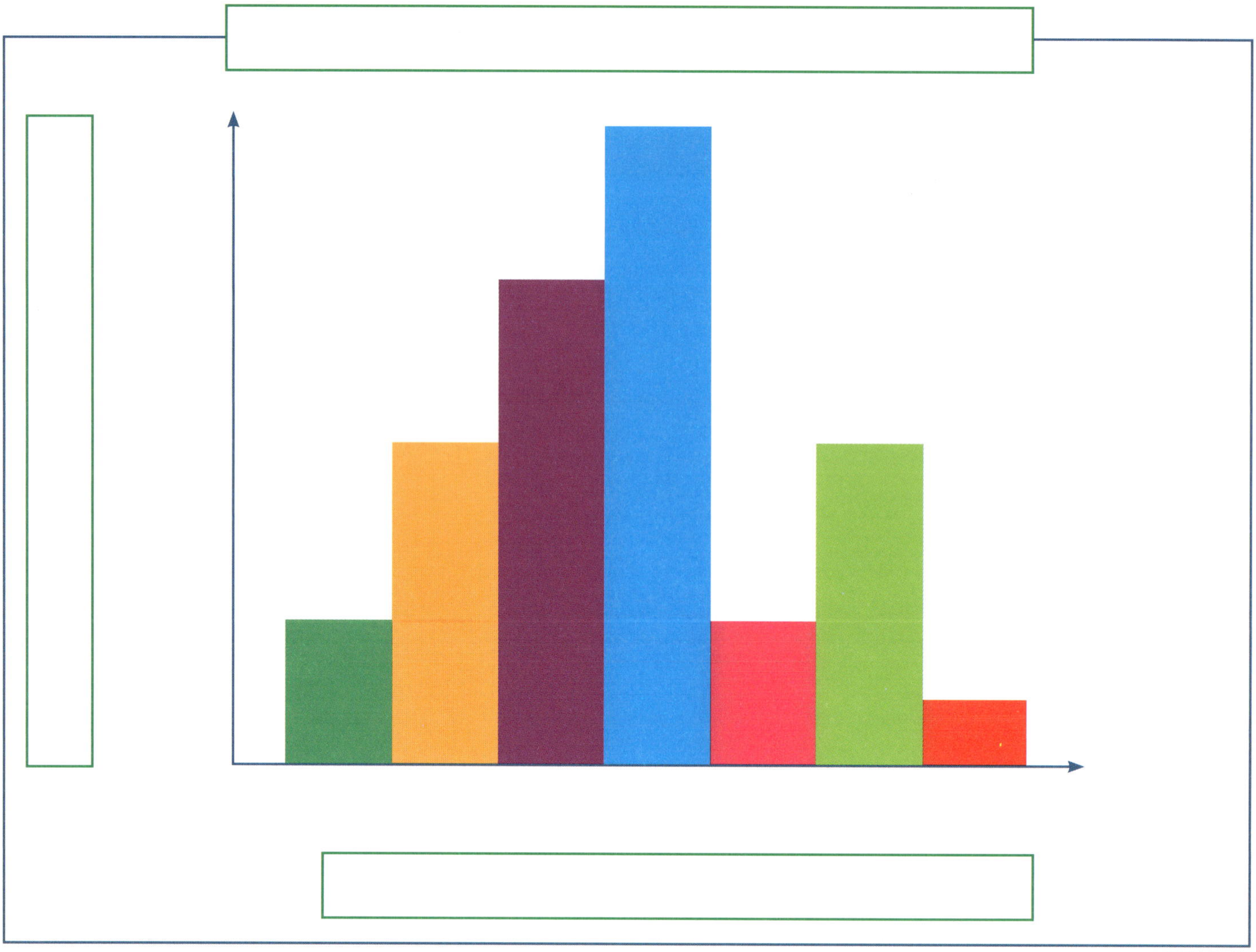

1 You decide what the graph is about.

2 Give the graph a title.

3 Label the axes and mark on their scales.

4 Make up 8 questions about your graph. Give them to a friend to answer.

a ______________________

b ______________________

c ______________________

d ______________________

e ______________________

f ______________________

g ______________________

h ______________________

Unit 29 Dot plots

Graphs

A dot plot uses dots to represent data.

Key ● = 1 student

Hair Colours of Year 4 Students

1 Use the dot plot to complete the table.

Hair colour	Brown	Red	Black	Blond	Grey
Number of students					

2 How many students were surveyed? ________

3 Which hair colour was least common? ________

4 Did more or less students have brown hair than blond hair? ______

5 Did more or less students have red hair than black hair? ______

6 Show the information in the table below on the following dot plot.

Goals kicked by Sam

Season	2018	2019	2020	2021	2022	2023
Number of goals	16	6	8	10	12	14

Key: ● = 2 goals

Unit 29 Interpreting data

Data

Meals	Boys	Girls
Steak	7	2
Chicken	3	8
Fish	2	3
Sausages	6	1
Pasta	2	6

This table is the result of a survey.

1 a Tick the best title.

Favourite meal

What I like to eat

What I will eat next Monday

b Give a reason for your choice. ______

______

Use the survey to answer these questions.

2 How many people were surveyed? ______

3 Were there equal numbers of boys and girls? ______

4 What was the favourite for:

a boys? ______ b girls? ______

5 How many chose:

a steak? ______ b fish? ______ c pasta? ______

6 Which meal was chosen:

a most often? ______ b least often? ______

7 a Does this survey show all food eaten by boys and girls? ______

b Why? ______

8 What 5 meals would you survey?

______

Challenge! Show this survey as a picture graph. Remember all the labels.

Unit 29 Spreadsheets

A spreadsheet has data organised into rows and columns.

This is a column

Rows

Bus trips to Uluru, January-June 2024

	A	B	C	
1	Month	Number of trips	Subtotal	This is a cell
2	Jan	609	609	= B2
3	Feb	413	1022	= C2 + B3
4	Mar	252	1274	= C3 + B4
5	Apr	595	1869	= C4 + B5
6	May	420	2289	= C5 + B6
7	Jun	159	2448	= C6 + B7

To get the **subtotal**, add the **column B** value to the previous **column C** value.

1 How many bus trips in these months?

a January ______ b March ______ c May ______

2 What is the value in these cells?

a C3 ______ b C5 ______ c C7 ______

3 What is the total number of bus trips:

a from January to March? ______ b from January to May? ______

4 In what month were there:

a 413 trips? ______________________

b 159 trips? ______________________

c 595 trips? ______________________

5 When was the lowest subtotal? ______________________

6 How many bus trips to Uluru were there altogether? ______

Mastery Checklist I can:
- ☐ collect, record and represent data
- ☐ interpret data in column graphs and dot plots
- ☐ interpret data in a table
- ☐ interpret data in a spreadsheet

Revision Term 3

1 Round to the nearest hundred. p 101

a 6874 ______

b 34 529 ______

2 Round to the nearest thousand.

a 4601 ______

b 64 259 ______

3 a

```
   7 6
   2 9
+  4 3
------
```

b

```
  6 2 8
+ 2 9 4
-------
```

c

```
  8 7 1
+ 4 8 3
-------
```

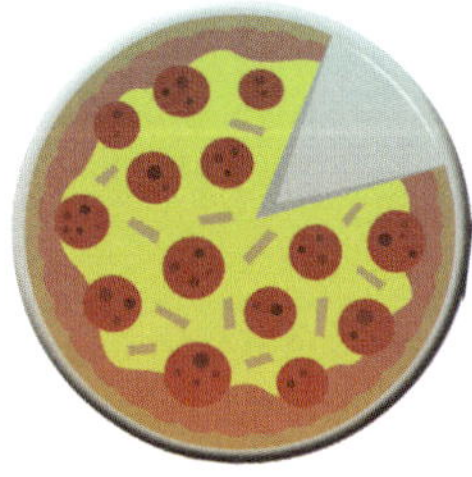

4 Farmer Brown had 329 sheep and 748 cows. How many animals altogether? p 102

5 p 104

a

H	T	O
	6	9
×		8

b

H	T	O
	7	2
×		3

6 A motorbike travelled 54 km on 1 litre of fuel. How far will it travel on 6 litres of fuel? p 105

Number sentence: ______

Answer: ______

7 p 106

a $6\overline{)36}$ b $7\overline{)28}$ c $9\overline{)63}$

d $4\overline{)52}$ e $6\overline{)72}$ f $3\overline{)69}$

8 Write the yellow part as a fraction. p 110

a b

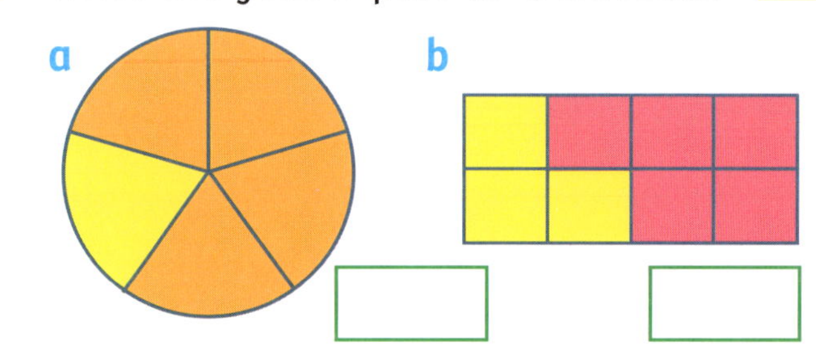

9 p 110

a $\frac{1}{4} + \frac{\square}{4} = 1$ b $\frac{\square}{10} + \frac{3}{10} = 1$

10 Colour to show: p 111

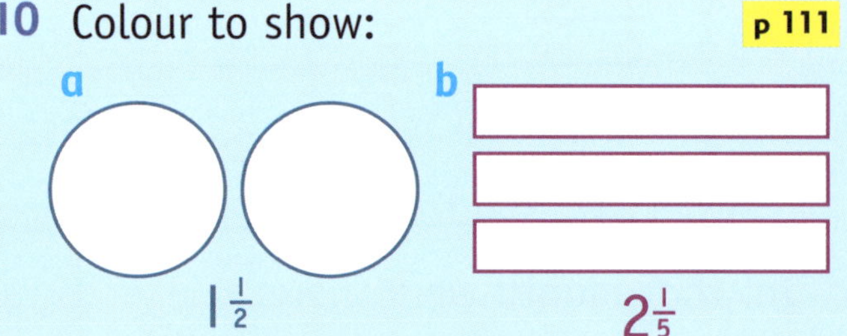

a $1\frac{1}{2}$ b $2\frac{1}{5}$

11 p 112

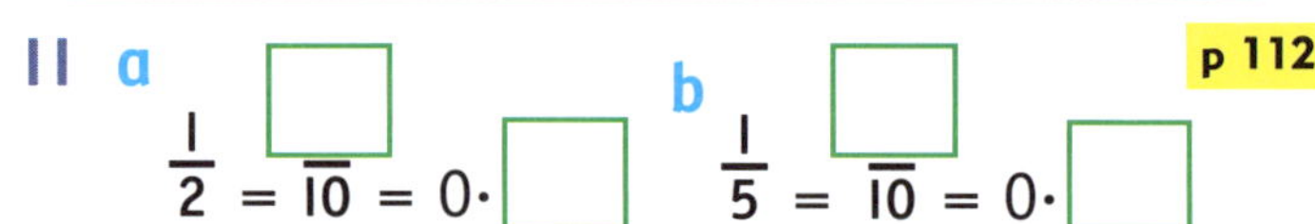

a $\frac{1}{2} = \frac{\square}{10} = 0{\cdot}\square$ b $\frac{1}{5} = \frac{\square}{10} = 0{\cdot}\square$

12 Write to the nearest whole number. p 113

a 7·1 ______ b 13·9 ______ c 10·5 ______

13 p 118

a 8 × ☐ = 32

b ☐ + 18 = 30 c 60 ÷ 2 ÷ ☐ = 10

d ☐ − 17 = 20 e 15 + 8 + ☐ = 32

Revision Term 3

14 a ✿ − 5 = 14 p 119

✿ = ______

b ♦ ÷ 7 = 7

♦ = ______

15 Circle the easiest fact to work first. p 121

8 × 13 × 5

Explain your answer. ______________

____

16 How many $5 notes make $100? ______ p 122

17 Make $10 in four different ways. p 122

a ______________________

b ______________________

c ______________________

d ______________________

18 Round to the nearest dollar. p 124

a $4.22_____ b $7.09_____ c $5.68_____

19 p 127

a Which is the lightest? ____________

b Which is the heaviest? ____________

c Which weighs $\frac{1}{4}$ of a kilogram?

____

d How much would 2 lemons weigh?

____

e How many oranges in 1 kg? ________

f How many strawberries in 100 g? _____

20 a 2 kg = ________ g p 127

b 9000 g = ______ kg c 3000 g = _____ kg

d 7·5 kg = ________ g e 1500 g = _____ kg

21 Colour to make a symmetrical pattern. Draw 2 axes of symmetry. p 132

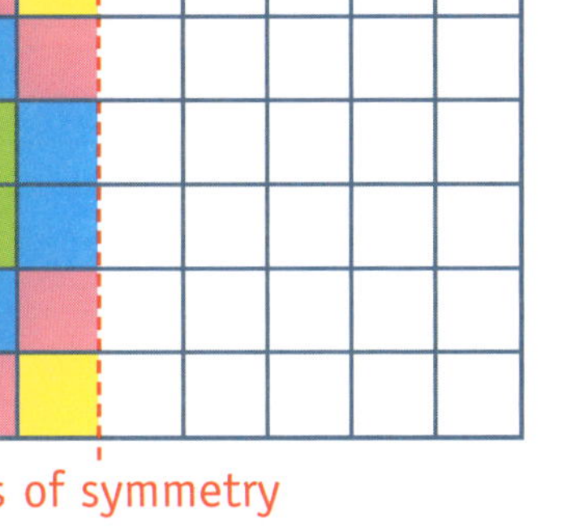

22 Cross out the shapes that do not tessellate. p 133

23 p 136

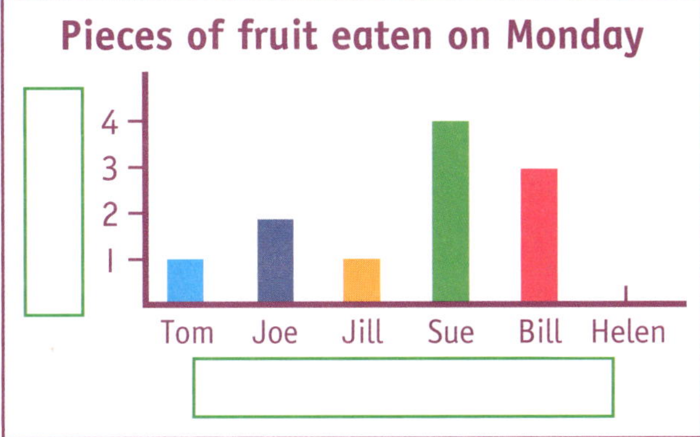

a Label the axes.

b How much was eaten by boys? ______

c Who ate no fruit? __________

d How many children were asked? ______

e How much fruit was eaten? ______

Unit 30 Estimation with division

REMEMBER
An estimation is **NOT** an exact answer.
eg 87 ÷ 3 [90 ÷ 3]
Estimation 30

1 Give estimations for these answers. Write what you did.

a 62 ÷ 3 [60 ÷ 3]
Est. [ ]

b 84 ÷ 4 [ ]
Est. [ ]

c 38 ÷ 2 [ ]
Est. [ ]

d 95 ÷ 5 [ ]
Est. [ ]

e 78 ÷ 6 [ ]
Est. [ ]

f 56 ÷ 4 [ ]
Est. [ ]

g 66 ÷ 3 [ ]
Est. [ ]

h 147 ÷ 7 [ ]
Est. [ ]

i 918 ÷ 9 [ ]
Est. [ ]

2 Now work out the exact answers.

a $3\overline{)72}$

b $4\overline{)84}$

c $2\overline{)38}$

d $5\overline{)95}$

e $6\overline{)78}$

f $4\overline{)56}$

g $3\overline{)66}$

h $7\overline{)147}$

i $9\overline{)918}$

3 Colour yellow the answers that are close to your estimates.

4 True or false?

a 56 is a multiple of 4. ____________

b 62 is a multiple of 3. ____________

c 87 is a multiple of 7. ____________

d 56 is a multiple of 6. ____________

e 130 is a multiple of 3. ____________

f 100 is a multiple of 20. ____________

Challenge!

a Who has more sweets? ____________

b By how many? ____________

I paid $1.05 for Chocolate buds.

I paid $1.08 for Strawberry balls.

Chocolate buds 3 for 7c

Strawberry balls 4 for 9c

AC9M4N06 • AC9M4N07 Number MA2-MR-01 Multiplicative relations A • Represent and solve problems involving multiplication fact families • Multiplicative relations B • Use known number facts and strategies

Unit 30 ÷ and × by 10, 100 and 1000

3-digit division

Multiply

Move the decimal point to the right when you multiply. Count the number of zeroes to check.

5 × 10 = 5·0· (1 zero) — Move the decimal point 1 place to the right.

5 × 100 = 5·00· (2 zeros) — Move the decimal point 2 places to the right.

5 × 1000 = 5·000· (3 zeros) — Move the decimal point 3 places to the right.

Divide

Move the decimal point to the left when you divide. 5 is the same as 5·0

5 ÷ 10 = 0·5· — Move the decimal point 1 place to the left.

5 ÷ 100 = 0·05· — Move the decimal point 2 places to the left.

5 ÷ 1000 = 0·005· — Move the decimal point 3 places to the left.

1 Multiply.

	×	×10	×100	×1000
a	4			
b	9			
c	10			
d	3			
e	12			

2 Divide.

	÷	÷10	÷100	÷1000
a	7			
b	19			
c	6			
d	14			
e	2			

Mastery Checklist I can:

- ☐ estimate with division
- ☐ identify multiples
- ☐ multiply and divide by 10, 100, 1000

Problem solving

Discover multiples

1 Complete this multiplication square neatly and lightly in pencil.

×

1	2	3	4	5	6	7	8	9	10	11	12
2											
3											
4											
5											
6											
7											
8											
9											
10											
11											
12											

2 Colour in the squares of all the multiples of 6. Do you see a pattern? Describe it.

____

____

3 Using different multiplication squares, colour the multiples of 3, 5, 8 or 9. Study the results. Comment on the patterns that you find.

____

____

4 On another multiplication square, circle all the 24s, 36s, 48s, 72s and 120s. What do you find?

____

____

I can solve problems by:

☐ using multiples ☐ describing number patterns.

AC9M4N09 Number **MAO-WM-01** Working mathematically • communicating thinking and reasoning coherently and clearly • **MA2-MR-01** Multiplicative relations B • Investigate number sequences involving related multiples • Use known number facts and strategies

Unit 31 Four-digit subtraction

1 Find the difference in price between:

a the Jeep and the Honda. ______________ b the Jeep and the Mercedes. ______________

c the Toyota and the Nissan. ______________ d the Ford and the Nissan. ______________

Working

2 Which car is:

a $1514 less than the Toyota? ______________

b $3110 more than the Nissan? ______________

c $2510 less than the Mercedes? ______________

3 Use a calculator to find which two cars have:

a the greatest difference. ______________ ______________

b the least difference. ______________ ______________

4 Estimate how much you would have left from $10 000 if you bought:

a the Mercedes. ______________ b the Ford. ______________

Unit 31 Trading tens

To trade down a ten
56 = 50 + 6
= 40 + 16

1 Trade down 1 ten.

a 46 = 40 + 6
= 30 + ____

b 72 = 70 + 2
= 60 + ____

c 85 = 80 + 5
= ____ + ____

d 27 = 20 + ____
= ____ + ____

e 51 = 50 + ____
= ____ + ____

f 34 = 30 + ____
= ____ + ____

g 48 = 40 + ____
= ____ + ____

h 93 = 90 + ____
= ____ + ____

i 61 = 60 + ____
= ____ + ____

j 36 = 30 + ____
= ____ + ____

k 69 = 60 + ____
= ____ + ____

l 87 = ____ + ____
= ____ + ____

m 45 = ____ + ____
= ____ + ____

n 78 = ____ + ____
= ____ + ____

2

a
	Tens	Ones
	2	12
	~~3~~	~~2~~
−	1	5

b
	Tens	Ones
	4	15
	~~5~~	~~5~~
−	2	8

c
	Tens	Ones
	5	13
	~~6~~	~~3~~
−	4	9

	Tens	Ones
	5	12
	~~6~~	~~2~~
−	2	7
	3	5

I can't take 7 from 2, so I traded down a ten.

d
	Tens	Ones
	6	14
	~~7~~	~~4~~
−	5	5

e
	Tens	Ones
	3	17
	~~4~~	~~7~~
−	1	8

f
	Tens	Ones
	7	18
	~~8~~	~~8~~
−	3	9

g
	Tens	Ones
	6	7
−	4	9

h
	Tens	Ones
	3	6
−	1	8

i
	Tens	Ones
	8	5
−	5	6

j
	Tens	Ones
	5	3
−	2	8

k
	Tens	Ones
	7	4
−	4	7

l
	Tens	Ones
	4	8
−	1	9

m
	Tens	Ones
	9	2
−	3	9

n
	Tens	Ones
	7	0
−	2	6

Unit 31 More subtraction with trading

1 a
```
   6 12
   7  2
 - 1  8
 ------
```
b
```
   5 3
 - 2 9
 -----
```
c
```
   8 0
 - 6 4
 -----
```
d
```
   6 5
 - 2 7
 -----
```
e
```
   4 4
 - 1 6
 -----
```

2

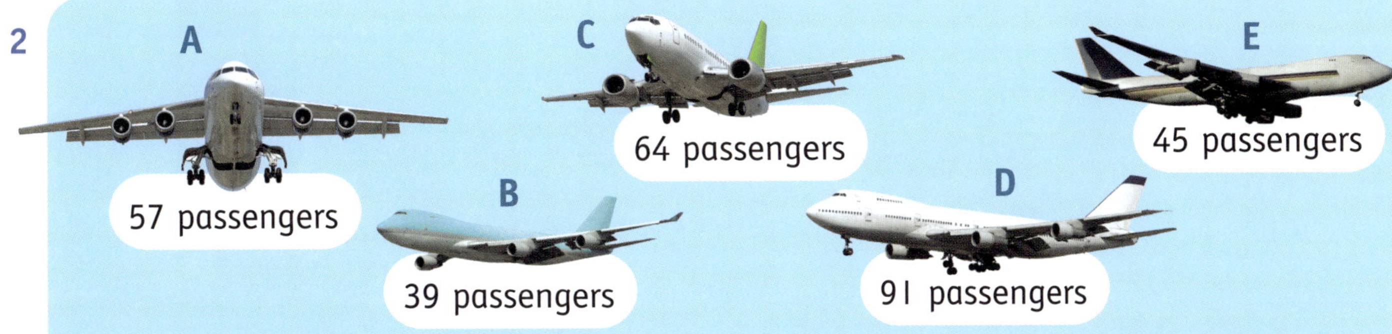

What is the difference in number of passengers between plane **D** and each other plane?

A
```
   9 1
 - 5 7
 -----
```
B
```
   9 1
 -
 -----
```
C

E

3 Which two planes have a difference of:

a 19? ______ b 18? ______ c 12? ______ d 25? ______

4 Which two planes have:

a the greatest difference? ______ b the least difference? ______

5 Complete these subtraction squares. Work mentally.

a

−		
62	14	
28	12	

b

−		
73	35	
25	19	

c

−		
58	23	
19	15	

d

−		
90	35	
59	24	

6 a There are 72 children in Year 4. 43 are boys.

How many girls? ______

b There are 81 apples.

How many are red, if 37 are green? ______

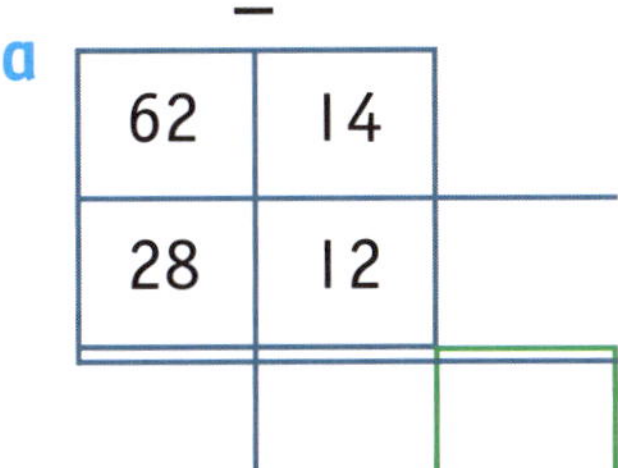

Unit 31 Algorithms using subtraction

Work out the answers to complete the crossnumber puzzle.

1 $24 - 13 =$ ____

2 $64 - 47 =$ ____

3 $94 - 19 =$ ____

4 $82 - 24 =$ ____

5 $70 - 47 =$ ____

6 $98 - 14 =$ ____

7 $90 - 41 =$ ____

8 $72 - 36 =$ ____

9 $81 - 18 =$ ____

10 $63 - 28 =$ ____

11 $95 - 41 =$ ____

12 $75 - 29 =$ ____

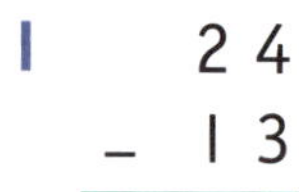

At the district pet show, there were 372 dogs, 490 cats, 138 rabbits and 257 guinea pigs.

Show your working.

Working

13 How many more:

a cats than rabbits? ☐

b dogs than guinea pigs? ☐

14 How many less:

a guinea pigs than cats? ☐

b rabbits than dogs? ☐

15 How many animals altogether? Estimate first.

Est. ☐

Ans. ☐

Trial and error

Two three-digit numbers have a difference of 628. The first number has 7 in the ones place. The second number has 2 in the hundreds place. What are the numbers?

☐

Mastery Checklist

I can:
- ☐ understand and find the difference
- ☐ subtract 4-digit numbers
- ☐ use trading to solve subtraction
- ☐ use subtraction to solve word problems.

Unit 32 Addition and subtraction

Hot-air Balloon Gala Day

1 What is the total distance travelled by:

a elephant and snowman? ______ b dog and cow? ______

c tiger and house? ______ d house and snowman? ______

2 What is the difference between the distances travelled by:

a elephant and snowman? ______ b dog and cow? ______

c tiger and house? ______ d house and snowman? ______

3 Which two balloons together travelled:

a 497 km? ______ b 658 km? ______

4 Which three balloons together travelled:

a 734 km? ______ b 1236 km? ______

5 a Which four balloons together travelled the greatest distance?

______

b Which two balloons had the least difference in distance travelled?

______

Unit 32 Patterns in addition and subtraction

Use subtraction to check addition

```
  2 9 3        8 7 1
+ 5 7 8      - 2 9 3
  8 7 1        5 7 8
```

1 a 3 + 8 = 11
30 + 80 = ____
300 + 800 = ____

b 6 + 9 = ____
60 + 90 = ____
600 + 900 = ____

c 5 + 7 = ____
50 + 70 = ____
____ + ____ = ____

d 4 + 8 = ____
____ + ____ = ____
____ + ____ = ____

e 7 − 4 = ____
70 − 40 = ____
700 − 400 = ____

f 9 − 5 = ____
____ − ____ = ____
____ − ____ = ____

g 8 − 6 = ____
____ − ____ = ____
____ − ____ = ____

h 8 − 1 = ____
____ − ____ = ____
____ − ____ = ____

2 From one fact write three more.

a 13 + 9 = 22, 9 + ____ = 22, 22 − ____ = 13, 22 − ____ = 9

b 16 + 7 = ____, ____ + ____ = ____, ____ − ____ = ____, ____ − ____ = ____

c 28 − 9 = ____, ____ − ____ = ____, ____ + ____ = ____, ____ + ____ = ____

d 23 − 6 = ____, ____ − ____ = ____, ____ + ____ = ____, ____ + ____ = ____

3 a

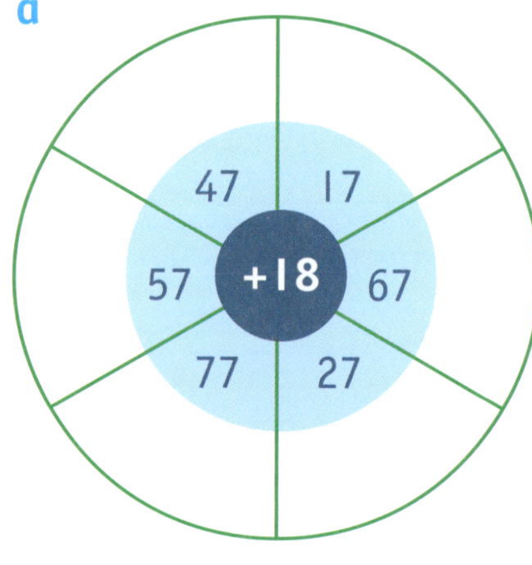

b

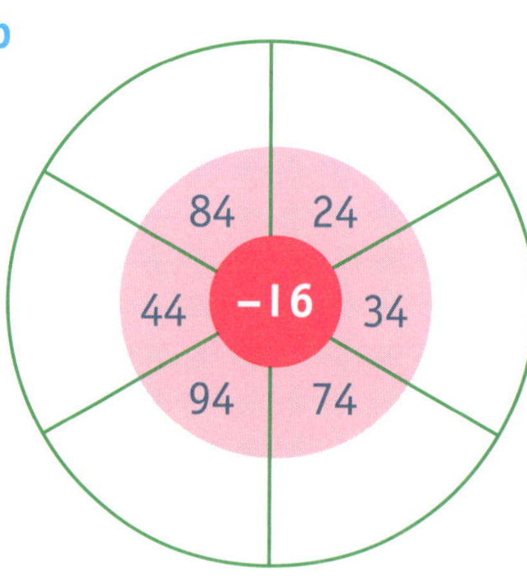

c

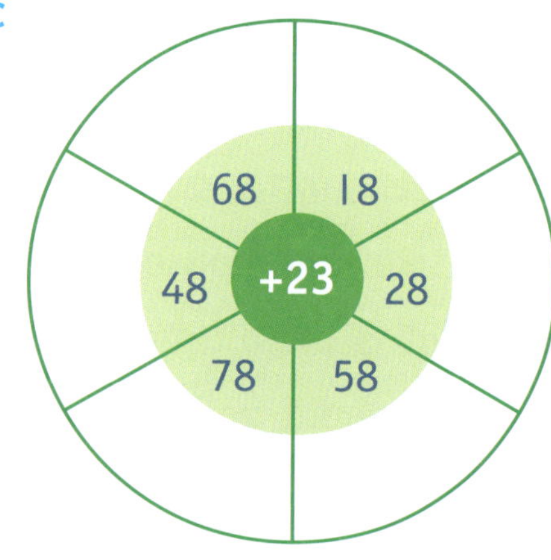

4 Add, then subtract to check your answers.

a
```
  3 7 2        ____
+ 2 1 9      − ____
  ____         ____
```

b
```
  5 6 4        ____
+ 3 5 8      − ____
  ____         ____
```

c
```
  7 5 5        ____
+ 3 7 9      − ____
  ____         ____
```

d
```
  6 0 9        ____
+ 3 8 6      − ____
  ____         ____
```

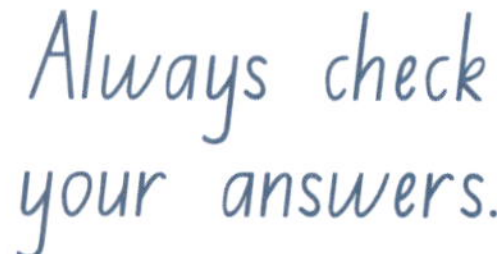

AC9M4N06 Number **MA2-AR-01** Additive relations A • Recognise and explain the connection between addition and subtraction • Additive relations B • Partition, rearrange and regroup numbers to at least 1000 to solve additive problems • **MA2-MR-01** Multiplicative relations A • Generate and describe patterns

Unit 32 Bar model for addition and subtraction

Related facts

Problem	Bar model	Equation
1 Aaina counted 353 fruit on Saturday, and then on Sunday she counted some more. If Aaina counted 536 fruit altogether, how many did she count on Sunday?	353 | ? 536 ? = 183	353 + 183 = 536 183 + 353 = 536
2 Nullah and Bindi collected 2682 wattle seeds. If Bindi collected 1365, how many did Nullah collect?	? | 1365 2682 ? = ____	____ + 1365 = 2682 1365 + ____ = 2682
3 Jiemba and Birrani were at the beach counting crabs. They each counted the same number and got 448 in total. How many did they each count?	? | ? 448 ? = ____ ? = ____	____ + ____ = 448 ____ + ____ = ____
4 Iluka saw two mobs of kangaroos. He saw 123 in the first mob and 84 in the second mob. How many kangaroos did he see altogether?	____ | ____ ? ? = ____	____ + ____ = ____ ____ + ____ = ____
5 Waru and his cousins drove 1184 km in August, 765 km in September and 2340 km in October. How many kilometres altogether?	____ | ____ | ____ ? ? = ____	____ + ____ + ____ = ____ ____ + ____ + ____ = ____
6 Ash counted 187 lizards in the rock garden and 168 more beside the creek. How many lizards altogether?	____ | ____ ____ ? = ____	____ + ____ = ____ ____ + ____ = ____

Unit 32 Estimation and calculation

This is a calculator display. 7629

1 What would you add to make:

a the 9 a 5? ______________

b the 2 an 8? ______________

c the 6 a 9? ______________

d the 7 an 8? ______________

e the 29 into 51? ______________

2 What would you subtract to make:

a the 9 a 5? ______

b the 2 a 6? ______

c the 6 a 3? ______

d the 7 a 1? ______

e the 29 into 12? ______

f the 629 into 420? ______

3 True or false?

a A + B is about 8000. ______________

b C + D is about 11 000. ______________

c B − C is about 500. ______________

d D is closer to 8000 than 7000. ______________

e B + C is less than A + D. ______________

f D − C is more than C − A. ______________

g Write two false statements about the numbers.

- ______________________________
- ______________________________

h Write two true statements about the numbers.

- ______________________________
- ______________________________

Challenge!

Complete the table.

Tree Survey Northside

Type of tree	Number	Number planted	Number cut down	Total
a gum	1736	2168	0	
b palm	3879	0	1274	
c fruit	958	1371	315	

Mastery Checklist

I can:
- ☐ choose the best strategy to solve problems
- ☐ recognise patterns in addition and subtraction
- ☐ use bar models to solve word problems
- ☐ use estimation to solve problems.

Problem solving

Think of a number

1 Find the pattern in this procedure so that you can make up a similar puzzle.

Try three different numbers. **a** **b** **c**

	a	b	c
Write down a number <30			
Add 15			
Subtract 8			
Add another 9			
Take away 19 this time			
Add 6			
Subtract 3			
That's your number!	Your number is	Your number is	Your number is

d What happens to make this answer?

CARD TRICK

2 Try this.

Ask a partner to choose a number card from a deck of cards. Instruct them to:

Add 12 to the value of the card

Subtract 8

Add a further 10

Take 16 from the total

Add 5

Subtract 4

Ask what their result is. Secretly add 1 and tell them the number of their card!

Work it out here

a Work out how you could tell their card was 1 more than their answer.

b Make up a similar puzzle of your own, using addition and subtraction.

I can solve problems by:

☐ using different operations ☐ finding patterns.

Unit 33 Decimal and fraction mates

Decimals and fractions have equivalents. They become good mates!

1 Find all the mates of:

a one tenth ______________________
b two tenths ______________________
c three tenths ______________________
d four tenths ______________________
e five tenths ______________________
f six tenths ______________________
g seven tenths ______________________
h eight tenths ______________________
i nine tenths ______________________
j ten tenths ______________________

2 Which fractions do not have any mates here? Circle them.

$\frac{1}{6}$ $\frac{2}{5}$ $\frac{1}{3}$ $\frac{1}{7}$ $\frac{5}{6}$ $\frac{1}{2}$ $\frac{23}{100}$ $\frac{90}{100}$ $\frac{3}{8}$ $\frac{5}{12}$

3 Choose three of those fractions and explain why they do not have mates here.

a ____

b ____

c ____

4 Place the following fractions and decimals in order on the number line.

0·9, $\frac{3}{5}$, $\frac{7}{10}$, $\frac{40}{100}$, 0·5, $\frac{1}{5}$, $\frac{80}{100}$, 1·0, $\frac{3}{10}$, 0·1

0 ——————————————————————————— 1

Unit 33 Fractions and decimals

1 What would you choose?

a 0·2 of the sweets supply or 0·75 of the sweets supply?

Why? ______

b To do 0·5 of the washing up or 0·05 of the washing up?

Why? ______

c To watch television for 0·1 or $\frac{5}{10}$ of the afternoon?

Why? ______

2 Use a calculator to write the decimal.

$\frac{2}{5}$ means $2 \div 5$

a $\frac{1}{5}$ = ______ b $\frac{1}{4}$ = ______ c $\frac{7}{10}$ = ______ d $\frac{4}{5}$ = ______

e $\frac{15}{100}$ = ______ f $\frac{9}{10}$ = ______ g $\frac{6}{100}$ = ______ h $\frac{3}{4}$ = ______

3 Add 0·1 to every decimal in question 2.

a ______ b ______ c ______ d ______

e ______ f ______ g ______ h ______

4 What place value changed number in question 3? Circle one.

ones **tenths** **hundredths**

5 True or false? Use a calculator.

a $\frac{2}{5} = \frac{4}{10}$ ______ Why? ______

b $\frac{600}{100} = \frac{3}{5}$ ______ Why? ______

6 a I earned $16 and saved 0·25 of it. How much did I save?

b Barb has 100 hens and 0·5 of them laid an egg. How many eggs?

c Bob gave 0·2 of his 30 marbles to Jenny. How many did he give her?

d Dad planted 50 vegetable seedlings. One tenth died. How many lived?

Challenge!

When sharing some lollies, I gave $\frac{30}{100}$ to Judy, $\frac{1}{5}$ to Bob and 0·5 to Meg.

How much is left for me?

Unit 33 Decimals everywhere

1 One metre is equal to 100 cm.

0 cm	10 cm	20 cm	30 cm	40 cm	50 cm	60 cm	70 cm	80 cm	90 cm	100 cm
0 m										1 m

Complete:

a 0·1 m = ______ cm b 0·2 m = ______ cm c ______ m = 50 cm d ______ m = 80 cm

2 One dollar is equal to 100 cents.

a 0·2 dollars = ______ cents = $__________ b 0·4 dollars = ______ cents = $__________

c 0·6 dollars = ______ cents = $__________ d 0·75 dollars = ______ cents = $__________

3 One kilogram is equal to 1000 grams.

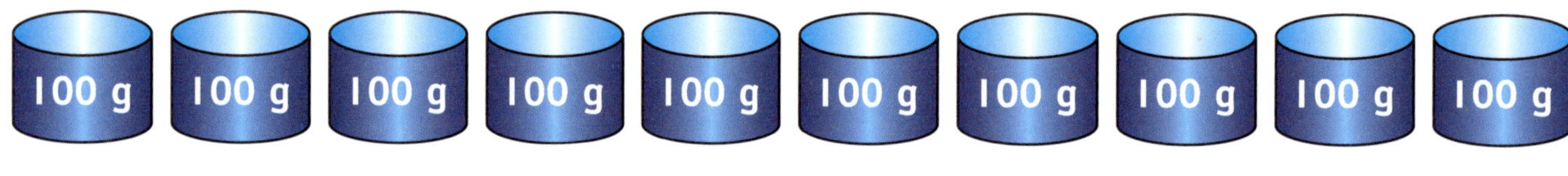

a 100 g = 0·_____ kg b 300 g = _____ kg c 450 g = _____ kg d 990 g = _____ kg

4 Using the letters a, b, c, d, place the following decimal measures on the number line.

a 0·3 m b 0·6 m c 0·32 m d 0·65 m

0 m ——————————————————— 1 m

5 Using the letters a, b, c, d, place the following dollar amounts on the number line.

a $0.55 b $0.45 c $0.15 d $0.05

0 ——————————————————— $1

6 Using the letters a, b, c, d, place the following decimal masses on the number line.

a 0·2 kg b 0·28 kg c 0·82 kg d 0·02 kg

0 ——————————————————— 1 kg

Mastery Checklist I can:
- ☐ identify equivalent fractions
- ☐ show fractions and decimals on a number line
- ☐ compare and make connections between fractions and decimals
- ☐ use real-world decimals.

Problem solving

Getting fit

There's a big get fit program happening. This is the schedule. Work out the distances you'd run and walk, weights lifted, food eaten and water drunk if you followed this program. Enter these amounts on the chart at the bottom of the page.

	Working
1 On the first morning of the get fit program, every person has to jog 1·5 km followed by a 1·2 km walk three times before lunch. What distance could you enter on your chart if you completed this task?	
2 Work your upper arms by lifting two 0·75 kg weights 20 times. What is the total weight lifted?	
3 Lunch is 0·2 kg of salad, 0·1 kg of bread and 0·1 kg of meat. How much of each food would you eat for lunch in 5 days?	
4 After each exercise session you drink at least 1·2 L of water. There are three exercise sessions a day. How much water would you drink in 5 days?	

GET FIT RECORD

Name: ______________________

Jog/walk distance: ______________________

Weights, kg lifted: ______________________

Food (5 days): ______________________

Drink (5 days): ______________________

I can solve problems by:

☐ understanding decimals and measurements ☐ writing algorithms.

Unit 34 Garden area

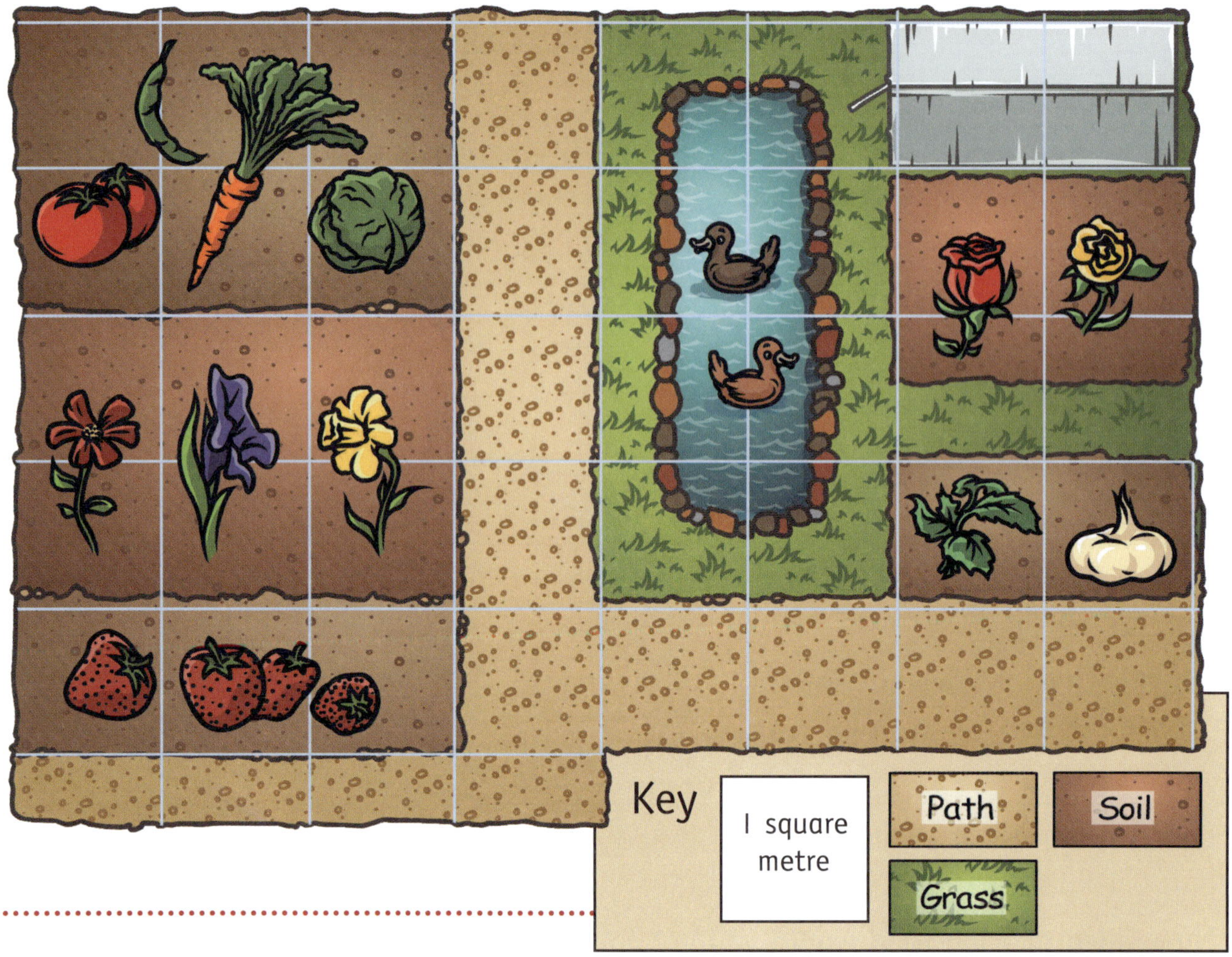

Key
1 square metre
Path
Soil
Grass

This is the Luu's garden. Study the key.

1 How many square metres is:

a the rose garden bed? ____________ b the shed? ____________

c the pond? ____________ d the strawberry patch? ____________

2 Which gardens have an area of:

a 3 square metres? ______________________________ and ______________________________.

b 6 square metres? ______________________________ and ______________________________.

3 What has an area the same as:

a the shed? ________________________ b the pond? ________________________

4 What is the area of the path? _______________

5 What is the area of the whole garden? _______________

Challenge!

How many square metres of grass are there? ☐

Unit 34 Area and perimeter

Look at page 158. Remember:

	1 square metre
1 m	
	1 m

Area is the size of a surface. Perimeter is the distance around the outside.

1 Find the perimeter of the:

a vegetable garden. ________ b herb garden. ________

c strawberry patch. ________ d flower garden. ________

e rose garden. ________ f shed and rose garden. ________

2 Estimate the perimeter of the pond. ________

3 These are 1 cm squares.

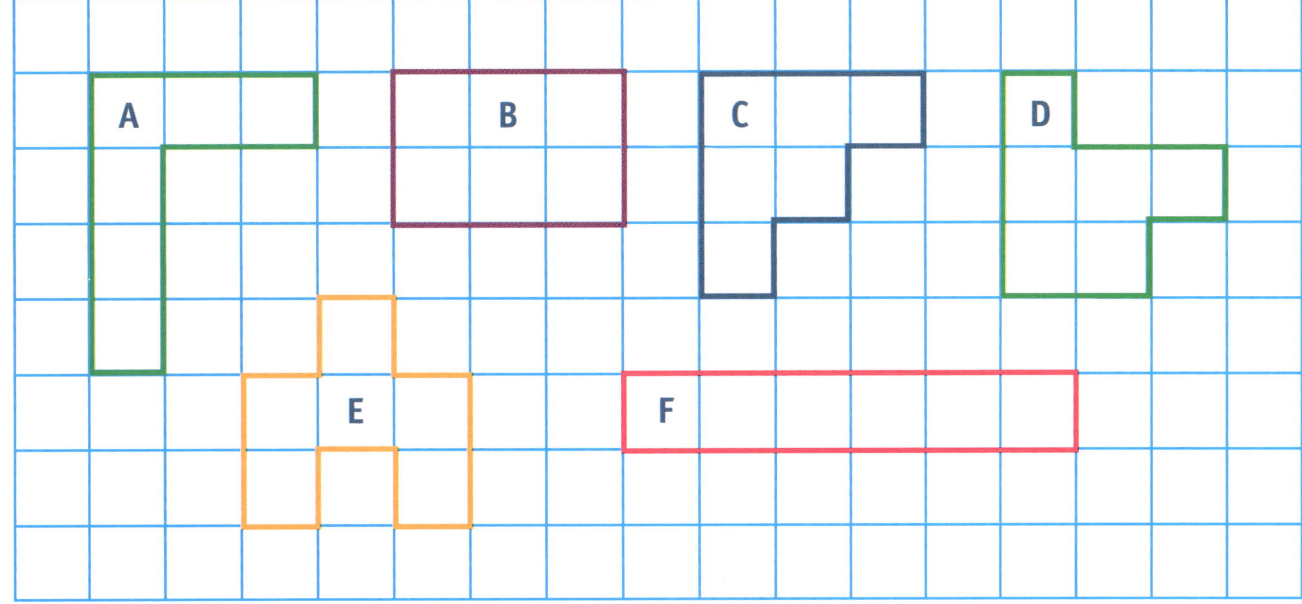

a Find the area of each in cm^2.

A ________ B ________ C ________ D ________ E ________ F ________

b Find the perimeter of each in cm.

A ________ B ________ C ________ D ________ E ________ F ________

c Write a statement about your answers.

____

____

____

Challenge!

On centimetre grid paper draw 6 different shapes, each with an area of 8 cm^2. Work out the perimeter of each shape. Write about what you discover.

Unit 34 Square metres

Area
is measured in squares.
1 square metre = 1 m^2
1 square centimetre = 1 cm^2

1 Work in a group of four.
Make a square metre by joining pieces of newspaper together.

Remember: It must be 1 m wide and 1 m long.

2 Use your square metre to measure five areas in your school. Estimate first. Answer in m^2.

Space to be measured	Estimate	Actual area
a		
b		
c		
d		
e		

3 Would you use square metres or square centimetres to measure the area of:

a a book cover? ________ b a park? ________

c a garage floor? ________ d a birthday card? ________

e a large rug? ________ f a face washer? ________

g a desk top? ________ h your bedroom floor? ________ i a DVD cover? ________

4 Name four things that are:

smaller than 1 m^2	about 1 m^2	more than 1 m^2

Draw a diagram

Use squared paper to draw a garden plan. Make 1 square = 1 m^2.
Label each part and state its area.

Unit 34 Area of rectangles and triangles

1

Area = 1 cm^2

1	2	3	4
5	6	7	8

Area = 8 cm^2

Area = 4.5 cm^2

1 Write the area of these rectangles.

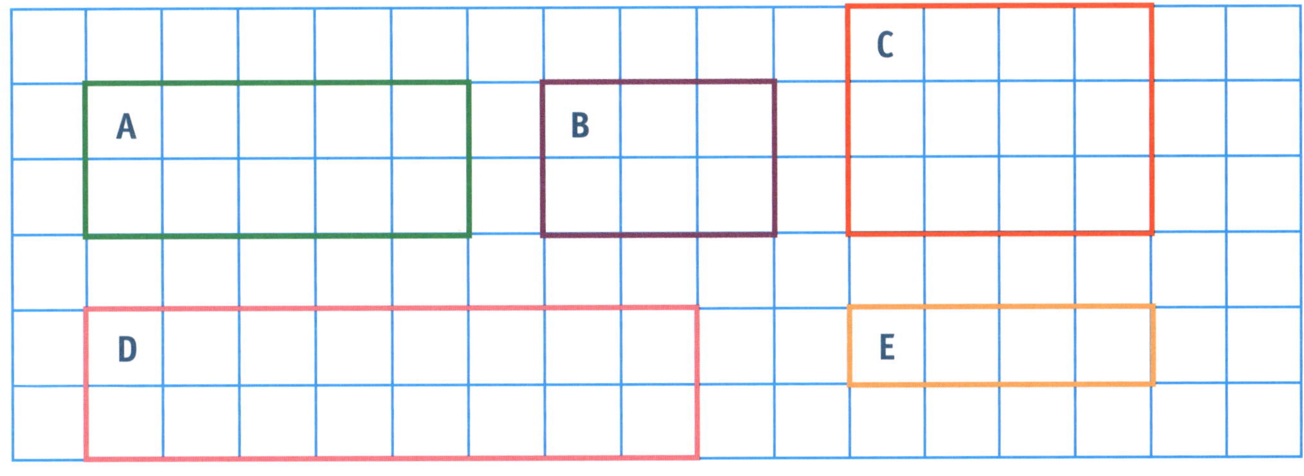

A ________ B ________ C ________ D ________ E ________

2 Which rectangle has: a the largest area? ________ b the smallest area? ________

c an area of 10 cm^2? ________ d an area of 6 cm^2? ________

3 Write the area of these triangles.

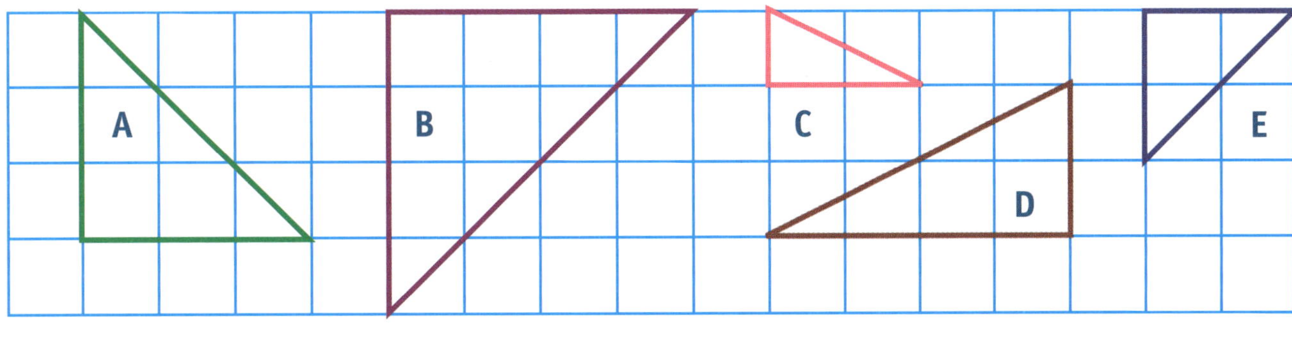

A ________ B ________ C ________ D ________ E ________

4 Which triangle has: a the largest area? ________ b the smallest area? ________

c an area of 8 cm^2? ________ d an area of 2 cm^2? ________

Mastery Checklist I can:

- ☐ measure area in square centimetres and square metres
- ☐ choose area units
- ☐ estimate areas
- ☐ find the area of rectangles and triangles.

Life in the Zoo

Investigation 4

Photographers want to photograph the animals of Wanderound Zoo in the morning. The Keepers made a list of times that the animals are awake. How can the photographers plan their timetable?

Keepers report for work at 5 am. They don't want their photos taken.
The elephant likes to sleep in and does not wake until $\frac{1}{2}$ an hour after the zebra.
The kangaroo wakes $\frac{1}{2}$ an hour before the zebra.
The giraffes wake up at 7 am every morning, $\frac{1}{2}$ an hour after the elephant.
Tigers wake half an hour after 7 am. Koalas always sleep in, so they will be last.
Monkeys get angry if disturbed before the tigers. The lion wakes before the tigers.
Zebras don't smile until 15 minutes after they wake. The keepers' break is at 8:30 am.
Wombats can be woken at any time of the morning, especially for photographs.

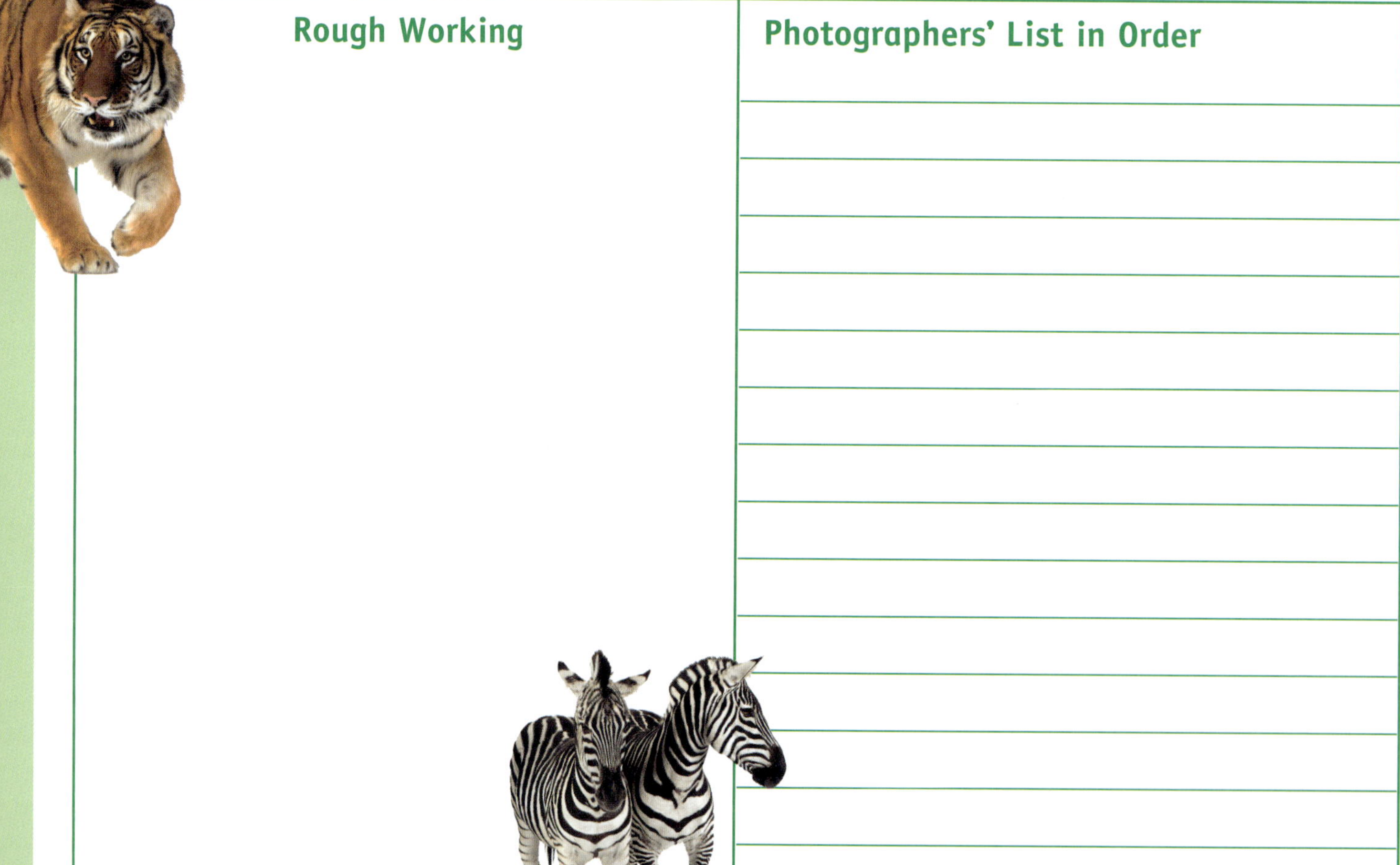

Rough Working	Photographers' List in Order

Photographers start at ______________________ and end at ______________________.

AC9M4M02 • AC9M4M03 Measurement MAO-WM-01 Working mathematically • exploring and connecting mathematical concepts • choosing and applying mathematical techniques to solve problems MA2-2DS-03 Two-dimensional spatial structure B • Area: Measure the areas of shapes using the grid structure • MA2-NSM-02 Non-spatial measure A • Time: Represent and read analog time

Life in the Zoo

Investigation 4

Zookeepers are planning some renovations to animals' areas. Large animals must have an area of about 60 squares. Small animals must have an area of about 30 squares. Choose two animals from the zoo and draw a plan (from above) of an enclosure for them. Use a ruler.

Plan a shelter for each one and a feeding place. **Draw** the front view of the shelter.

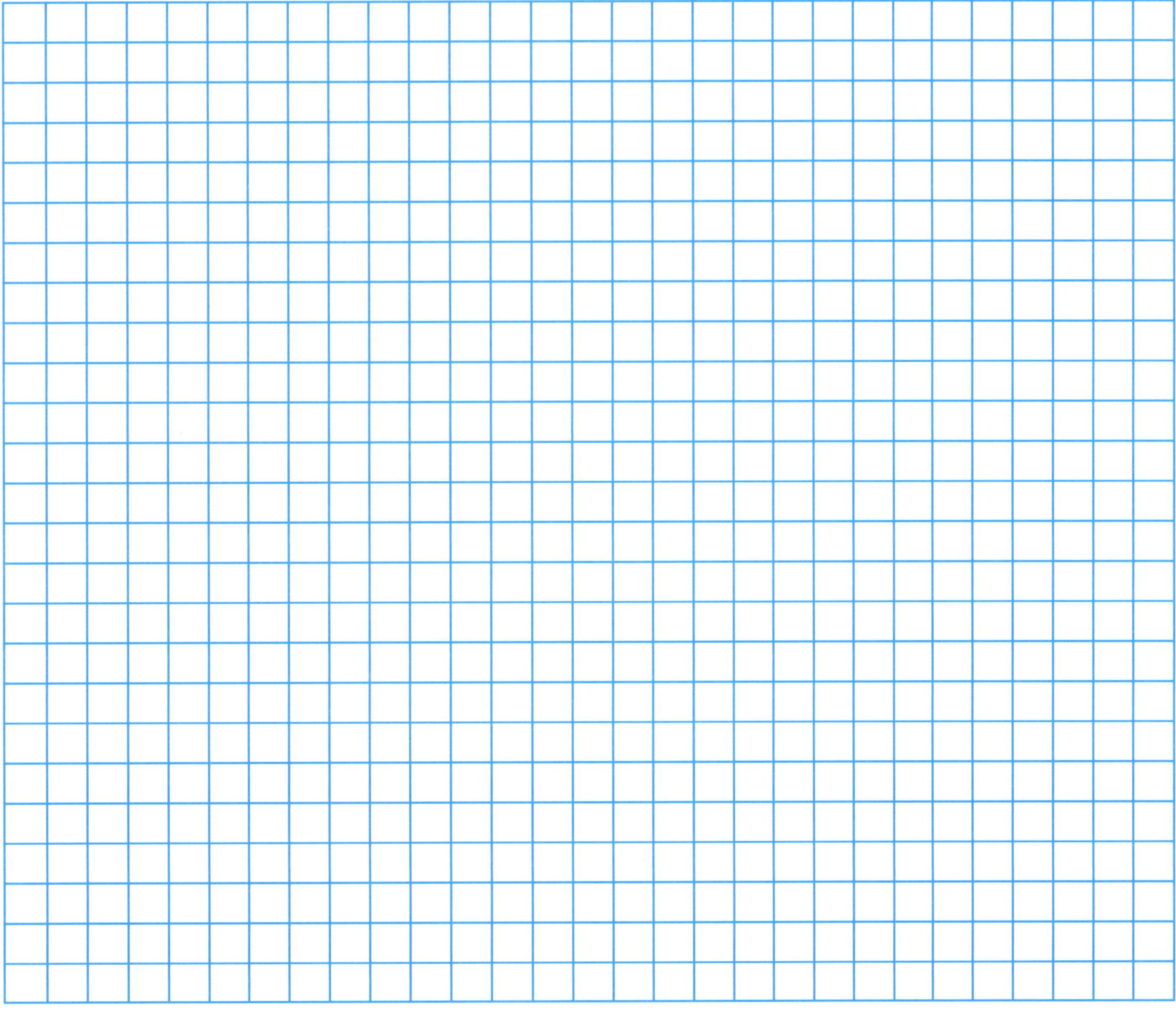

To carry out these tasks, I need to:

- ☐ work backwards to solve problems of time
- ☐ make a list of tasks
- ☐ use a grid for an area
- ☐ create a simple plan drawing
- ☐ use measurements in squares.

I enjoyed this task! ☆☆☆☆☆

Revision

Shade one bubble.

1 Find the difference in price.

$3950 $7250

$11 200 ◯ $2300 ◯ $3300 ◯ $10 200 ◯

2 What is the total distance they cycled?

539 km 113 km 872 km

1514 km ◯ 1298 km ◯ 1524 km ◯ 1498 km ◯

3

$$2\overline{)58}$$

24 ◯ 25 ◯ 26 ◯ 29 ◯

4

$$6 \div 1000 = \square$$

$\square = 6$ ◯ $\square = 0{\cdot}6$ ◯ $\square = 0{\cdot}06$ ◯ $\square = 0{\cdot}006$ ◯

5

$$\begin{array}{r} 92 \\ -\ 39 \\ \hline \\ \hline \end{array}$$

67 ◯ 64 ◯ 53 ◯ 121 ◯

6 What is the area of the garden?

Shade one bubble.

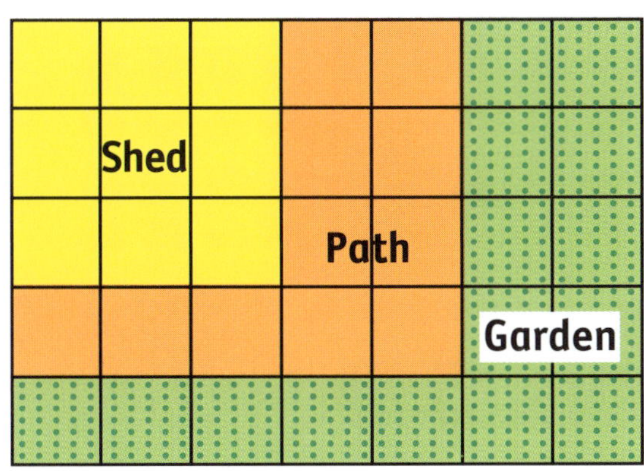

Key

□ = 1 square metre

9 m^2 ◯   11 m^2 ◯   15 m^2 ◯   35 m^2 ◯

7

$$\begin{array}{r} 284 \\ +\ 465 \\ \hline 749 \\ \hline \end{array}$$

The check using subtraction is:

$$\begin{array}{r} 749 \\ +\ 465 \\ \hline \\ \hline \end{array}\qquad \begin{array}{r} 749 \\ -\ 465 \\ \hline \\ \hline \end{array}\qquad \begin{array}{r} 465 \\ +\ 284 \\ \hline \\ \hline \end{array}\qquad \begin{array}{r} 465 \\ -\ 749 \\ \hline \\ \hline \end{array}$$

  ◯ ◯

8

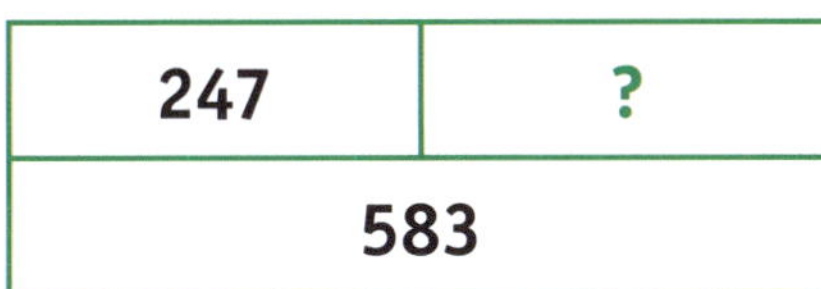

334 ◯   335 ◯   336 ◯   830 ◯

Unit 35 Square and triangle numbers

Number patterns

Pattern A Square Numbers

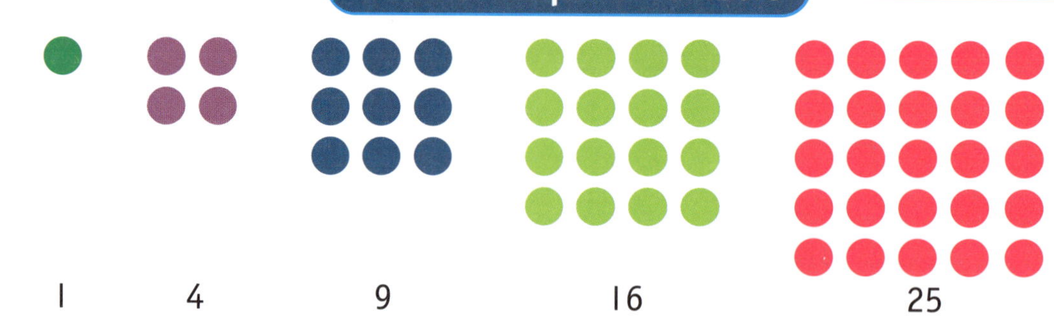

1 4 9 16 25

Pattern B Triangular Numbers

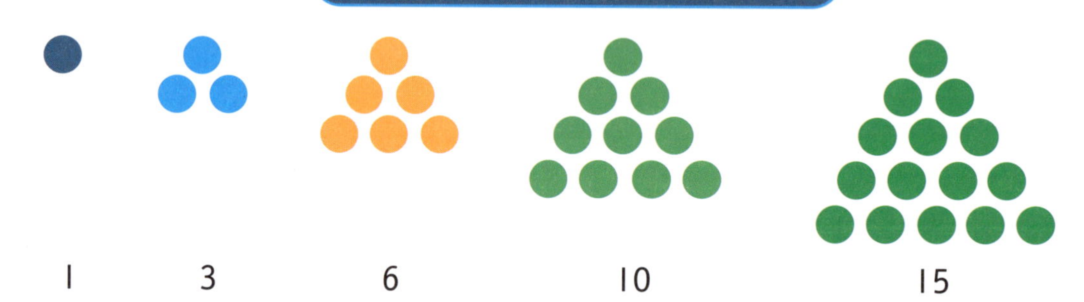

1 3 6 10 15

1 Pattern A

a Why are the numbers called square numbers? ______________________

b Complete the table.

Order of term	1	2	3	4	5	6	7	8	9
Term									

c How many dots would be in the 10th term? ____________

2 Pattern B

a Why are the numbers called triangular numbers? ______________________

b Complete the table.

Order of term	1	2	3	4	5	6	7	8	9
Term									

c Complete this pattern.

1 = ____

1 + 2 = ____

1 + 2 + 3 = ____

1 + 2 + 3 + 4 = ____

d Write the next four lines for the pattern.

1 + 2 + 3 + 4 + ____ = ____

____

____

____

____

Unit 35 Triangular numbers

Number patterns

1 Look at **Pattern A** on page 166.

a Draw the 12th term.

b How many dots does it have? ______

c 12 squared = ______

2 Look at **Pattern B** on page 166.

a Draw the 12th term.

b How many dots does it have? ______

3 Three people shake hands with each other.

a How many handshakes? ______

How many handshakes for:

b 4 people? ______

c 5 people? ______

d 6 people? ______

e What type of numbers are your answers? ______

f Predict how many handshakes for 9 people. ______

g Act it out with 8 friends. Were you correct? ______

4 Write as many multiplication facts as you can for each of these numbers.

a 

b 12

c 36

5 True or false?

a $6 \times 4 = 8 \times 3$ ______

b $6 \times 6 = 12 \times 2$ ______

c $9 \times 4 = 12 \times 1$ ______

d $4 \times 3 = 6 \times 6$ ______

e $9 \times 4 = 6 \times 6$ ______

f $4 \times 3 = 6 \times 2$ ______

Unit 35 Multiple patterns

1	2	3	4	5	6	7	8	9	10
11	12	13	14	15	16	17	18	19	20
21	22	23	24	25	26	27	28	29	30
31	32	33	34	35	36	37	38	39	40
41	42	43	44	45	46	47	48	49	50
51	52	53	54	55	56	57	58	59	60
61	62	63	64	65	66	67	68	69	70
71	72	73	74	75	76	77	78	79	80
81	82	83	84	85	86	87	88	89	90
91	92	93	94	95	96	97	98	99	100

You may use a calculator.

1 Colour [1] red.

2 Starting at [4] colour every number divisible by 2, blue.

3 Starting at [6] colour the rest of the numbers that are divisible by 5, green. (**Hint:** They end in a 5.)

4 Starting at [4] colour the rest of the numbers that are divisible by 3, yellow.

5 Starting at [8] colour the rest of the numbers that are divisible by 7, orange.

6 Write a list of the numbers which are left.

____

____

____

Mastery Checklist I can:
- ☐ identify patterns in square numbers
- ☐ identify patterns in triangular numbers
- ☐ identify multiples of 2, 3, 5 and 7.

Unit 36 Angle types

A B C D E F G H I J K L M N O

1 Mark one angle in each picture.

2 Name the types of angles (right angle, acute angle, obtuse angle).

A acute ______ B ______ C ______

D ______ E ______ F ______

G ______ H ______ I ______

J ______ K ______ L ______

M ______ N ______ O ______

Unit 36 Acute, right, obtuse

right angle is 90°

acute angle is less than 90°

obtuse angle is more than 90° and less than 180°

1 Colour the right angles **red**, acute angles **blue**, obtuse angles **green**.

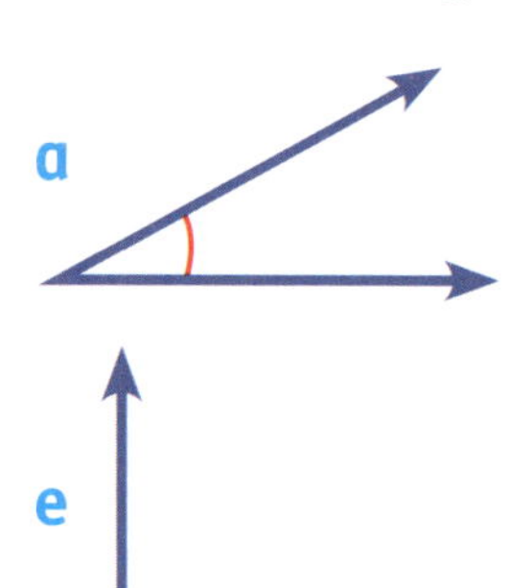

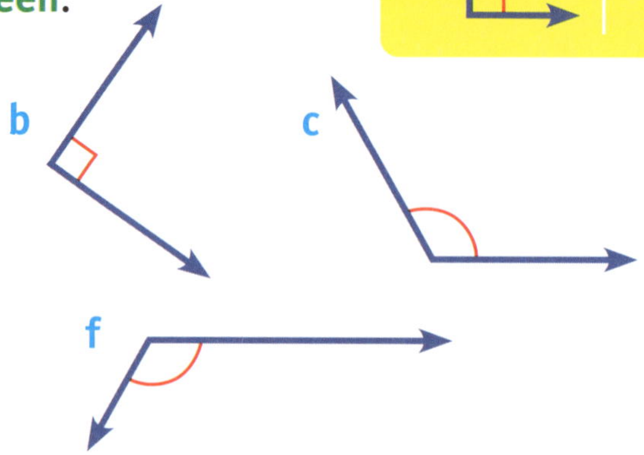

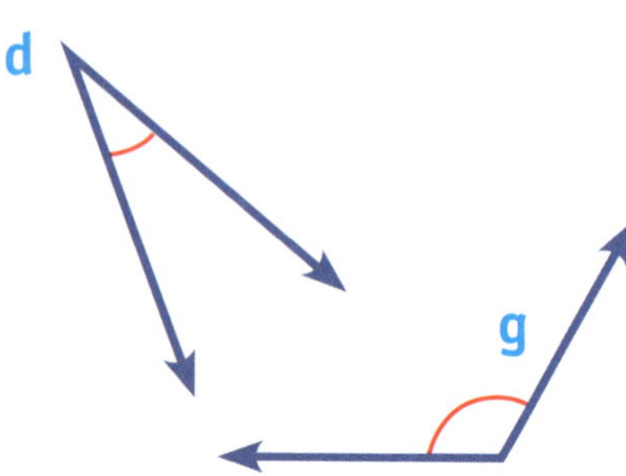

2 Name 6 right angles you can see in your classroom.

a ______________ b ______________ c ______________

d ______________ e ______________ f ______________

3 Name 6 acute angles you can see in your classroom.

a ______________ b ______________ c ______________

d ______________ e ______________ f ______________

4 Name 6 obtuse angles you can see in your classroom.

a ______________ b ______________ c ______________

d ______________ e ______________ f ______________

5 Draw:

a 2 acute angles.	b 2 right angles.	c 2 obtuse angles.

Unit 36 Vertex and arms

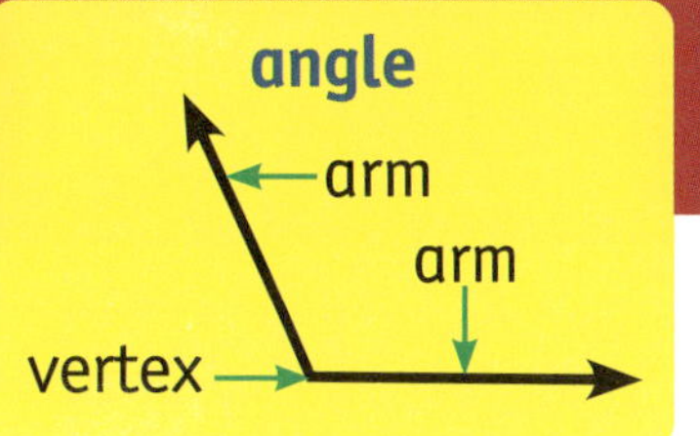

1 a Put a red dot at the vertex.

b Colour the arms of the acute angles green.

c Colour the arms of the obtuse angles blue. d Colour the arms of the right angles yellow.

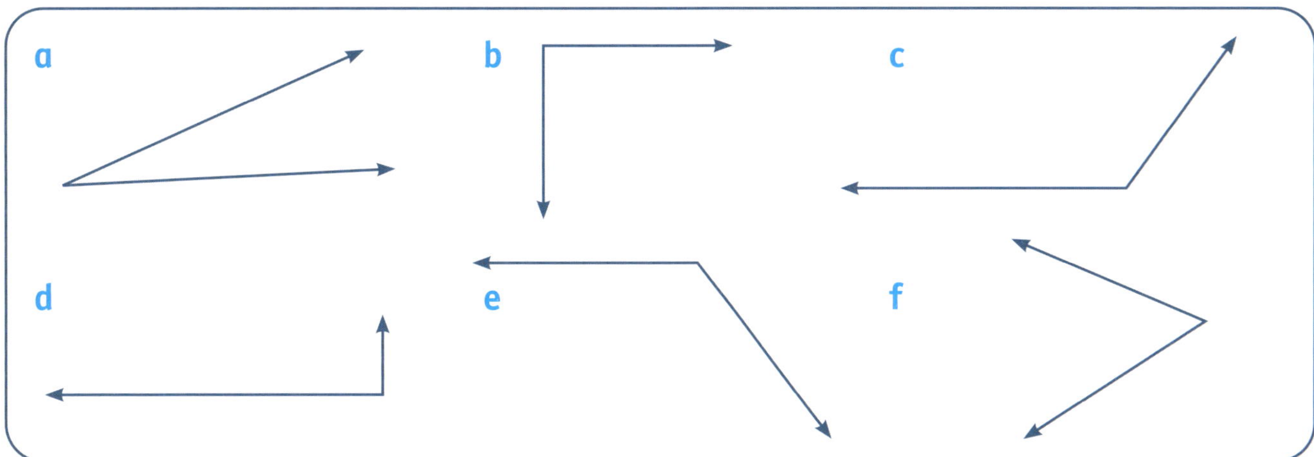

2 Write **R** on the right-angled triangles, **A** on the acute-angled triangles and **O** on the obtuse-angled triangles.

Triangles

One right angle = right-angled triangle

All acute angles = acute-angled triangle

One obtuse angle = obtuse-angled triangle

Challenge!

Draw the time on the clocks and write the type of angle the hands make.

a 9 o'clock

b 10 past 4

c 20 to 3

Mastery Checklist can:

- ☐ identify right, acute and obtuse angles
- ☐ find examples of angles in the real world
- ☐ draw different angles
- ☐ identify the vertex and arms on an angle.

Problem solving

Making new shapes

Use pattern blocks.

1 Show how you can draw a trapezium using only the acute-angled triangle to draw around.

2 Show how you can use another pattern block to draw other 2D shapes.

3 Use any two pattern blocks to draw around and make a third shape.
Describe what you have done and the angles you started with and ended with.

eg 1 triangle + 1 trapezium = 1 parallelogram

5 acute angles + 2 obtuse angles = 2 acute and 2 obtuse angles

I can solve problems by:

☐ understanding angles and 2D shapes ☐ drawing diagrams.

AC9M4M04 Measurement **MAO-WM-01** Working mathematically • communicating thinking and reasoning coherently and clearly • **MA2-GM-03** Geometric measure B • Angles: Compare angles to a right angle • **MA2-2DS-02** Two-dimensional spatial structure B • 2D shapes: Create two-dimensional shapes that result from combining and splitting common shapes

Unit 37 Timetable

1

A 12:15 pm	lunch
B 8:25 am	arrive at school
C 9:40 pm	go to bed
D 1:55 pm	afternoon sport
E 10:40 am	morning break
F 7:45 pm	watch television
G 7:20 am	wake up
H 5:05 pm	homework
I 7:55 am	breakfast
J 6:50 pm	dinner
K 3:40 pm	walk home

This is Tina's timetable for Monday. She has not written it in order.

a Use the timeline to help put her activities in order.

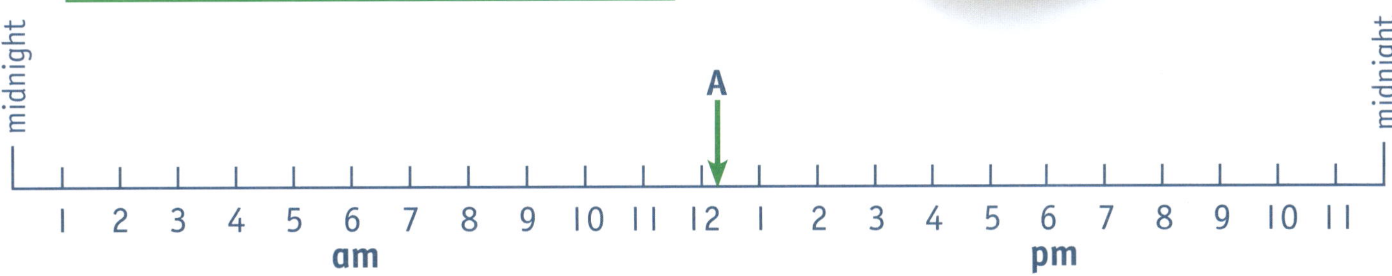

b Draw the times on the clocks.

A 
F 
H 
K 

B [:]
C [:]
H [:]
I [:]

2 Choose the best unit to measure:

a how long it is until the end of the month.

b the time it takes to blink.

c the length of a movie.

d how long it is until you are 15.

e the time from Easter to Christmas.

f the length of a school term.

seconds
minutes
hours
days
weeks
months
years

Problem solving

Timetabling the carnival

Mrs Mato has to finish the timetable for the athletics carnival.
Each activity must be completed by all three classes: 4T, 4K and 4P.

Activities

- Year 3–6 rotations
- 50-metre sprints
- 100-metre sprints
- 200-metre sprints
- Relay
- Shotput
- Discus
- Javelin
- Rest stop

Rules checklist:

- ☐ Everyone has lunch 12–1 pm.
- ☐ Everyone has break time 2.00–2.15 pm
- ☐ Everyone has 3–6 rotations for 1 hour after lunch and before break time.
- ☐ All other activities take 30 minutes, and none can be done at the same time, not even rest stops.
- ☐ All sprints must be done by 10.30 am.
- ☐ Everyone has one 30-minute rest stop before noon.
- ☐ No shotput after break time.

Time	Class		
	4T	4K	4P
9.00–10.00 am	50 m sprints	200 m sprints	
	100 m sprints		200 m sprints
10.00–11.00 am	200 m sprints	Rest stop	
	Javelin		
11.00–12.00 noon	Shotput		
	Rest stop		
12.00–1.00 pm	Lunch		
1.00–2.00 pm	3–6 rotations		3–6 rotations
2.00–2.15 pm	Break time	Break time	
2.15–3.15 pm	Discus	Javelin	Relays
	Relays		

I can solve problems by:
☐ understanding time and duration of events ☐ guessing and checking.

AC9M4M03 Measurement **MAO-WM-01** Working mathematically • choosing and applying mathematical techniques to solve problems • communicating thinking and reasoning coherently and clearly • **MA2-NSM-02** Non-spatial measure B • Time: Represent and interpret digital time displays

Unit 37 Map reading

Position

Skull Cave
Pirate Cemetery
Cramer Castle
N
Crocodile River
Mount Ispy
Quicksand Marsh
Darkheart Woods
Jolly Dodger
Lake Eerie
Safehaven Beach

Green Beard is at the top of Mt Ispy with his telescope.

1 What can he see when he looks:

a East? __________ b South? __________

c West? __________ d North-west? __________

e South-east? __________ f North-east? __________

g North? __________ h South-west? __________

2 He is facing the Pirate Cemetery. What will he see when he turns through a right angle:

a clockwise? __________ b anti-clockwise? __________

3 If you are standing on the Jolly Dodger, in what direction is:

a Lake Eerie? __________ b Safehaven Beach? __________

c Skull Cave? __________ d Mt Ispy? __________

4 If you are at the cemetery, in what direction is:

a Lake Eerie? __________ b the Jolly Dodger? __________

c Darkheart Woods? __________ d Skull Cave? __________

Unit 37 Grids

Position 

E					
D					
C					
B					
A					
	1	2	3	4	5

For position on a grid read the column (bottom) first then the row (side).

2nd	C			3C
	B		2B	
	A	1A		
		1	2	3
			1st	

1 Write the position of the:

a basket. ________ b lamp. ________ c armchair. ________

d teapot. ________ e wooden chest. ________ f vase. ________

g bath. ________ h plate. ________ i bell. ________

2 Draw:

a a pencil in 1C. b a spoon in 3A. c an eggcup in 2E.

d a cup in 5B. e a bed in 4D. f a book in 3B.

g a mat in 1A. h a jug in 2C. i a broom in 5C.

3 Name all the blank spaces.

____

Challenge!

Use centimetre grid paper. Outline an 8 × 8 grid and label the rows and columns.
Draw 10 symbols (eg ● ■ ✱) on the grid.
Swap with a friend. Name the position of each symbol on your friend's grid.

Unit 37 Plotting points

To plot a point, use two numbers — the bottom number first, then the side number. Use brackets and a comma. (1, 3)

1 The red dot is the point (1, 5). Name these points.

a  ____________ b  ____________

c  ____________ d ____________

e  ____________ f ____________

g ____________ h ____________

2 Draw the dot at each point.

a (2, 6) b (4, 1)

c  (1, 5) d (6, 2)

e (3, 3) f (5, 4)

g  (4, 6) h (0, 0)

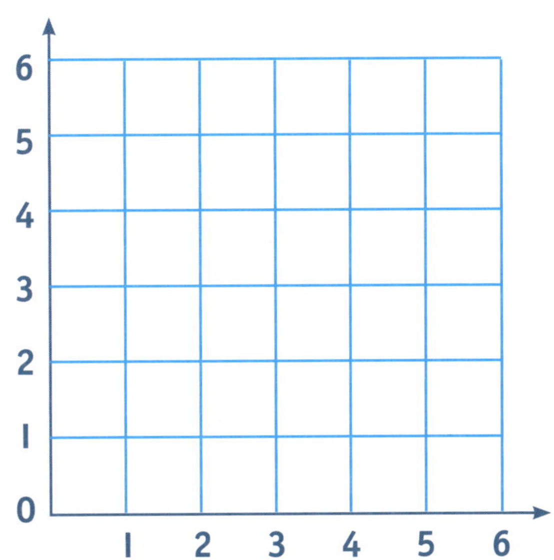

Draw a diagram

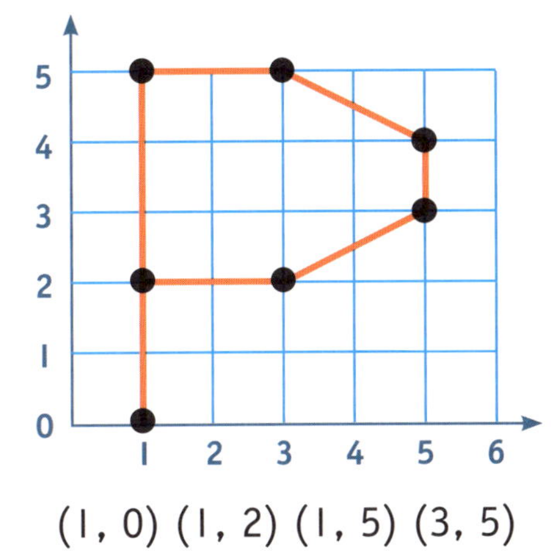

(1, 0) (1, 2) (1, 5) (3, 5)
(5, 4) (5, 3) (3, 2) (1, 2)

a Write your first initial.

b Name the points you used.

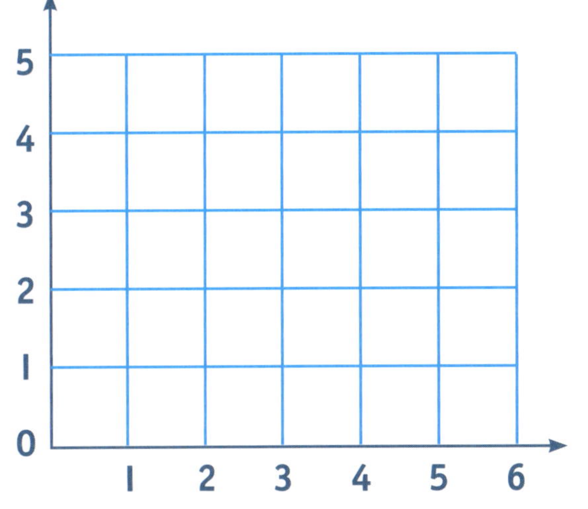

Unit 37 Follow the path

Position 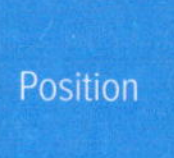 

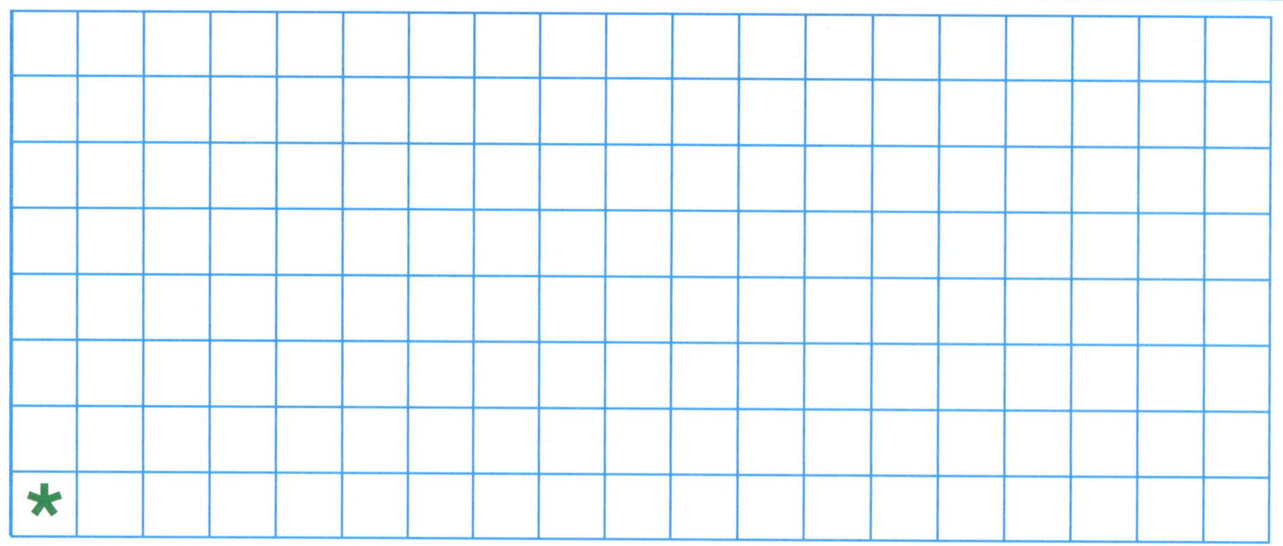

1 Sam the clown steps out his initials. He starts at *. Each square is a step. Follow the directions to colour his path.

a 5 steps east
b 3 steps north
c 4 steps west
d 3 steps north
e 6 steps east
f 6 steps south
g 4 steps east
h 6 steps north
i 2 steps east
j 6 steps south
k 4 steps east

l What are his initials? 

2 Draw Santa's path to the present. Write the directions he travelled eg E, S, E, W.

Directions:

Mastery Checklist I can:

- ☐ use am and pm
- ☐ understand timetables
- ☐ choose the best unit of time
- ☐ complete a timetable
- ☐ locate items on a map
- ☐ locate items on a grid
- ☐ find and plot points using coordinates
- ☐ follow and write directions for a path.

Unit 38 Outcomes

Chance 

Carl's Ice-cream Combos

SPECIAL
Any two scoops for $2

CARL

Vanilla
Chocolate
Strawberry
Mango
Lime

1 Draw all possible two-scoop combinations on these cones.
Hint: Vanilla and lime is the same as lime and vanilla.

2 How many combinations did you find? ________

Unit 38 Predicting outcomes

Chance

chance experiment

John tossed a coin 10 times. These are the results.

1 a Who is correct? ________________

b Why? ____

____

2 Work with a partner. Toss a coin 10 times.

a Record your results.

b Totals. Heads = __________ Tails = __________

c Which occurred more often? __________

3 a Repeat with a different coin.

b Totals. Heads = __________ Tails = __________

4 a Are both results the same? ________________

b Why? ____

Unit 38 Certainty of events

Bart has a small puppet collection in a box.

1 He opens the box and looks for the mouse. Is it certain he will get the mouse? ________

2 He closes his eyes and picks a puppet.

Is it certain he will get the mouse? ________ Why? ________________________

____

3 What is meant by selecting at random? ________________________

____

For all these questions, Bart has his eyes closed.

4 What chance does he have of selecting the cat puppet? ________

5 a He selected the cow puppet and the chicken puppet and left them out of the box.

What chance does he have now of selecting the cat puppet? ________

b Why has the chance changed? ________________________

____

6 How many goes must he have to be certain of getting the cat puppet? ________

7 On this line draw a blue arrow to show the chance of Bart selecting the penguin puppet when all the puppets are in the box.

impossible ———————————————— certain

8 He removes the cow, the mouse and the cat puppets. Draw a red arrow to show the chance he now has of selecting the penguin puppet.

Mastery Checklist I can:
- ☐ identify possible outcomes
- ☐ complete repeated chance experiments
- ☐ understand certainty
- ☐ understand how one event can affect the chance of another event happening.

Revision Term 4

1 p 142

a $2\overline{)58}$ b $4\overline{)92}$ c $7\overline{)84}$

2 p 143

a 7 ÷ 10 = ______

b 6 ÷ 100 = ______

c 8 ÷ 1000 = ______

d 9 × 10 = ______

e 8 × 100 = ______

f 3 × 1000 = ______

3 p 144

a Write three multiples of 12.

______ ______ ______

b Write three multiples of 8.

______ ______ ______

4 What is the difference between: p 147

a 19 and 11? ________

b 52 and 38? ________

5 p 147

a
```
  7 5
– 3 7
-----
```

b
```
  9 3
– 6 8
-----
```

c
```
  6 4
– 1 9
-----
```

d
```
  8 3
– 4 5
-----
```

6 Complete. p 147

a –

64	16
30	14

b –

53	27
34	8

7 Alastair had $74 saved but he spent $49 on a chess set. How much did he have left? p 147

[ ]

8 Complete the fact families. p 150

a 76 – 8 = ______

76 – ______ = 8

______ + ______ = ______

______ + ______ = ______

b 19 + 12 = ______

______ + ______ = ______

______ – ______ = ______

______ – ______ = ______

9 a   b p 150

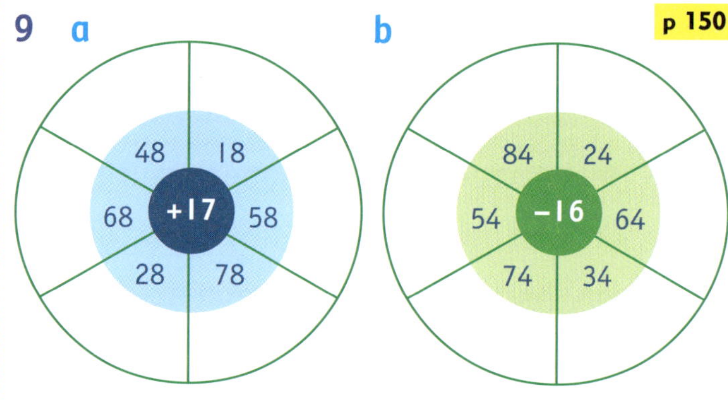

10 Add, then subtract to check your answer. p 150

a

b

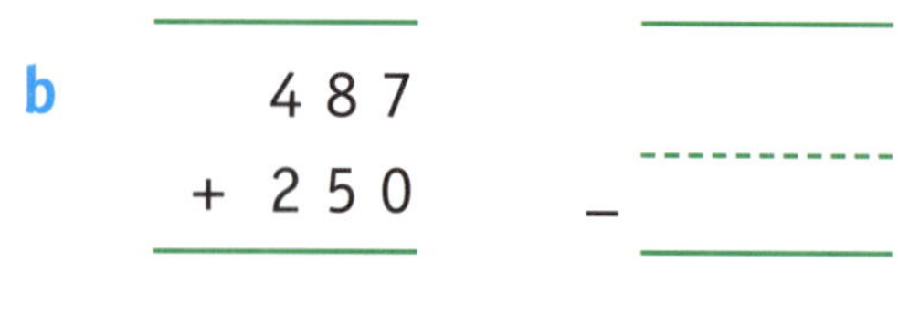

11 p 151

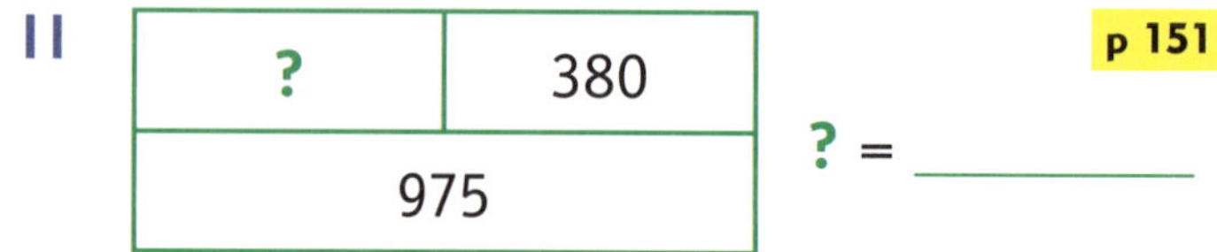

Revision Term 4

12 This is a calculator display. p 152

What would you add to make the:

a 5 a 7? ________

b 6 a 9? ________

What would you subtract to make the:

c 2 a 0? ________

d 9 a 4? ________

13 If you add 7 and 8 to any number, then subtract 9 and take away 6, why do you end up with the number you started with? p 153

____

____

14 Match equivalent fractions by joining with a line. p 154

$\frac{5}{10}$	$\frac{10}{10}$
$\frac{3}{5}$	0·6
0·8	$\frac{80}{100}$
$\frac{90}{100}$	0·9
1·0	0·7
$\frac{70}{100}$	$\frac{1}{2}$

15 Circle the tenths numeral. p 155

a 4·78 b 62·09

16 Would you use m^2 or cm^2 to find the area of: p 160

a your garden? ________

b this page? ________

c a book cover? ________

d the playground? ________

17 What is the area of the triangle? p 161

____

18 These are 1 cm squares. p 161

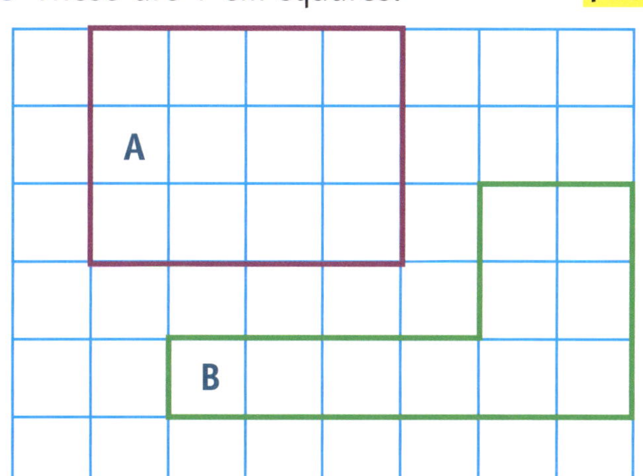

a Area A = _____ b Perimeter A = _____

c Area B = _____ d Perimeter B = _____

19 Colour the acute angles blue, the obtuse angles red and the right angles yellow. p 170

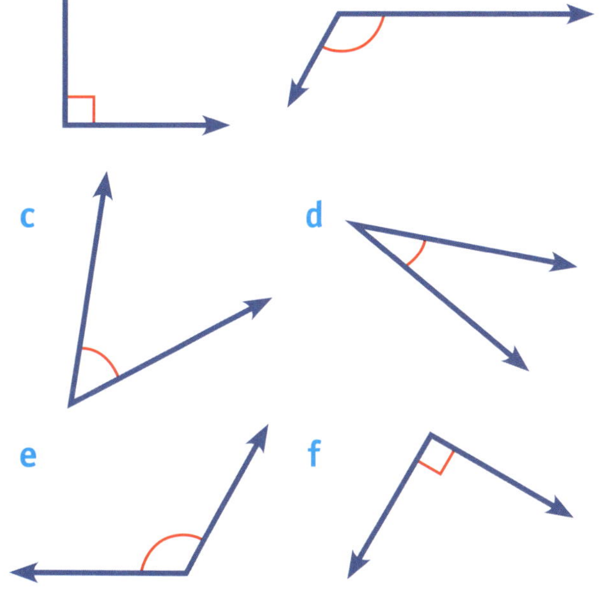

Revision Term 4

20 p 177

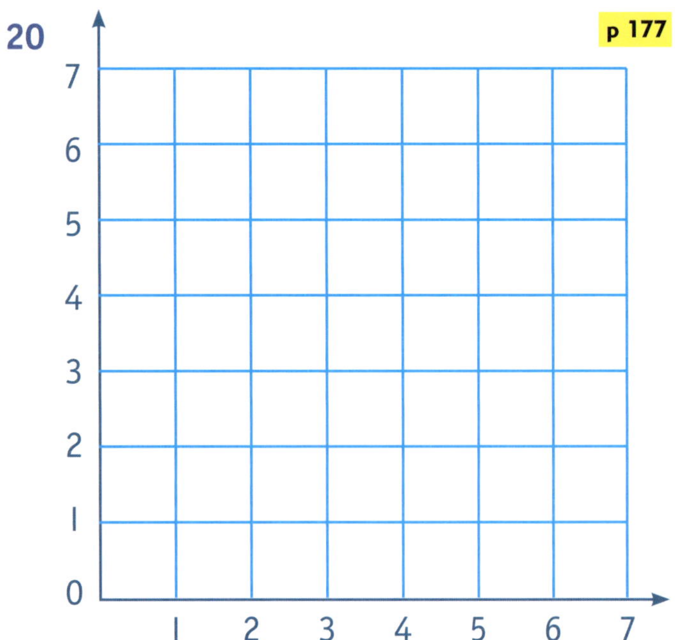

Plot these points.

a ● (1, 1) b ● (5, 4)
c ● (2, 7) d ● (6. 6)
e ● (3, 5) f ● (7, 2)

21 p 178

Kev looked for his bone. Start at * and draw his path.

a 1 up	b 3 right	c 2 up
d 3 left	e 3 up	f 6 right
g 1 up	h 2 right	i 3 down
j 3 left	k 2 down	l 2 right
m 2 down	n 2 left	

22 In her pencil box, Sue has 2 red pens, 2 green pens and 2 black pens. p 179

(R = red, G = green, B = black)

a If she selects one pen, what are the possible outcomes? ______________

How many outcomes are there? ______

b If she selects two pens, what are the possible outcomes? ______________

____

How many outcomes are there? ______

c How many goes must she have to be certain of getting a red pen? ______

d She removes the black pens.
How many goes must she have now to be certain of getting a red pen?

______

23 True or false? p 181

a It has rained for the last 3 Saturdays.

So this Saturday it will definitely rain.

____

b I have 4 girls but the next baby might be a boy.

____

c I know I will win a prize in the raffle.

Because I always do.

____